la cocina de mamá

Also by Penelope Casas

Paella! Spectacular Rice Dishes from Spain
¡Delicioso!: The Regional Cooking of Spain
Discovering Spain: An Uncommon Guide
Tapas: The Little Dishes of Spain
The Foods and Wines of Spain

BROADWAY BOOKS NEW YORK

LA COCINA DE MAMÁ

The Great Home Cooking of Spain

PENELOPE CASAS

Color photography by Shimon and Tammar

ADDITIONAL PHOTOGRAPHY BY LUIS CASAS

PRINTED IN CHINA

BROADWAY BOOKS and its logo, a letter B bisected on the diagonal, are trademarks of Random House, Inc.

Visit our Web site at www.broadwaybooks.com

First edition published 2005

Book design by Elizabeth Rendfleisch
Map by David Cain

Library of Congress Cataloging-in-Publication Data

Casas, Penelope.
    La cocina de mamá : the great home cooking of Spain / Penelope Casas.
        p.   cm.
    1. Cookery, Spanish.   I. Title.
    TX723.5.S7C3575 2005
    641.5946—dc22   2004051835

641.5946

ISBN 0-7679-1222-5

10 9 8 7 6 5 4 3 2 1

To Luis

Since the first time we shared
tapas several decades ago,
your unlimited faith in me
and your extraordinary love
for your Spanish homeland
have been my beacon and
my strength

FOREWORD

I have said many times that for me my mother is the best cook in the world. I am sure many supposed my words were spoken carelessly and I was simply seeking to pay homage to her. Nothing could be further from the truth: the culinary memory embodied within our mothers is incalculable. By honoring all mothers who cook and have cooked for centuries for their families, we acknowledge their great importance not only for our daily nutrition and even the education of our palates, but also for the survival of our culinary traditions. Women at home have always taken on the task of transmitting recipes that they learned from their own mothers in an endless chain going back to the beginning of time.

Personally, I owe to my mother—and all mothers—gratitude for two fundamental reasons: First, for their capacity for selfless sacrifice and love, and the patience with which, day after day, from morning till night, they take upon themselves the responsibility for thinking about feeding their families, going to market, and cooking. And second, because mothers are the reason why all of us are able to know, to taste, to eat, and to enjoy all the recipes that comprise our culinary heritage.

—Ferran Adrià

CONTENTS

Roasting sardines, Málaga

ACKNOWLEDGMENTS

All my thanks to the following cooks, both humble and grand, and all my many Spanish friends, family, and acquaintances whose cooking has inspired me over the years.

• Juan Mari Arzak and his mother, Francisca Arratibel • Elena Arzak • Pedro Subijana and his father, Pedro Subijana • Ferran Adrià and his mother, Josefa Acosta • Pilar Vico and her mother, Pilar Monteoliva • Mari Carmen Martín, her mother, Carmen Pastor, and Chalo Peláez • Carmen Serrano and Pepe González • Cinta Gutiérrez and the Gutiérrez family • Ruperto and Josefa Blanco • José Manuel Caro • Cándida Acebo • Digna Prieto • Irene España and Andrés Vidal • Pepita Alía • Fernando and Paco Hermoso • Tomás Herranz • Paco Patón and his mother, Antonia Belmar • Marisé Zubizarreta • Gonzalo Córdoba • Reme Domínguez and Ximo Boix • Aurora Sánchez • Pilar del Olmo • Rafaela Ortiz • Bartolomé Rodrigo • Elisa Tello • Julia and Lucía Piñedo • Concha López-Viota • Félix Durán • Rufino López • Ramón San Martín • Alexia Ballesteros • Charito de Pablo

Although my immediate family—my mother, Toni; husband, Luis; daughter, Elisa, and her husband, Steve—and my dear friend Marsha Stanton did not contribute recipes to this book, their moral and practical support were incalculable. And I salute my young granddaughter, Ruby, who, to our amusement, learned in Spain the fine art of "deconstructing" food a la Ferran Adrià.

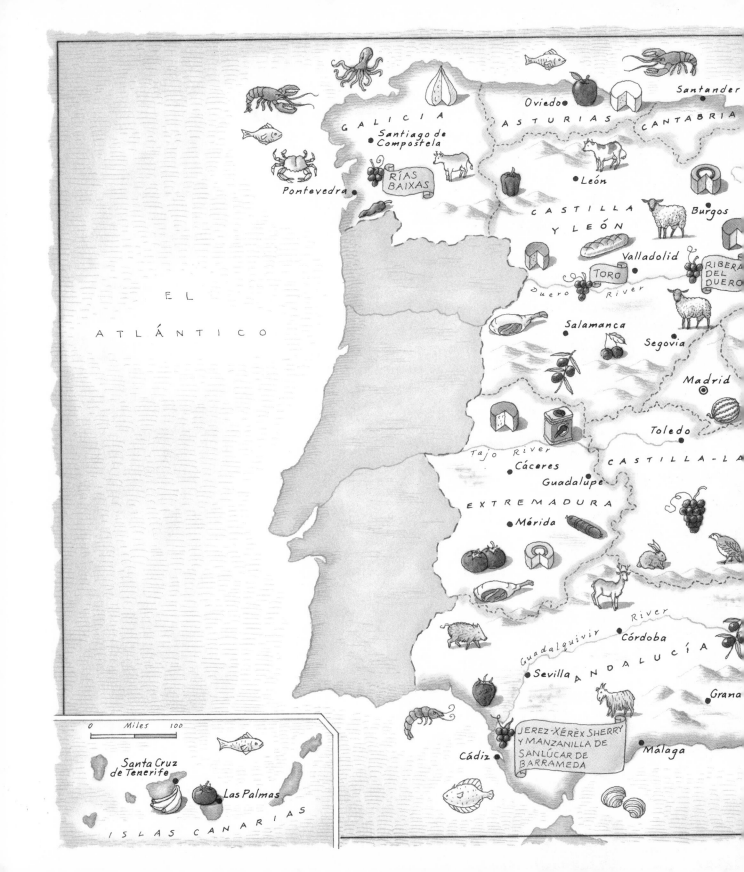

EL ATLÁNTICO

GALICIA

Santiago de Compostela

Pontevedra

RÍAS BAIXAS

ASTURIAS

Oviedo

León

CANTABRIA

Santander

CASTILLA Y LEÓN

Burgos

Valladolid

TORO

Duero River

RIBERA DEL DUERO

Salamanca

Segovia

Madrid

Toledo

CASTILLA-LA

Tajo River

Cáceres

Guadalupe

EXTREMADURA

Mérida

Córdoba

Guadalquivir River

Sevilla

ANDALUCÍA

Grana

Málaga

Cádiz

JEREZ-XÉRÈZ SHERRY Y MANZANILLA DE SANLÚCAR DE BARRAMEDA

0 Miles 100

Santa Cruz de Tenerife

Las Palmas

ISLAS CANARIAS

Bilbao
San Sebastián
PAÍS
VASCO

Pamplona
NAVARRA
NAVARRA

roño
RIOJA

Zaragoza
ARAGÓN
Ebro River

CATALUNYA
Girona
CAVA
Barcelona
PENEDÈS
Tarragona
PRIORATO

Teruel
Cuenca
MANCHA

COMUNIDAD
VALENCIANA
Castellón
de la Plana
Valencia
Turia River

Palma de
Mallorca

ISLAS BALEÁRICAS

MURCIA
Murcia
Alicante

N

Miles
0   100

MAR

MEDITERRÁNEO

introduction

THE NIGHTLY SCENE AT CASA LUCIO IN OLD MADRID IS controlled chaos as royalty, celebrities, top executives, and politicians rub shoulders in cramped quarters. There is no pretentiousness here—coats are strewn everywhere, table settings are plain, and guests so crowded together that it is a challenge for anyone, even waiters, to move about. And yet even the king of Spain dines here. Why? Because the mood is convivial and the simple, homespun food, prepared with pristine ingredients, reminds everyone of home and hearth. The baby lamb chops, succulent garlic chicken, rib-sticking bean stews, and fried eggs are for every Spaniard comfort foods beyond compare—a welcome relief from the dizzying flavors and exotic ingredients in so many of Madrid's trendsetting restaurants.

Even Spain's greatest chefs in their leisure time prefer the dishes passed down to them by their *mamás* and *yayas*. They are invariably simple and down-to-earth foods (a Spanish chef I know once gathered garlic, onion, tomato, and peppers on his chopping board and declared, "This is Spanish cooking"). Indeed, what could be more basic than one of Spain's most beloved dishes, *tortilla española*, made from nothing more than egg, potato, and olive oil, or irresistible *tortas de aceite*, short wafers with just two principal ingredients: flour and olive oil.

But it is the special touches that each cook imparts to even the most tradition-bound dishes that spark my interest—because traditional does not imply uniformity and lack of variety. And although I have been exploring Spanish cooking for thirty-five years, I am surprised that many of the family recipes I have recently collected from Spanish friends and family are not merely variations on dishes I have loved for years, but recipes firmly rooted in the past that have never crossed my path before.

Take the stewed potatoes with pork ribs that Antonia Rollón prepared for a group of American gourmets who traveled with me to the Bodegas Fariña winery. It was a dish Antonia learned at her grandmother's knee, and my travelers were swept away by these potatoes, heaping their plates with seconds and thirds. We were nearing the end of a trip that had included some of Spain's most fashionable and renowned restaurants, and yet this peasant dish was the meal that all agreed was the most memorable.

Here at home my friend Pilar Vico, who hails from Albacete in La Mancha, shared with me her mother's handwritten recipe collection. Several recipes caught my eye—one, an intriguing preparation of pork loin simmered in sweet sherry and another, a fish soup seasoned with cumin, both of which show the lingering influence of the long Moorish domination of Spain.

Another good friend in Spain, Mari Carmen Martín, loaned me a treasured volume inherited from her mother, who grew up in the region of Valencia; Paco Nuñez de Prado, who comes from a long line of estate olive oil producers, gave me his heirloom recipes, which naturally rely on the family's sublime olive oil. A Spanish monk in the town of Guadalupe in the western region of Extremadura, in charge of the kitchen for his order and the inn of the sixteenth-century monastery, gave me several recipes passed down from his priestly elders; Juan Mari Arzak, who two decades ago began the creative food movement in Spain, graciously showed me his mother's recipes that inspired his celebrated cooking. Even our travel group's bus driver, Jesús Muñoz, told me about his favorite recipe: sautéed bread bits with chorizo sausage and hot green peppers *(migas)* that his grandmother made, and he described how the family would sit around a table and partake from a common dish. And Ferran Adrià, whose culinary innovations have brought him world acclaim, still loves to go home to eat his mother's simple foods. Surprisingly, the recipes he gave me were among the simplest I received, like this one from his mother: "Break open and hull baby lima beans. Eat raw, alternating with strips of dried salt cod, and accompany with a glass of Priorato wine."

Historically, Spain was a poor country, and as I collected these recipes I was constantly amazed to see how home cooks so brilliantly coaxed flavor from the simplest foods. They created wonders from a paucity of ingredients—infinitely more difficult than when products from all over the world are at your beck and call. That to me is cooking at its finest, and such ingenuity born of necessity is what makes Spanish cooking so wonderful.

I have always been fascinated by the ancient origins of so many of Spain's great dishes. Some recipes come straight from Greek and Roman cooking, like *garum* (see page 27) and *alioli* (see page 186). Other dishes were influenced by ingredients introduced to Spain by the conquering Moors who ruled the country for almost eight hundred years. They brought rice, saffron, nutmeg, cumin, and oranges, for example, and were fond of sweet and savory mixtures. Sometimes they used such unusual combinations of ingredients that the dishes could be mistaken for creations of an imaginative modern-day chef.

When the Jews and Moors were expelled in the fifteenth century, a wave of religious fervor gripped Spain and translated into a proliferation of convents and monasteries, institutions known in the past—and many even today—for their fine cooking. To this day, nuns are the guardians of many of Spain's finest sweet confections ("Spanish cooking is filled with garlic and religious preoccupations," says Spanish writer Julio Camba). At about the same time, tomatoes, peppers, potatoes, corn, and chocolate were brought to Spain from the New World. So many great Spanish dishes would be unthinkable without these products.

Indeed, history, as well as climate and geography, accounts for the great diversity of foods and food preparations in Spain. Spain encompasses soaring snowcapped peaks, vast plains, thick forests, deserts, and wetlands, all in a country no larger than Texas. Because of the imposing mountain ranges that crisscross the country and physically carve up Spain, each of the country's seventeen regions is a cultural and culinary world unto itself. The cooking of Castilla is based on beans and baby roasts; the Basque Country is famed for its fine fish in unique sauces; in Galicia the emphasis is on savory pies and shellfish; in Valencia, paellas and other rice dishes reign supreme; in Catalunya, pasta takes on greater importance (Barcelona was the port of entry in the sixteenth and seventeenth centuries for products coming from Spain's Italian possessions); and Andalucía is noted for its tapas and gazpachos. Everywhere, however, cooking is market based, and central food markets continue to play an important role in everyday life.

La Cocina de Mamá compiles treasured family recipes collected from my Spanish friends, family, and acquaintances, as well as recipes I uncovered in centuries-old cookbooks—recipes, in many cases, remarkably similar to those made today. The number of recipes I received for chicken, pork loin, and soups, for example, are indicative of the foods eaten most often in Spanish homes (except for fish, which is indeed eaten at home but most often simply grilled or fried). My task was never merely to transcribe. Many recipes came to me in the crudest forms—in all but indecipherable script and with the most rudimentary instructions—a pinch of this, a handful of that, no weights, no specific quantities. To develop coherent recipes I needed to use intuition and rely on my general knowledge of Spanish cooking.

Patterns began to emerge. Time and time again I was given recipes that included ñoras—dried sweet red peppers—to intensify flavors of stews and sauces. Although I have always said that pasta plays a minor role in Spanish cooking, pasta dishes appeared in regions in which I had no idea they existed. It also became evident that just about every Spanish home cook relies on the mortar and pestle to extract an extra measure of flavor. Take my word: there is nothing like a mortar and pestle to put you in the mind-set of the past and to achieve the authentic taste of Grandma's cooking.

Spanish cooking is based on olive oil, and plenty of it is used—to sauté, to fry, to marinate, and even to use in making desserts. Please do get over your fear of frying. Olive oil is a monounsaturated fat and Spain has the third highest life expectancy in the world. Deep-frying is common all over the country, but when the frying is done with olive oil and the temperature is controlled, the oil absorption is minimal. Lard, a nasty word to many cooks, is another fat preferred in Spain and, in fact, it has less saturated fat than butter and creates wonderfully flaky pastries, pastry doughs, and cookies, while also subtly imparting its characteristic flavor.

I have accompanied many recipes with profiles or casual chats with those who contributed recipes. Their fond remembrances of their native land, family traditions, holiday meals, and the importance of food in their upbringing make this much more than an impersonal collection of recipes. Family recipes, indeed, give a portrait of a society and of a way of life. A deep-seated appreciation and respect for quality ingredients is obvious even at humble tables. Everyday meals continue to be special occasions for family and friends to gather, and an extraordinary amount of time is spent over lunch and dinner. I might add that Spanish wines are, naturally, an integral part of every meal.

Undoubtedly a revolution has taken place in Spanish restaurants and in Spanish attitudes toward food. Creative cooking has taken the country by storm—and by surprise—in recent years, and in so doing, revived a yearning for the past and for tradition. Unquestionably, most Spaniards still prefer the country's hearty country cooking, clearly evident at restaurants like Casa Lucio. When my husband and I travel to Spain we are irresistibly drawn to such down-to-earth restaurants and to simple tapas bars.

Travel to Spain by Americans has increased by leaps and bounds in recent years. Those of you who enjoy using my cookbooks as travel guides will find many vignettes of people and places that I have collected during my travels. On the tours that my husband and I lead, we see the passion that Spain and its foods inspire in our travelers. They return home with a desire to reproduce the wonderful flavors of Spain in their own kitchens. Not surprisingly, Spanish food products imported to the United States have increased dramatically, including ingredients that I could not have recommended in my previous books. Artisan cheeses, boutique olive oils, regional wines, exceptional Serrano ham and chorizo sausage, unique smoked paprika, Spanish *piquillo* red peppers, and Valencian rice, to give a few examples, are now relatively easy to find.

Spanish cooking is a compendium of dishes spanning millennia. To me it is a universal truth that traditional foods are those that everyone turns to for comfort and appealing taste that never become tiresome. Great chefs, after all, do not emerge from thin air. Rather, they are the products of long years of learning, albeit unconsciously, at the knee of their mothers and grandmothers—caretakers of Spanish culinary traditions. In short, I am sure that these recipes will appeal to even the most sophisticated among us.

GREAT WINES FROM SPAIN: EXCITEMENT IN A BOTTLE

In the two-thousand-year history of Spanish wine making, never has there been a moment like now for the wines of Spain. A revolution is under way, and perhaps the most exciting wines in the world today are coming from Spain. Wine critics agree that Spain is on the move, setting incredibly high standards and producing wines of a quality and variety beyond compare. Spanish wines today are hot—red hot—and Americans are finally taking notice of the exploding Spanish wine scene.

Although Rioja and Ribera del Duero wines—and it goes without saying, sherry wines, among the world's oldest—have long been the aristocrats of Spanish wines, they are facing stiff competition from once laid-back regions that have suddenly come alive. A good case in point are the wines of La Mancha, traditionally crudely made jug wines served in Madrid taverns by the glass for pennies and used to make sangría. Seemingly overnight, quality bodegas have sprouted everywhere in La Mancha, and its wines compete with the finest. Similarly, the wines of Rías Baixas and Ribeira Sacra in Galicia, the wines of the Priorat region of Catalunya, and Toro wines from Zamora in Castilla were once strictly for local consumption and have all become serious contenders in the world wine market. Even Aragón's red Cariñena wines, which used to be so robust (over 14 percent alcohol) they were not deemed fit for ladies, have been significantly refined. I remember twenty-five years ago my husband, Luis, and I entered a bar in the town of Cariñena and asked for two glasses of wine; he was given a glass of red but I got a sweetish white wine. The reds, the bartender insisted, were only for men.

Indeed, no region of Spain has been left untouched, and there are so many outstanding wines on the market today from up-and-coming wineries that I have trouble keeping track. It seems as if every day a new bodega emerges to rave reviews. Controlled conditions and advanced technical know-how are responsible for this dramatic development. And because of the care with which Spanish wines are made, today there are an astonishing sixty-three wine regions worthy of the Spanish government's Denomination of Origin status, when just fifteen years ago there were a mere thirty-six. Best of all, Spanish wines have maintained their uniquely earthy Spanish taste that I have always loved.

While Spanish wineries have always been partial to blending grapes, the blends today are often of great native Spanish grapes, like Garnacha, Tempranillo, and Graciano, with popular foreign varietals, like Chardonnay, Merlot, and Cabernet Sauvignon. To experience Spanish wines at their finest, however, seek out those that stubbornly stick to traditional varietals and use traditional methods. That generally means barrel aging and at least two more years in bottle in the bodegas before release to the public. If the wines are the highly prized *reservas* and *gran reservas*, aging could extend another five years or more.

Every day there are more Spanish wines available to the American public, and prices generally remain more than reasonable. And yet, local wine shops most often have a pitiful selection and restaurant menus ofttimes do not list even one Spanish wine—or at best offer one or two (that's your cue to order them—more likely than not, they will be excellent wines at reasonable prices). In the meantime your best bet for finding a good selection for your home bodega is to purchase online (see Sources, page 293).

When it comes to pairing wines with food, rules have been thrown to the wind. The days of white wine with fish and red wine with meat are long gone. Whatever pleases you is more than acceptable. But to my taste nothing complements Spanish cooking like the wines of Spain that spring from the very same earth. Seek out in particular elegant Albariño whites from Rías Baixas in Galicia from, for example, Filaboa and Fefiñanes bodegas; rosés *(rosados)* from Navarra, such as those made by Chivite; extraordinary reds from such bodegas as Montecillo, Artadi, and Marqués de Cáceres in La Rioja; wines of Ribera del Duero in northern Castilla from bodegas like Mauro, Vega Sicilia, Pesquera, and a host of others. In the Toro Denomination of Origin in the Castilian province of Zamora, Gran Colegiata from Bodegas Fariña is tops, as is L'Ermita in the Priorat region of Catalunya.

Adding to the variety of wines produced in Spain are Cavas, as the exceptional sparkling wines made by the *méthode champenoise* are called. Some of the best come from Freixenet.

Uniquely Spanish sherry is in a category of its own. A fortified wine, it ranges from bone-dry manzanilla and fino, served chilled as an aperitif, to medium-dry amontillado, medium-sweet oloroso, and syrupy sweet Pedro Ximénez cream sherry, appropriate with or after dessert. All of these sherries are made by such fine bodegas as Osborne and Gonález Byass, and since the wines are a blend of vintages, quality is uniformly excellent.

Take this opportunity to explore the wines from Spain, and I am sure you will agree that they are well worth your while. I have no doubt that you will become as big a fan of Spanish wines as I have been for the past thirty years. *¡Salud!*

Neverías INGENIOUS SUBTERRANEAN FREEZERS

I always enjoy visiting the town of Alcañiz in Aragón. Its elegant Plaza de España, uniquely built on uneven terrain to conform to the steep rise of the land, is surrounded by exceptional structures. The lovely Renaissance Town Hall, a fine example of austere and harmonious Aragonese civil architecture, and the galleried fifteenth-century Commodities Exchange (La Lonja) both face the square. Rising above the town, the parador, a magnificent twelfth-century walled castle, is one of my favorite places to stay in this unusual part of Aragón, known as El Maestrazgo, an isolated area of abrupt mountains, dramatic gorges, and startling precipices. Strange rock formations take familiar and fantastic shapes and are almost impossible to distinguish from man-made stone villages and ruined castles.

When I returned to Alcañiz recently, an intriguing new attraction had been uncovered: ancient subterranean passageways, carved from living rock, that connect the town's historic buildings. Accessed by way of the Town Hall, this veritable labyrinth, which most likely dates to Moorish times, was used as a place of refuge, as a city water cistern, and also as a *nevería*.

The Moors, a desert people, were fascinated by snow and ice. In the mid-sixteenth century, well over a century after the Moors were expelled from Spain, chilled drinks, sherbets (the word is of Arab origin), and ice cream continued to be all the rage in the wilting heat of Spanish summers. Thanks to deep underground storage areas, such as the *nevería* in Alcañiz and others near the tiny village of Fuendetodos (birthplace of Francisco Goya) that are freestanding stone structures, mountain snow, compacted into ice bars, would stay frozen well into the summer. Ice was also important medicinally for its ability to alleviate fever, hemorrhage, and inflammation.

A flourishing trade developed carrying snow and ice, covered with straw to maintain the temperature, from the surrounding mountains to be stored in the *nevería* (you can still see the chutes where the snow was channeled underground). By 1726 a city ordinance decreed that these tradesmen must "give neighbors and travelers all the ice they need . . . and they have to sell it day and night during the months of June, July, and August from dawn until eleven at night, and for sick people at any hour." The *neverías* remained in use until the nineteenth century.

The recipes for spiced wine and lemonade that follow are delicious, refreshing reminders of the Moorish and Renaissance passion for ice-cold refreshments.

ALOJA DE NIEVE ❧ SPICED LEMONADE

makes 7 cups

1 cup honey

2 cups freshly squeezed lemon juice

2 peeled quarter-size slices fresh ginger

4 cloves

A generous grating of nutmeg

1 cinnamon stick

Place the honey in a pitcher and gradually add 4 cups water, stirring to blend. Add the lemon juice, ginger, cloves, nutmeg, and cinnamon. Cover and refrigerate overnight. It keeps refrigerated for weeks and gains in flavor the longer the ingredients marinate together. Before serving, strain.

HIPOCRÁS ❧ SPICED CHILLED WINE

Emperor Charles V (King Charles I of Spain), like his contemporary Henry VIII of England, enjoyed lavish meals ending with desserts and a spiced wine called Hipocrás. It later became known in Spain as garrapiñado, which was most likely the refreshing precursor of sangría, albeit with the addition of wonderful aromatics from medieval times, like ginger, cloves, nutmeg, cinnamon, and orange blossom water. Hipocrás can be made with either red or white wine, although I think it is much finer with white. It will keep for months in the refrigerator and gains in flavor the longer it is kept. **serves 4**

One 24-ounce bottle dry white or red wine

2 peeled quarter-size slices fresh ginger

5 cloves

2 tablespoons sugar

2 tablespoons orange blossom water (available in Italian delicatessens)

1/2 teaspoon freshly ground nutmeg

1 cinnamon stick

2 lemon slices

1 small ripe peach, nectarine, or apple, cut into wedges

Combine all the ingredients in a large glass jar or plastic container. Let sit overnight, but preferably longer, in the refrigerator. To serve, strain, returning the fruit pieces to the wine. Serve very well chilled—no ice cubes, please.

THE SPANISH PANTRY

To purchase any of these food products or cooking equipment, see Sources (page 293).

ALIOLI   An emulsion of olive oil and garlic, sometimes with a touch of egg. You can make your own (page 186) or buy bottled.

ALMONDS, MARCONA   Spain's rounded almonds—the aristocrats of almonds—distinctively sweet with a delicate flavor. Buy already roasted in olive oil or blanched and fry them yourself.

ANCHOVIES   Anchovies vertically packed in olive oil and in bottles are usually superior to those in tins. Spain's best anchovies come from the north—from the Mediterranean in Catalunya and the Cantabrian Sea in the Basque Country. When anchovies are fresh they are known as *boquerones* (see page 48) and if marinated in vinegar, they become a popular tapa called *boquerones en vinagre*.

ASPARAGUS, WHITE   The region of Navarra has long been celebrated for its white asparagus, painstak-ingly grown by covering young shoots with earth to prevent them from turning green. Spaniards insist that canned or bottled white asparagus is far superior to fresh—which is often the case, since fresh white asparagus rapidly loses quality, and factory-processed asparagus are cooked at their peak of freshness and flavor. White asparagus is most often served with a vinaigrette or mayonnaise as a salad course or used as a salad ingredient.

BACALAO   Spaniards adore salt cod, even though fresh fish in Spain is extraordinary. I don't recommend cod that has been sitting around for months in local greengrocers or delis (just because the cod is dried no one has a license to mistreat it). Look for cod that is white, not yellow, and desalt according to recipe instructions. The loin section is considered choice. Dried cod can also be bought vacuum sealed.

BEANS, DRIED   Spanish dried beans are of the highest quality and are grown in several varieties you are not likely to find on supermarket shelves. Chick-peas (*garbanzos*) are among Spain's favorite beans and a key ingredient in Spain's *cocido* (page 118).

Oversized kidney-shaped beans (*judiones*) and other large white beans like *fabas asturianas* are favored in Spanish bean stews. Beans the size of a pea are popular in Catalunya and sometimes served as a vegetable side course (page 80), and red beans (*caparrones*) are preferred in the Basque Country. Spanish lentils are not processed for fast cooking but are superior in taste and texture to lentils found in supermarkets. They will need an overnight soaking, like any other dried beans.

CANELONES   Dried pasta squares, which in Spanish cooking are boiled, then filled, typically with meat, and rolled.

CAPERBERRIES   The fruit of the caper bush that forms once the flowers have faded. They make great tapas.

CAPERS   The flower buds of the caper bush that proliferates in warm Mediterranean climates. When the buds are at their smallest they are known as nonpareil capers and are very attractive in salads and marinades. But the quality is no different from larger, less expensive capers.

Capers are typically bottled in brine but are also available dried in sea salt. Chefs prefer the salted capers because when desalted they are more flavorful.

CHEESES   The variety of Spanish cheeses, many of which are imported to the United States, is remarkable. Among the most popular are:

Queso Manchego A unique sheep's milk cheese that is quickly finding a niche in America (I can even find it in my suburban butcher shop and in local supermarkets). It may be semicured and relatively mild, or well cured and slightly sharp.

Queso Cabrales and Queso de Valdeón Blue cheeses that are less pungent than Roquefort and perhaps most similar to Gorgonzola. They are made with a mixture of sheep's, goat's, and cow's milk and are naturally blue from aging in caves in the mountains of the Picos de Europa. Cabrales comes from the northern, damper side of the mountains and is a softer cheese, while Valdeón is made in the drier western face of the mountain range and has a more solid consistency.

Queso Torta del Casar and Queso Torta de La Serena Two very similar cheeses from Extremadura, soft and runny—mild but with a bite—made with sheep's milk and unlike any other cheese you have ever tasted. Both have caused a sensation among cheese experts the world over.

Queso Roncal Made in the Spanish Pyrenees from sheep's milk. It is somewhat similar to Manchego and can be semicured or well cured.

Queso de Maó (Mahón) A cow's milk cheese from the island of Menorca—semisoft with a unique flavor, but somewhat like Gouda.

Queso de Tetilla Cow's milk cheese from Galicia in the shape of a woman's breast (thus its name) that is mild and creamy but with a slight pungency.

Queso Idiazábal Made in the Basque Country from sheep's milk, semicured and usually smoked.

CLAMS AND MUSSELS, CANNED Among other wonderful Spanish fish products are cockles in brine *(berberechos al natural)* and pickled mussels *(mejillones en escabeche),* both of which make tasty tapas.

HAM, CURED Spaniards have a love affair with *jamón*—simply thin sliced as a tapa or as an ingredient in everything from sautéed vegetables to bean stews. Serrano ham *(jamón serrano)* from the domestic white pig, is Spain's everyday cured ham, but its flavor

is rich and its texture excellent. It is now available imported from Spain.

Most ham lovers agree that no other cured ham in the world can compare to *jamón ibérico* made from free-range native Iberian pigs that feast on acorns (the ham acquires a slightly nutty flavor). Efforts are in progress to bring this exquisite ham to the United States. Let's hope that time is not far away.

LARD Don't even think about using commercially produced, supermarket lard. It is hydrogenated and has an unpleasant taste—a far cry from the real thing. Spanish cookies and savory pie crusts are generally made with lard, and they are flaky and irresistible.

MARÍA BISCUITS Spain's favorite cookies, which are not overly sweet and are appropriate to eat on their own, dunk in coffee or hot chocolate, or use to make refrigerator dessert logs (page 277).

MEMBRILLO Quince preserves are well loved in Spain as a dessert, typically accompanied by Manchego cheese. Also popular as an afternoon snack for children with bread.

Seductive Iberian Ham

Rarely have I eaten a meal in Spain that does not begin with a communal plate of thinly sliced *jamón ibérico,* which typically disappears in the blink of an eye. And invariably that ham brings to mind our first face-to-face encounter many years ago with a free-range Iberian pig. While driving through the mountains of Aracena, an area in western Andalucía covered with cork and holm oak trees, we spot an Iberian pig and stop to admire it. For this is no ordinary pig, mind you. This pig is perfectly clean and—dare I say—beautiful. Taupe colored with a pronounced snout, long floppy ears, and a muscular compact body with long slim legs that taper to black hooves, this noble and ancient breed native to Spain retains many characteristics of its wild boar ancestors.

The pig rushes to greet us without a trace of fear, as docile and friendly as a pet dog, and in no time dozens of pigs in a snorting frenzy appear from the bushes and surround us. We wonder why we are the objects of such desire, when out of nowhere a man in blue overalls with the weathered face of a Spanish field worker appears. Crestfallen, we realize the pigs had mistaken us for their keeper and have now lost all interest in us. With a long stick he shakes an oak tree, knocking down acorns for the ravenous pigs. In the fall acorns are the steady diet of the Iberian pig and are responsible for the faintly nutty taste of Iberian ham.

Some years ago we saw a Spanish film entitled *Jamón Jamón* in which a muscle-bound young man named Raúl, who delivers cured hams for a living, overtakes deliciously sultry Silvia and attempts to seduce her with the line "You are more luscious than ham." Not very romantic, you may say, but this farce, intertwining ham with love, life, and death (the movie ends when Raúl bludgeons Silvia's fiancé with a whole ham) is not so far-fetched, at least from a Spanish point of view. Spaniards, you see, have an ongoing love affair with *jamón*—in particular salt-and-air-cured *jamón ibérico* with its sensual earthiness and multifaceted flavor. To them, it is to die for.

OLIVE OILS   I consider olive oils from Spain to be the world's finest. Ideal growing conditions and a vast variety of terrains, be it to the north in Catalunya or in southern Andalucía, produce so many varietals that tasting Spanish oils is a never-ending trip of discovery. There are oils for every taste and every purpose—olive oils from deep green and incredibly fruity to golden and mild. Not surprisingly, each region of the country prefers its locally produced oil—after all, it springs from the same earth as its foods and seems to create the perfect balance of flavors.

In Andalucía the oils of choice are green and wonderfully fruity, like those made from the *picudo, picual,* and *hojiblanca* varietals (most agree that *hojiblanca* is perfect for gazpachos, and all three are great for salads and marinades). In Catalunya, fragrant but mild *arbequina* oils are preferred, and there are also great olive oils from Aragón and Castilla. Try as many as possible, and find those that suit you best.

Contrary to popular belief, olive oil is ideal for deep-frying. It quickly coats foods to prevent the oil from penetrating and has a high smoking point. For frying and for general cooking needs, use mild olive oil (those oils labeled "pure") rather than extra virgin, since heat destroys the lovely nuances of top-quality virgin oils. Save your finest extra virgin oils for salads and marinades.

OLIVES   Olive varietals that make the best oils do not always produce great table olives. A case in point are *manzanilla* olives—those we commonly find in supermarkets—which are generally not used to make oil. There is no reason, however, to limit yourself to well-known *manzanilla* olives (although I do especially like them stuffed with anchovies). Tiny *arbequinas* are also great eating olives, and although the variety of Spanish table olives available here is not extensive, when in Spain be sure to try olives wherever you travel.

PAPRIKA (PIMENTÓN)   An extremely important flavor in Spain's cooking—far from being a mere color accent sprinkled on food. Smoked paprikas from Extremadura, which have their own Denomination of Origin (see page 71), are prized by serious cooks for their pronounced earthy flavor and range from sweet (*dulce*) to bittersweet (*agridulce*) to hot (*picante*). Using the authentic product will give added zest to stews, paellas, and grilled meats.

PEPPERS, DRIED RED   There are many kinds of dried red peppers in Spain. *Ñoras, pimientos romescos,* and *pimientos choriceros* are sweet, not hot, and one of the secrets of great Spanish home cooking. They may be mashed in a mortar, added to a stew pot after the core is removed with kitchen shears and the seeds shaken out, or presoaked before the flesh is scraped from the skin. Their taste can be roughly reproduced with a combination of paprika and pimiento, but I strongly recommend purchasing the real thing.

Guindillas are dried chile peppers—hot but not fiery and akin to Mexican *guajillo* chiles. In Spanish cooking hot peppers are used only as an accent, as in *Clams in Garlic Sauce* (page 53).

PEPPERS, JARRED OR CANNED Tops in this category are *pimientos del piquillo*, grown in a small microclimate in Navarra with its own Denomination of Origin and wood roasted. Small with a delicate flesh and slightly piquant, they are often stuffed with meat or fish, but are extraordinary simply cut in strips and combined with olive oil and garlic. If you substitute ordinary pimientos, you can greatly improve the flavor by rinsing off the brine, covering them with olive oil, and letting them sit an hour or more. Less known but also excellent are *guindillas vascas,* moderately hot, pencil-thin green peppers bottled in wine vinegar. They are a great accompaniment to Basque bean dishes.

RICE Spanish cooking calls for short-grain rice, which comes from three principal regions: Valencia, in the area between the Turia and Júcar rivers; Calasparra, near the Segura River in the mountains of Murcia; and from the silted land near the mouth of the Ebro River in the Tarragona region of Catalunya. Each of these regions also produces celebrated *arroz bomba*, a grain that needs very special care to grow but resists overcooking and has a remarkable texture. This rice needs about $3/4$ cup more liquid for every 3 cups rice than other short-grain rice.

SAFFRON The world's costliest spice, introduced to Spain by the Moors in the eighth century, is made from the stigmas of the purple saffron crocus. Saffron gives color as well as unique flavor to foods, and besides its use in paellas, it is an ingredient in many Spanish stews. In Spain the best saffron comes from a microclimate in La Mancha around the village of Membrilla. Always buy saffron in strands to better judge quality (the strands should be uniformly deep red) and most important, buy from a reputable source.

SALT, KOSHER AND SEA Get used to using these coarse salts—they really do make a difference. In Spanish cooking meats and fish are usually salted before cooking to bring out flavor—especially important to bring back the briny taste of the sea to fish and shellfish. When sprinkled over food, coarse salt distributes more evenly and does not penetrate like fine salt.

SAUSAGES, CURED   Spaniards dearly love their sausage products, and each region has its specialties. Chorizo, a sausage seasoned with paprika and garlic, is found all over the country. When well cured it is simply sliced and eaten as a tapa, or it can be sautéed and speared on bread cubes. Semicured chorizo, also known as cooking chorizo, gives wonderful flavor to stews and hearty soups.

Two subcategories of chorizo are semicured *chistorra*, a Basque sausage eaten sautéed for breakfast or as a tapa (page 50), and *sobrasada*, a delicious soft spreadable chorizo from the Balearic Islands that also makes a magnificent tapa (page 30) and a filling for pork cutlets (page 226). *Lomo embuchado*, although not in fact a sausage, is a delicious cured pork loin seasoned like chorizo.

In Catalunya *salchichón de Vic* and *fuet* are popular salami-like sausages, and *morcilla* black sausage is found all over the country, typically seasoned with onion or mixed with rice. It can be sliced and fried as a tapa or used in stews like *cocido* (page 118).

SHERRY   Besides being an outstanding drinking wine, sherry—in its full range from dry to sweet—lends a unique flavor to Spanish sauces and desserts.

TOMATE FRITO   A popular item in the Spanish pantry, this canned cooked tomato sauce includes sugar to counteract the tomato's acidity and olive oil for flavor.

TUNA, CANNED AND JARRED   White tuna (bonito) from Spain is of extraordinarily high quality and packed in solid pieces with nothing more than olive oil and salt. Salt-cured tuna loin (*mojama*) is prized in salads or on its own.

TURRÓN   Spain's almond and honey nougat candy that may be crackling hard (Alicante style) or soft (Gijona style). Other varieties are made with chocolate, toasted egg yolk, and coconut. Gijona style is exceptionally good sprinkled over or incorporated into vanilla ice cream.

VINEGARS   In the Spanish kitchen, two kinds of vinegar are commonly used: sherry vinegar, among the

An Ode to Love

Spain has been devoted to pigs ever since the end of the fifteenth century, when the sign of a good Christian was the consumption of pork products. Jews and Moors, both of whom rejected pork in their diets, had been expelled from Spain and a religious fervor gripped the country. Today the love for pork products continues unabated. Cured ham is a national obsession, and chorizo sausage is an integral part of Spain's traditional cooking. Pork can even inspire verse, as in this graffiti on a stone wall in Villanueva de Los Infantes in the region of La Mancha, dedicated to a girl named Merche:

Merche—	Merche—
Si el amor que puse en ti,	If the love I gave to you,
Lo hubiese puesto en un gorrino,	I had given to a pig,
Ahora estaría comiendo,	I could be eating today,
Buenas tajadas de tocino	Nice thick slabs of bacon

But my favorite pig tale takes place in La Alberca in Salamanca province, an incredibly beautiful mountain village declared a national monument in its entirety, in a region with a long tradition of curing hams and sausages. It is a glorious autumn day, and we leave our car to take a stroll through the village. In the cobbled main square we pause to admire its stone porticoes and flower-laden wood balconies, from which peppers are hanging to dry. Our attention turns to a sign over a doorway that reads "Public Jail"—a place undoubtedly centuries old and no longer in use. To our surprise, in front of the prison a decidedly well-fed charcoal gray Iberian pig lolls contentedly, soaking up the afternoon sun. He occasionally arises and takes a casual stroll through town, like, as they say in Spanish, *"Pedro por su casa."* We find out that he belongs to the entire village, a gift from City Hall, and everyone contributes to his well-being.

But, alas, Pedro's days are numbered, for at Christmas he will be raffled, then sent off to pig heaven—to the delight of the winner, who can look forward to ham, pork chops, and sausage for many months to come.

world's greatest vinegars, wonderful in gazpachos and in salads when its assertive flavor is what you are looking for; and an inexpensive mild white wine vinegar found in every Spanish home and used when the bite of a concentrated vinegar is not desired.

SPANISH COOKING EQUIPMENT

CAZUELAS   Earthenware casseroles are ubiquitous in Spain, used both for cooking—in the oven or on top of the stove—and for serving. They come in many sizes, from individual tapa size to large casseroles. Before using for the first time, soak in water for several hours. You might also want to use a flame tamer when placing over direct heat. Foods undoubtedly cook more evenly in *cazuelas* and liquids do not evaporate as easily as in metal cookware. Some say *cazuelas* impart a distinctive flavor to foods. In any case, their rustic look is charming for serving tapas and roasted and simmered dishes, and they retain heat much better than other cookware. Do not subject earthenware to sudden changes in temperature—heat gradually and cool slowly.

CHURRO PRESS   A traditional metal device, like a pastry tube but larger and wider, to make Spanish breakfast fritters *(churros)*.

MORTARS   A mortar holds a place of honor in every Spanish kitchen—be it a rustic village kitchen or a high-tech city kitchen. Nothing beats the mortar and its companion the pestle to unlock flavor, especially from herbs, spices, and garlic. Its purpose is not just to mince and mix but to commingle ingredients in a way that a food processor can never do. If there is any one item you should have to cook Spanish style, it is without question the mortar. The one most commonly used in Spain is charming—bright yellow ceramic, dabbed with green.

PAELLA PANS   The typically wide flat pans with handles are specifically designed to make authentic paellas. Use the inexpensive steel pans (rather than stainless steel) that are used in Valencia, paella's homeland. True, these pans will discolor with use, but because they heat so rapidly, give the best results.

Paella pans at La Pepica, Valencia

CHAPTER 1

TAPAS
the little dishes of spain

ON MY FIRST VISIT TO SPAIN SO MANY YEARS AGO, I lost my heart in Madrid—to Luis, whom I later married, and to tapas. The two events really went hand in hand, beginning that first night when I joined Luis and his friends in making the rounds of the tapas bars and taverns that line the evocative dimly lit streets of Old Madrid. Such tapas as Serrano ham and potato omelet (*tortilla española*) were an integral part of the long, fun-filled evenings I spent in Spain that first summer, and my love for tapas has never diminished. They are what I crave the minute I touch down on Spanish soil.

Tapas to me are a vivid symbol of Spanish spontaneity and the carefree life that so captivated me long ago. In tapas bars (it is said that Spain has more bars than the rest of the European Community combined) food and drink help to create an atmosphere of instant camaraderie. It is always a thrill for me to enter a lively tapas bar and let my eyes take in the spectacular array of tapas on display in earthenware casseroles and on platters along the length of the bar. Just as important as eating the food is becoming engulfed in the warmth and gaiety of a tapas bar, be it in the company of friends or the people you meet while standing at a crowded bar.

Although many a time I have made a meal of tapas, Spaniards generally regard them as appetizer food, and once the midday tapas hour has passed, bars fall into a cheerless silence. Clients return home for lunch—the main meal of the day—or head to restaurants to continue socializing. Bars come to life again around 7:00 P.M. then empty once more as the 10:00 P.M. dinner hour approaches.

Tapas have an uncertain origin, although it is generally thought that they began at least a century ago in western Andalucía's sherry country. Since sherry is a fortified wine, served as an aperitif, it cries out for an accompanying nibble. The custom developed of serving a slice of ham, some olives, or other tidbits on a little plate that covered the mouth of the sherry glass. A cover or lid in Spanish is called a *tapa*, and thus the word became associated with appetizer food.

From this humble beginning, an enormous variety of tapas emerged, and each region of Spain has its specialties. In Galicia, empanadas (pizza-size savory pies), tiny fried green peppers, and octopus bathed in olive oil and sprinkled with paprika appear time and time again in tapas bars. In the Basque Country, *pintxos*—complex and beautifully crafted little bites—are labor-intensive wonders. As the capital of Spain, Madrid unites tapas from every region, and they coexist with local favorites like spicy *patatas bravas* and batter-fried cod *(soldaditos de Pavía)*, and in Sevilla—tapas heaven to be sure—exquisite little fish fried to crunchy perfection and foods bathed in cooling vinaigrettes reign supreme. You can serve tapas with any kind of wine or beer. Nevertheless, there is nothing better with tapas than dry fino sherry, the drink that started it all.

Tapas were at first slow to catch on in America. Certainly they were not the boom that was predicted in 1985, the year my book *Tapas: The Little Dishes of Spain* was published. Rather, acceptance was a gradual process that took place over decades. Today tapas have finally become a significant food trend, and tapas bars are sprouting across the nation.

Many of the tapas recipes in this chapter do not, in fact, come from *mamá* but from tapas bars around Spain. Tapas are street food, easy to find anywhere and not likely to be served at home. But tapas are really about portion size—just about any food in small amounts becomes a tapa—so many tapas can become first courses or even main courses. The possibilities are endless. Make several tapas and you have a lively tapas party (a good selection might include one tapa that is marinated, one fried, another in a sauce, and yet another with bread or pastry). Perhaps supplement them with a few instant tapas like those described on the following page. Select one tapa and serve it as a first course, like Clams with Ham and Artichoke Hearts (page 35) or Breaded Mushrooms with *Alioli* (page 42). Or increase the portions of Old-Fashioned Spanish Potato and Tuna Omelet (page 39) or Mini Meatballs in Saffron Garlic Sauce (page 55), and you've got a meal. The beauty of tapas is their enormous flexibility.

Instant Tapas from the Spanish Pantry

Tapas can be as easy as opening a can or a jar. In fact, there are tapas bars in Spain that do nothing more than that, placing the contents on a plate or spearing a variety of these first-rate conservas on toothpicks. Although professed gourmets may scoff at anything from a can, in Spain these products are top notch and treated as delicacies. Here are some suggestions to effortlessly supplement any tapas menu.

- Fry blanched almonds, preferably marcona almonds from Spain, in olive oil. Drain and sprinkle with salt. Or purchase marcona almonds already fried. Watch them disappear in the blink of an eye.
- Top wedges of Manchego cheese with slices of quince preserves *(membrillo)*.
- Make *banderillas* (so called because of their resemblance to their counterparts in the bullring) by spearing on toothpicks or small skewers such jarred products as pitted olives, cocktail onions, pickles, anchovies, pimiento or marinated hot red pepper, and chunks of tuna.
- Slice *piquillo* peppers into strips, combine with minced garlic and extra virgin olive oil, and sprinkle with parsley.
- Open a can of cockles in brine and add a generous squeeze of lemon juice.
- Serve pickled mussels from the can, just as they are.
- Spread green or black Spanish olive pâté on rounds of garlic toast and top with strips of *piquillo* peppers or anchovy fillets.
- Lightly sauté slices of chorizo and spear with a toothpick onto pieces of bread.
- Place a Spanish sardine on a slice of garlic toast (cut from a French-style loaf), top with strips of bottled hot red peppers, and sprinkle with parsley.
- Bring out anchovy-stuffed olives—always a big hit.
- Present a plate of delicious caperberries.

PIQUITOS DE ENRIQUE DACOSTA ❧ ENRIQUE'S BREAD BITES

These small flatbreads serve the same purpose as bread sticks. They are crisp and flaky, and because of the olive oil (use your finest) and salty edge can easily be addictive. Based on centuries-old *tortas de aceite*, they are the specialty of young chef Enrique Dacosta, whose restaurant Poblet in Denia, Alicante, is the best regarded in the region. They are great with tapas.

Instead of making bread dough for this recipe, I simplify by buying pizza dough from my local pizzeria, and the results are excellent.

makes about 15 bites

1/4 pound pizza dough, at room temperature
Kosher or sea salt
4 tablespoons extra virgin olive oil plus more for brushing
About 8 tablespoons flour

Place the dough in a bowl and knead in 1/4 teaspoon salt. Add 1 tablespoon of the oil and 2 tablespoons of the flour and work with your hands to fully incorporate. Repeat three more times for the remaining oil and flour, adding 1 tablespoon oil and 2 tablespoons flour at a time. Turn out on a floured work surface and knead lightly until smooth, adding more flour if the dough is too sticky.

Preheat the oven to 375°F. Roll the dough on a floured surface to 1/8 inch thick and cut with a cookie cutter into crescents or other shapes. Place on a greased cookie sheet, brush with olive oil, and sprinkle lightly with salt. Bake for 15 to 16 minutes, until lightly golden. Turn off the oven and leave in the oven for another 10 minutes to fully crisp.

PAN CON TOMATE Y ANCHOA ❧
GARLIC, OLIVE OIL, AND FRESH TOMATO ON TOASTED BREAD

Nothing could be more simple and down to earth than this tapa, but its appeal is universal. It originated in Catalunya, but can now be found all over Spain. In fact, I will never forget a breakfast of exceptional *pan con tomate* and steaming *café con leche* at an outdoor café overlooking the mountains of Granada in Galera, a town of cave dwellings. The recipe that follows has the advantage of last-minute assemblage, so the bread doesn't get soggy. Since ingredients are few, it goes without saying that the very best tomatoes, extra virgin olive oil, and anchovies are essential.

If last-minute preparation is not a problem, I suggest the even simpler traditional method of toasting the bread, rubbing it with a cut clove of garlic, then rubbing with a cut tomato, squeezing the tomato gently as you rub. Drizzle with oil and sprinkle with salt.   serves 4

1^{1}/2 pounds very ripe and flavorful tomatoes, preferably plum tomatoes, split in halves crosswise

2 large garlic cloves, mashed to a paste

4 tablespoons best-quality fruity extra virgin olive oil, plus more for drizzling

Kosher or sea salt

Good-quality French-style loaf, split in half and halves cut into 4-inch lengths

8 to 16 best-quality anchovy fillets, preferably jarred, optional

With a coarse grater held over a bowl grate the tomatoes down to the skin. Pour off any excess liquid. Add the garlic, olive oil, and salt to taste (the mixture should be well seasoned). Let sit for a few minutes to meld flavors.

Lightly toast the split bread and drizzle with olive oil. Pour the tomato mixture into a serving bowl and arrange the bread and anchovies, if using, on plates. Let each guest spread the tomato mixture on the bread and top it off with one or two anchovy fillets.

QUESO MANCHEGO CON ACEITUNAS Y PIQUILLOS ❧
MANCHEGO CHEESE CANAPÉS WITH OLIVES AND *PIQUILLO* PEPPERS

An extremely easy tapa to assemble that comes straight from El Corregidor, the most delightful bar and restaurant in the region of La Mancha, where Manchego cheese is made and windmills from the times of the Errant Knight Don Quixote still stand.

makes 24 canapés

One $1^3/_4$-inch wedge (about $^1/_2$ pound) Manchego cheese

30 cured black olives, pitted and chopped

$^3/_4$ cup chopped *piquillo* peppers (see Pantry, page 15), or pimientos

6 anchovy fillets

1 tablespoon extra virgin olive oil

Minced fresh parsley

Cut the wedge of cheese lengthwise into $^1/_8$-inch slices to form triangular pieces. In a mortar or mini processor, mash to a paste the olives, *piquillos*, anchovies, and oil.

Spread about $^3/_4$ teaspoon of the mixture on each cheese slice. Sprinkle with parsley and arrange attractively on a serving dish.

CANAPÉ DE GARUM DE CINTA GUTIÉRREZ ⚜
CINTA'S CANAPÉ OF OLIVE, ANCHOVY, AND CAPER PASTE

Our friend Cinta is from the town of L'Escala, just a stone's throw from the impressive ruins of the ancient Greek city of Empúries on the Mediterranean coast. "With a few differences," explains Cinta, "the Romans and the people of the ancient city of Empúries used this mixture as a condiment. We like to spread it on toast rounds as an appetizer." Garum, in fact, was made all over the ancient world and generally refers to a condiment made by fermenting fish in brine. It fell into disuse in Europe but has been reintroduced today into Spanish cooking in a modified form.

Local anchovies, in any case, continue to be a principal ingredient in the Spanish version of garum. Indeed, among the ruins of Empúries are the remains of a factory where anchovies from local waters were salted and preserved. The process continues unchanged today, and the anchovies of L'Escala are famous throughout Spain for their high quality and fine flavor.

makes 16 to 20 canapés

40 small cured black olives, pitted and chopped

4 large anchovy fillets, preferably jarred in olive oil

1 teaspoon capers

1 garlic clove, minced

1 1/2 teaspoons Dijon mustard

1 teaspoon red wine vinegar

1 hard-boiled large egg yolk

4 teaspoons rum

Freshly ground pepper

2 tablespoons extra virgin olive oil

Kosher or sea salt

16 to 20 bread slices, 3/8 inch thick, cut from a French-style loaf

Narrow strips of *piquillo* peppers or pimientos (see Pantry, page 15), optional

In a large mortar, mash to a paste the olives and anchovies, then mash in the capers, garlic, mustard, vinegar, egg yolk, rum, and pepper. Gradually incorporate the olive oil and taste for salt.

Place the bread slices on a cookie tray in a 350°F oven and bake for about 5 minutes, turning once. They should be crusty but not browned. Cool. Spread the olive mix on the bread. Garnish, if you wish, with strips of pimiento.

ESPARDENYES DE PILAR DEL OLMO ⚜
PILAR'S TOMATO, EGGPLANT, PIMIENTO, AND ANCHOVY CANAPÉ

This was the beginning of our perfect meal at El Robost de la Cartoixa in Scala Dei. For this tapa, toast is rubbed with garlic and tomato, as in Pan con Tomate (page 25), and covered with eggplant slices, pimiento strips, and anchovy fillets.

makes about 8 canapés

2 baby eggplants

Kosher or sea salt

Extra virgin olive oil

Freshly ground pepper

8 bread slices, $3/8$ inch thick, cut from a long but not too narrow French-style loaf

1 large garlic clove, cut in half crosswise

1 ripe and flavorful medium tomato, cut in half crosswise

Pimientos, preferably *piquillos* (see Pantry, page 15), cut into sixteen $1/2$-inch strips

16 anchovy fillets

1 tablespoon minced fresh parsley

Preheat the oven to 400°F. Partially remove the skin from the eggplants with a potato peeler. Cut into $1/4$-inch crosswise slices. Place in a colander, sprinkle well with salt, and let drain for 1 hour. Dry between paper towels. Arrange on a baking sheet greased with olive oil, brush the eggplants with olive oil, and sprinkle with salt and pepper. Roast for about 10 minutes, turning once. Cool.

Lightly toast the bread slices. Rub well with the cut edge of the garlic, then rub with the cut tomato, squeezing gently, till the toast has a pink color. Drizzle with olive oil and sprinkle with salt.

Arrange on each toast first the slices of eggplant, then 2 strips of pimiento and 2 anchovies. Sprinkle with parsley and serve.

The village of
Albarracín, Teruel

TOSTADA DE SOBRASADA ✧ SOBRASADA SAUSAGE CANAPÉ

Sobrasada is a soft spreadable chorizo typical of the island of Mallorca. I have always loved it, especially in a grilled sandwich. In tapas bars it was simply spread on a slice of bread and sometimes run under a broiler, as at Bar Cervantes in Madrid. Then suddenly I began to find it in combination with somewhat unlikely ingredients. In Catalunya it appeared in a truly spectacular rendition, drizzled with honey and vinegar and topped with a fried quail egg (the union of *sobrasada* and honey, in fact, was first described by an Augustinian friar from Mallorca in the eighteenth century). In Zaragoza I thoroughly enjoyed *sobrasada* on toast, melted with a slice of soft *Torta del Casar* cheese (a unique Spanish cheese, somewhat similar to Brie or Camembert). In this book, you will also find *sobrasada* in an exceptional main course dish (page 226), sandwiched between breaded pork cutlets.

makes 10 canapés

Version 1

Ten $3/8$- to $1/2$-inch bread slices, cut from a French-style loaf

$1/2$ pound *sobrasada* (see Pantry, page 16), or a soft semi-cured chorizo like Bilbao style, skinned, cut into $1/4$-inch slices

Version 2

Ingredients from Version 1

$2^1/2$ teaspoons honey

$1^1/4$ teaspoons vinegar

Mild olive oil for frying, optional

10 quail eggs, optional

Version 3

Ingredients from Version 1

5 ounces *Torta del Casar* (see Pantry, page 11), Brie, or Camembert, cut into $1/4$-inch slices

To make Version 1, on each slice of bread, spread the *sobrasada*. Place in a 450°F oven for about 4 minutes, until the *sobrasada* is warm and gives off its oil.

To make Version 2, on each slice of bread, spread the *sobrasada*. Combine in a cup the honey and vinegar. Drizzle over the *sobrasada*. Place in the oven, as directed above. If making the fried eggs, keep the bread warm until the eggs are ready.

Pour olive oil into a small skillet to a depth of at least $1/4$ inch and heat until the oil quickly browns a cube of bread. Crack several quail eggs at a time into the skillet. Quickly spoon some hot oil over them to cook and puff the tops. Remove with a pancake turner and hold over paper towels to drain. Place an egg on top of each tapa.

To make Version 3, on each slice of bread, spread the *sobrasada*. Top with a slice of the cheese and place in the oven as directed in Version 1.

PATATERA EXTREMEÑA ❧ SMOKED PAPRIKA AND POTATO SPREAD

I have enjoyed this tasty tapa at the Parador of Plasencia in the region of Extremadura, as well as at the tapas bar La Fábrica in Madrid, although you are not likely to find this regional specialty elsewhere in Spain, and few Spaniards even know it exists. Although in this recipe I have used chorizo, *patatera* is not, in fact, made with chorizo but with cured pork fat (and unless you happen to have a Serrano ham, you are not likely to find that ingredient), so I have substituted chorizo, and the results are just as good.

makes 8 to 10 canapés

$1/2$ medium baking potato, peeled

Kosher or sea salt

1 tablespoon minced onion

1 garlic clove, minced

$1/4$ pound soft semicured chorizo (see Pantry, page 16), skinned and finely chopped

$1/4$ teaspoon paprika, preferably Spanish smoked bittersweet (see Pantry, page 14)

$1/8$ teaspoon hot paprika, preferably Spanish smoked (see Pantry, page 14)

$1/8$ teaspoon dried oregano

8 to 10 bread or toast rounds

Boil the potato in salted water to cover until tender. Cool. In a mortar, mash to a paste the onion, garlic, and $1/8$ teaspoon salt. Add the chorizo and continue to mash, then mash in the potato, the bittersweet and hot paprikas, and the oregano. Spread about 2 teaspoons of the mixture on each of the bread rounds.

PATATAS "ALIÑÁS" DE SALVADOR LUCERO &
SALVADOR'S MARINATED POTATOES WITH TUNA AND EGG

I have known Salvador and his unassuming Bar Bahía in Cádiz for almost three decades, and I am always impressed by his innate good taste and the ease with which he prepares his delicious tapas in a closet-size kitchen. These marinated potatoes are a case in point, a dish served as a tapa and for which he selects a special local vinegar that gives the flavor he looks for and, in fact, makes all the difference. I could never quite capture the taste at home until a friend, Carm Hakan, who was with me in Cádiz, suggested that the vinegar tasted very much like seasoned Asian rice vinegar, which, indeed, is similarly light with a hint of sweetness. It did the trick, and now I taste Cádiz each and every time I prepare this tapa. The potatoes are best when served at room temperature, and of course are also excellent as an accompaniment to a summer meal.

serves 4

$3/4$ pound small to medium white potatoes

Kosher or sea salt

2 tablespoons seasoned rice wine vinegar, or white wine vinegar lightly seasoned with salt and sugar

3 tablespoons extra virgin olive oil

Freshly ground pepper

2 scallions, finely chopped

1 tablespoon minced fresh parsley

1 large hard-boiled egg, sliced

About 2 tablespoons dark- or light-meat tuna in olive oil, preferably Spanish, broken into chunks

Bring the potatoes to a boil in salted water, cover, and cook until tender. Cool slightly, peel, and roughly cut into $1/4$-inch slices. Place in a bowl, and while the potatoes are still hot, fold in the vinegar with a rubber spatula and let sit until the potatoes have cooled.

Fold in the remaining ingredients and leave for at least 1 hour at room temperature before serving.

ALCACHOFAS MARINADAS CON ANCHOAS Y PIQUILLOS
MARINATED ARTICHOKES WITH ANCHOVIES AND *PIQUILLO* PEPPERS

We tasted this simple but exceptional tapa in the local bar in the town of Las Pedroñeras—a totally ordinary place were it not for Manuel de la Osa's top-rated Las Rejas restaurant located there and the town's distinction as the "Garlic Capital of Spain." Indeed, in summer the aroma of garlic greets you as you approach, and braids of garlic are everywhere, drying in the searing sun.

Surprisingly this tapa has no garlic, but it does include several other typically Spanish ingredients like olives, anchovies, and *piquillo* peppers. It can be assembled in minutes from pantry ingredients but is best when left to marinate overnight.   **serves 4 to 6**

Two 6-ounce jars marinated artichoke hearts with their
   marinade
12 small cured black olives
4 large anchovy fillets, cut crosswise in halves or thirds
2 *piquillo* peppers (see Pantry, page 15), or 1 small pimiento,
   cut into long narrow strips
2 tablespoons minced fresh parsley

In a bowl, combine all the ingredients with a rubber spatula. Cover and refrigerate, preferably overnight, to meld flavors.

ALMEJAS CON ALCACHOFAS Y JAMÓN ✤
CLAMS WITH HAM AND ARTICHOKE HEARTS

A delightful marriage of ingredients, each perfectly complementing the others, this dish makes an outstanding first course. Elisa, wife of our cousin, Rafa Salgado, provided the recipe, which comes from her family.   serves 4

Kosher or sea salt

Dried bread crumbs or cornmeal for sprinkling

1^1/2 dozen littleneck clams, smallest available

Juice of 1 lemon plus 2 tablespoons

1 teaspoon flour

6 baby artichokes, 1^1/2 to 2 inches in diameter, or
    6 quartered frozen artichoke hearts

8 tablespoons fruity extra virgin olive oil

1 tablespoon minced fresh parsley

1 tablespoon minced scallion (white part only)

1^1/2 teaspoons chopped fresh rosemary, or ^{1}/4 teaspoon
    dried

1 teaspoon minced fresh dill

^{1}/4 cup Serrano ham or prosciutto cut into julienne strips ^{1}/8
    inch thick, about 1^1/2 inches long

Freshly ground pepper

To remove any impurities from the clams, soak several hours or overnight in the refrigerator in salted water sprinkled with bread crumbs or cornmeal. Rinse well before using.

In a saucepan combine the juice of the one lemon and the flour. Cut off the artichoke stems and remove the thick outer leaves around the base. Clip the tips of the remaining leaves with scissors and rub with 1 tablespoon lemon juice. Cut the artichokes in quarters, place in a pot, and add water to cover. Bring to a boil, cover, and cook over medium heat for 10 to 15 minutes, until the artichokes are tender. For frozen artichokes, cook according to package instructions. Drain and cool. Remove the remaining leaves, leaving only the artichoke hearts.

Rinse the clams and place in a skillet with 3 tablespoons water. Cover and boil until the clams open. Drain the clams, leaving 4 in their shells and saving only the meat of the rest.

In a salad bowl, combine the oil, the remaining 1 tablespoon lemon juice, the parsley, scallion, rosemary, dill, and ham. With a rubber spatula fold in the artichoke hearts and clams and season with salt and pepper to taste. Refrigerate for 1 hour before serving.

To serve, arrange on 4 salad plates and garnish each with a clam in its shell.

PUDIN DE SALMÓN DE MARISÉ ZUBIZARRETA ⚬ MARISÉ'S SALMON PÂTÉ LOAF

Fish "pudin," as these dishes cooked *"al baño maría"* with eggs and milk or cream are called, are a popular first course in Spanish households. Earlier versions often included some bread as a filler—that's how Clara, my Spanish mother-in-law, used to make her "pudin," and it was always a summertime favorite of mine. The fish she used was hake, and in the Basque Country scorpion fish *(krabarroka)*—an ugly fish that looks like a prehistoric monster—is the fish of choice. But my friend Marisé lives in Asturias on the banks of the Cares, an outstanding river for trout and salmon in Asturias, and cooks at the family restaurant, Casa Julián. Her recipe calls for salmon, and it certainly gives the dish a lovely color. It may be garnished with shrimp and is typically served with mayonnaise—in this case I have used Juan Mari Arzak's outstanding mayonnaise made with sherry vinegar.   serves 6 to 8

Butter for greasing

Dried bread crumbs for sprinkling

1 cup dry white wine

2 cups clam juice or water

1 small carrot, scraped and cut into several pieces

1 small leek, well washed and cut into several pieces

2 fresh parsley sprigs

1 bay leaf

Kosher or sea salt

$1/4$ pound medium shrimp in their shells, optional

$3/4$ pound salmon fillet, scorpion fish fillet, or scrod

6 large eggs

2 cups heavy cream

Freshly ground pepper

$2/3$ cup tomate frito (see Pantry, page 16), or canned stewed tomatoes, pureed

Juan Mari Arzak's Sherry Vinegar Mayonnaise

$1^1/2$ tablespoons lightly beaten large egg

1 tablespoon sherry vinegar (see Pantry, page 18)

$1/8$ teaspoon salt

1 cup peanut oil

Grease a $9^{1}/_{4}$ x $5^{1}/_{4}$ x $2^{3}/_{4}$-inch loaf pan with the butter and sprinkle with a light coating of bread crumbs. In a deep skillet, combine the wine, clam juice, carrot, leek, parsley, bay leaf, and salt to taste and bring to a boil. Cover and simmer for 10 minutes. If using the shrimp add them to the skillet and cook for a minute or so, until just cooked through. Shell and reserve.

Add the salmon to the skillet and simmer until just done, about 8 minutes to an inch of thickness. Preheat the oven to 350°F. In a large bowl, whisk the eggs, then whisk in the cream, salt and pepper to taste, and tomato. Flake the fish and stir into the bowl. Pour the fish mixture into the loaf pan and place in a pan of hot water (bain-marie). Transfer to the oven and cook until set, about 1 hour and 20 minutes, or until a toothpick inserted comes out clean. Cool.

To make the mayonnaise, place in a food processor the egg, vinegar, and salt and beat for a minute. With the motor running, drizzle in the oil, stopping occasionally to scrape down the sides if necessary.

Unmold the loaf onto a serving platter. Garnish with the shrimp, if using, and chill. Slice and serve with the mayonnaise.

Tortilla on the Train

My husband, Luis, has fond memories of train rides with his grandfather when they traveled to the coast of Galicia in northwestern Spain for summer vacation or to visit family and friends scattered around the country.

"In the forties, train travel was elegant and the first-class wagons were exquisitely appointed," explains Luis. "Grandfather Victorino and I would dress in our finest and preparation was meticulous. As was the custom, my nanny Pilar would pack a lunch in a large wicker basket. In it was everything we needed for a refined meal-on-the-go, from a tablecloth to glassware, napkins, plates, and cutlery. The menu was immutable: breaded veal cutlets, hake sautéed in a light egg coating a *la romana, tortilla española,* cold cuts like Serrano ham and chorizo, good crusty bread, vine-ripe tomatoes, and fruit at its peak, all of which not only kept well at room temperature, but, as I recall, the cooked foods tasted much better than right out of the skillet.

"When lunch hour arrived, we opened the folding table next to the train window, spread the tablecloth, and set up our repast, which to me was—and still is—food for the gods. Proper etiquette required us to ask fellow riders, 'Would you like some?' although the proper response was always, 'No, thank you. Please enjoy.' However, local sweets, like cookies from Astorga and candied egg yolks from Ávila, purchased from vendors who flooded the stations when the trains refueled or changed tracks, were another story. These were generously passed around for all to partake.

"These stops were also occasions to meet friends and family who lived in nearby towns and villages. They would show up for a quick hello, a brief chat, and a good-bye embrace. By the time we reached our destination our fine clothes were covered in soot—I can still smell the smoke, as if it were yesterday, from the burning coal that fueled the train. These trips were for me unforgettable adventures that I know contributed to my lifelong love for trains and train travel."

ANTIGUA TORTILLA ESPAÑOLA ✿
OLD-FASHIONED SPANISH POTATO AND TUNA OMELET

Tortilla española bears no resemblance to the so-called Spanish omelet—made with peppers and tomatoes—that commonly appears in American cookbooks and on coffee shop menus. And its only connection with Mexican tortillas is its round shape. Although easy to make, it requires a certain technique that you will easily master following the recipe instructions.

Tortilla española is one of the most beloved and ubiquitous dishes in Spain, and it has always been my husband's favorite. We frequently eat it for supper, accompanied by sautéed Spanish piquillo peppers. If you cut out the tuna and herbs from the recipe (and add one more potato), you have the simplest and best-known version of Spain's potato omelet. I often serve it to guests, cut in small squares and speared with toothpicks, as a tapa.

Potatoes, of course, came to Spain by way of America, and I am sure that Spaniards quickly discovered that potatoes and eggs were made for each other. A Spanish food writer who describes Parmentier's experiments with egg and potato dishes in the eighteenth century quips, "It makes me wonder if he was actually trying to make a tortilla española that turned out badly."

serves 8 to 10 as a tapa or 4 for supper

1 cup plus 4 teaspoons mild olive oil

3 medium-large potatoes, peeled and cut into $^1/_8$-inch slices

1 medium-large onion, thinly sliced

Kosher or sea salt

5 large eggs

1 tablespoon minced fresh parsley

1$^1/_2$ teaspoons fresh thyme or chopped rosemary, or $^1/_4$ teaspoon dried

4 ounces good-quality canned white- or light-meat tuna, broken into small pieces

Heat 1 cup of the oil in an 8- or 9-inch skillet (or use a deep-fryer set to 320°F) and add the potato slices one at a time to keep them from sticking together, alternating them with the sliced onion. Sprinkle with salt. Cook over medium heat (the potatoes will "boil" rather than fry in the oil and should not brown), lifting and turning the potatoes occasionally with a pancake turner until they are tender. Drain the potatoes in a colander (or in the deep-fryer basket). Wipe out the skillet.

In a large bowl, beat the eggs lightly with a fork and season with salt. Mix in the parsley, thyme, and tuna, then add the potatoes, pressing them down with a pancake turner to submerge them in the egg. Let sit for 10 minutes at room temperature.

Heat 3 teaspoons of the remaining oil in the skillet

until it reaches the smoking point (the skillet must be very hot). Add the potato and egg mixture and spread it out rapidly in the skillet with the aid of the pancake turner. Lower the heat to medium-high and shake the pan often to prevent sticking. When the tortilla begins to brown, slide it onto a dinner plate, invert another plate over it, and turn the tortilla onto the second plate. Add the remaining teaspoon of oil to the skillet, heat until very hot, reduce the heat to medium, then slide the tortilla back into the skillet. Continue shaking until the tortilla is brown underneath, using the back of the pancake turner to neatly tuck in the edges. Turn once or twice more (the tortilla should remain juicy within). Transfer to a platter and cut into wedges, or for tapas, into small squares.

TORTILLA DE ALCACHOFAS DE JOSEFA ACOSTA ✿
JOSEFA'S ARTICHOKE OMELET

Who would have imagined that a simple omelet of artichoke hearts would leave us hungry for seconds? Master Chef Ferran Adrià, the undisputed world master of revolutionary cooking, waxes poetic over his mother Josefa's artichoke omelet. Despite its few ingredients, it does have its subtleties: the artchoke hearts are briefly sautéed, then left to sit in the beaten egg before the omelet is made. And Ferran advises, "Be sure the omelet remains juicy inside. That's the way my brother and I always liked it." **serves 1**

1 tablespoon olive oil

2 cooked artichoke hearts, quartered

Kosher or sea salt

2 eggs, at room temperature

2 teaspoons minced fresh parsley

Heat the oil in a 6-inch skillet. Sauté the artichokes over medium heat for a minute or so, until they are lightly browned. Sprinkle with salt. Remove the artichokes to a dish to cool, leaving the oil in the skillet.

In a bowl, beat the eggs lightly with a fork and salt to taste. Add the artichokes and let the mixture sit for 5 minutes. Reheat the skillet over high heat, pour in the egg mixture, and spread it evenly in the pan. When the eggs are no longer runny but not completely set, fold the omelet in half, cook a few seconds more (it should remain juicy within), then serve, sprinkled with the parsley and more salt if necessary.

SETAS EMPANADAS CON ALIOLI ❧ BREADED MUSHROOMS WITH *ALIOLI*

These breaded and fried mushrooms are ethereal—a thing of beauty that you couldn't imagine as so special looking at the simple ingredients. I couldn't stop eating them at the Buenaventura tavern in Madrid, and I continue to crave them, although now I am able to reproduce them at home.

Oyster mushrooms are by far the most popular kind of mushroom in Spain, and they are common on tapas menus, simply grilled and sprinkled with garlic and parsley. You can make this recipe with other kinds of mushrooms, but none can compare to the crisp, light, and tender results from oyster mushrooms. At one time they were a somewhat exotic item, but I now find oyster mushrooms at my local greengrocer. Fan shaped when separated from the clusters in which they grow, their flatness is one reason why they are perfect in this recipe, and, of course, a touch of *alioli* makes them that much better.   **serves 4**

2 large eggs

$1/2$ teaspoon dried parsley flakes

1 teaspoon grated cheese

6 ounces oyster mushrooms, stems well trimmed and separated into individual ears, or other thin flat mushrooms, stems removed

Dried bread crumbs, preferably mixed with Japanese-style panko crumbs

Mild olive oil for frying

Kosher or sea salt

Alioli, homemade (page 186) or bottled

Beat together in a deep dish the eggs, parsley, and cheese. Coat the mushrooms with the egg mixture, then cover with the crumbs, shaking off any excess. Dry on a wire rack for 20 minutes.

Pour oil to a depth of 1 inch in a skillet, heat to the smoking point (or better still, use a deep-fryer set at 360°F), and fry the mushrooms, turning once, until lightly golden on both sides. Drain on paper towels and sprinkle with salt. Serve with *alioli*.

TORTITAS DE CAMARONES DE LUISA OSBORNE ❧
LUISA OSBORNE'S SHRIMP PANCAKES

The Osborne family, famed for their fine sherry, arrived in Spain from England at the end of the eighteenth century and established Bodegas Osborne, today among the oldest and most prestigious sherry companies in Spain. Although many sherry companies in the city of Jerez in southwestern Spain bear the names of Englishmen, over the centuries the families have become very Spanish, although they never forget their English roots. So when Luisa Osborne set out to write a cookbook, her recipes were for the most part Spanish, such as this outstanding recipe for shrimp pancakes, so typical in this part of Spain. This version includes the shrimp shells, which give additional shrimp flavor and extra crispness to the pancakes.

makes 20 pancakes

Kosher or sea salt

$1/4$ pound very small shrimp in their shells

2 tablespoons minced onion

1 garlic clove, minced

2 tablespoons minced fresh parsley

$1/8$ teaspoon sweet paprika, preferably Spanish smoked (see Pantry, page 14)

$1/2$ cup flour

Mild olive oil for frying

Bring to a boil in a small saucepan about 1 cup water with $1/2$ teaspoon salt. Add the shrimp and cook briefly until just opaque. Remove with a slotted spoon and measure the liquid to $1/2$ cup plus 2 tablespoons (boil down if there is more). Transfer the liquid to a bowl and cool.

Chop the shrimp with their shells into approximately $1/8$-inch pieces. Add to the cooled liquid with the onion, garlic, parsley, paprika, flour, and salt to taste and stir until smooth. Let sit for 1 hour at room temperature. The mixture should have the consistency of a thin pancake batter.

Pour the oil to a depth of $1/4$ inch into a large skillet and heat to the smoking point. Drop the batter by the tablespoon into the oil, spreading and pricking with the edge of a spoon into thin, lacy-textured pancakes. Fry until golden, then flip them over to brown the other side. Drain on paper towels. Keep warm in a 200°F oven while preparing the rest of the pancakes. Transfer to a platter and serve.

CROQUETAS AL VINO DE CARMEN SERRANO ❧
CARMEN'S WINE AND HAM CROQUETTES

These crunchy little croquettes, unlike most, do not rely principally on a milk- and butter-based bechamel, but on a bechamel made also with white wine and olive oil. Look for a light white wine—anything more will be overpowering because the taste of the wine does come across. The morsels of Serrano ham add texture and give great flavor as well.   makes 18 to 20 croquettes

3 tablespoons mild olive oil plus more for frying

3 tablespoons unsalted butter

6 tablespoons flour

$1/2$ cup mild-flavored white wine, such as a white from Catalunya

$1/4$ cup chicken broth

$1/4$ cup milk

A generous grating of pepper

$1/4$ teaspoon grated nutmeg

$1/3$ cup Serrano ham or prosciutto, cut from a $1/8$-inch slice and finely diced

1 tablespoon minced fresh parsley

Kosher or sea salt

1 large egg, lightly beaten

1 cup dried bread crumbs, preferably mixed with Japanese-style panko crumbs

In a medium saucepan, heat the oil and the butter. Add the flour and cook for 3 minutes, stirring constantly. Gradually stir in the wine, broth, milk, pepper, and nutmeg and cook over medium heat, stirring constantly, until the mixture begins to thicken. Add the ham and parsley and continue cooking and stirring for 5 minutes more. Taste for salt. Cool, stirring occasionally.

Spread the mixture out on a dinner plate, cool, then refrigerate for 1 to 2 hours, until the mixture has solidified. Shape into 1-inch balls, dip in the egg, and coat with the crumbs. Let sit for 20 minutes. Pour oil into a skillet to a depth of about 1 inch (or better still, use a deep-fryer set at 360°F) and heat until it quickly browns a cube of bread. Fry the croquettes, in several batches if necessary, until golden brown, turning once, and drain on paper towels. You can keep the croquettes warm for up to 30 minutes in a 200°F oven. Arrange on a platter and serve.

San Salvador
de Valdediós church,
Villaviciosa, Asturias

MINI CROQUETAS DE PERDIZ Y JAMÓN DE LA FAMILIA NÚÑEZ DE PRADO ⚜
THE NÚÑEZ DE PRADO FAMILY'S PARTRIDGE AND HAM MINI CROQUETTES

I sampled these bite-size croquettes as part of a feast prepared at the Núñez de Prado olive oil estate, and I have never tasted better. Of course, when the Núñez de Prado family fries these extraordinary croquettes they use only their exceptional olive oil, but at the risk of being accused of heresy, I daresay that any good-quality olive oil should work just as well.

Partridge is hard to come by in the United States (although very common in Spain, a country famous for its game birds and fine hunting) but quail, which is an excellent substitute, is easy to find. You could also use chicken, but I'm afraid you will lose some of the exquisite taste of these croquettes.

makes about 60 croquettes

1 partridge or 2 quail (equivalent to about $1/2$ cup finely chopped raw quail, partridge, or chicken meat)

3 tablespoons plus 1 teaspoon olive oil

1 tablespoon unsalted butter

6 tablespoons flour

$3/4$ cup milk

$1/4$ cup chicken broth

Kosher or sea salt

Freshly ground pepper

A generous grating of nutmeg

$1/4$ cup minced Serrano ham or prosciutto, cut from an $1/8$-inch slice

2 large eggs, lightly beaten

Dried bread crumbs, preferably mixed with Japanese-style panko crumbs

Mild olive oil for frying

With a sharp thin knife, remove as much meat as possible from the partridge or quail (if you wish you can simmer the bones to enrich the chicken broth). Finely chop.

Heat the oil and butter in a saucepan until the butter is melted. Add the flour and cook for 2 minutes over medium heat, stirring constantly. Gradually stir in the milk and broth and season with salt and pepper to taste and nutmeg. Cook, stirring constantly, until thickened and smooth. Add the boned meat and the ham and cook for 5 minutes more. Check the seasoning. Cool for a minute, stirring to release the steam. Spread out on a dinner plate and let sit until completely cool. Refrigerate for 1 to 2 hours, until firm enough to handle.

Shape $\frac{1}{2}$ teaspoon at a time with your hands either into balls or into ovals. Dip in the egg, then coat with the crumbs and allow to dry on a wire rack for 20 minutes. Pour the oil into a skillet to a depth of at least 1 inch (or better still, use a deep-fryer set at 360°F) and heat until it quickly browns a cube of bread. Add as many croquettes as will comfortably fit and brown on both sides. Drain on paper towels and serve immediately—or keep warm for up to 30 minutes in a 200°F oven.

BOQUERONES FRITOS ✤ BATTER-FRIED FRESH ANCHOVIES

Visitors to Spain invariably fall in love with *boquerones fritos*—fried fresh anchovies, generally served as a tapa or as part of a mixed fish fry. In this version an egg white coating makes them light as air. It is of course best to use fresh anchovies (recently they have begun to appear in my local fish market), but otherwise use other very small fish.

serves 4

Mild olive oil for frying

12 fresh anchovies or other fish of a similar size, cleaned, heads off, butterflied, and boned

Flour for dusting

1 large egg white, lightly beaten with a fork

Kosher or sea salt

Lemon wedges

Pour oil into a skillet to a depth of at least $1/2$ inch (or better still, use a deep-fryer set at 365°F) and heat until it quickly browns a cube of bread. Dust the butterflied fish on both sides with flour, coat with the egg white, and transfer directly to the hot oil. Fry until lightly golden, turning once. Drain on paper towels, sprinkle with salt, and serve right away with lemon wedges for garnish.

CAZÓN EN ADOBO ❧
FRIED FISH BITES MARINATED IN GARLIC, VINEGAR, OREGANO, AND CUMIN

This wonderful tapa generally appears in An- *2 tablespoons wine vinegar, preferably mild Spanish white*
dalucía as part of a mixed fish fry, and the flavor
and succulence given by the marinade is a nice
counterpoint to the simply fried fish. Although
typically made with tope shark—a fish greatly
appreciated in southern Spain—it works equally
well with other firm-fleshed fish like halibut or
swordfish. This tapa is also excellent made with
skinless chicken breast instead of fish.

serves 4 to 5

2 tablespoons wine vinegar, preferably mild Spanish white
    vinegar (see Pantry, page 18)

2 garlic cloves, mashed to a paste

$1/2$ teaspoon dried oregano

1 tablespoon fresh thyme, or $1/2$ teaspoon dried

$1/2$ teaspoon ground cumin

1 bay leaf, crumbled

1 pound shark, halibut, or swordfish steaks, cut into 1-inch
    cubes

Kosher or sea salt

A mixture of flour and cornmeal for dusting

Mild olive oil for frying

Stir together in a bowl the vinegar, garlic, oregano, thyme, cumin, and bay leaf. Add the fish and coat well. Cover and marinate for a couple of hours at room temperature or overnight in the refrigerator.

Drain and dry the fish on paper towels. Sprinkle with salt and dust with the flour mixture. Pour oil into a skillet to a depth of $1/2$ inch (or better still, use a deep-fryer set at 365°F) and heat until it quickly browns a cube of bread. Fry the fish for about 5 minutes, until just done, turning once. Drain on paper towels. Keep warm, if necessary, for up to 30 minutes in a 200°F oven.

CHISTORRA EN FRITO DE MAÍZ ⚬ BASQUE CHORIZO AND CORNMEAL FRITTERS

Rarely will you find corn or cornmeal used in Spanish cooking, and when it does appear, it is almost always in a dish from Galicia or the Basque Country. Corn, native to America, found ideal conditions in the damp cool regions of northern Spain. Galicia's wonderful dense moist breads are made with cornmeal, and in the Basque Country, a cornmeal batter for a long skinny chorizo called *chistorra* forms a distinctive crunchy coating.

makes about 35 fritters

$^3/_4$ cup cornmeal

$^1/_4$ cup flour

$^3/_4$ cup sparkling water

1 tablespoon minced fresh parsley

$^1/_2$ teaspoon Kosher or sea salt

1 tablespoon extra virgin olive oil

Mild olive oil for frying

Chistorra sausage (see Pantry, page 16), cut into $^1/_2$-inch slices, or chorizo cut into $^1/_2$-inch cubes

Combine in a bowl the cornmeal, flour, sparkling water, parsley, salt, and extra virgin olive oil and mix until smooth. Pour the oil into a skillet to a depth of at least 1 inch (or better still, use a deep-fryer set at 365°F) and heat until it quickly browns a cube of bread. Dip each piece of *chistorra* in the batter and transfer immediately to the hot oil. Fry until golden on all sides. Drain on paper towels (the fritters can be kept warm in a 200°F oven for up to 30 minutes).

GAMBAS AL AJILLO MAMÁ PEPA ❧ MOTHER PEPA'S GARLIC SHRIMP

I received an e-mail from María Jesús Davis, who resides in Washington, D.C., but is inordinately proud to be a native of Jerez de la Frontera in Andalucía. Writing in charming Andalusian colloquial Spanish, she says, "I am Jerezana to the bone, and I hope you like my mother's recipe, which is very simple and easy to understand—because I get bored when cooking gets complicated."

Gambas al ajillo, a staple in most tapas bars, takes on a new twist and a haunting flavor with the addition of medium-dry amontillado sherry, which also comes from María Jesús's hometown. She advises, "Be sure to provide plenty of bread to sop up the sauce. It's to die for!"   serves 5 to 6

3/4 pound small shrimp, shelled

Kosher or sea salt

5 tablespoons extra virgin olive oil

3 tablespoons minced garlic

2 tablespoons minced fresh parsley

2 tablespoons amontillado (medium-dry) sherry

Sprinkle the shrimp with salt and let sit for 10 minutes. In a shallow casserole, preferably earthenware, heat the oil with the garlic and parsley until the garlic begins to sizzle. Add the shrimp and stir until they are opaque. Add the sherry, salt to taste, and cook over medium heat for a minute or two until the sherry evaporates and the sauce thickens slightly. Serve immediately, in the casserole.

Fishing boats, Castro
Urdiales, Cantabria

ALMEJAS A LA MARINERA DE LUISA OSBORNE ⚜
LUISA OSBORNE'S CLAMS IN GARLIC SAUCE

Clams in garlic sauce, one of Spain's most appealing tapas, found all over the country, typically calls for white wine, but as might be expected from the matriarch of the Osborne sherry family, her outstanding version is made with dry fino sherry, which gives the sauce a distinctive flavor.

serves 4 to 5

3 tablespoons extra virgin olive oil

3 tablespoons minced onion

2 garlic cloves, minced

1 bay leaf

One 1-inch piece medium-hot dried red chile pepper, such as Spanish *guindilla* or *guajillo* (see Pantry, page 15)

3 dozen Manila clams or cockles (about 1^1/$_2$ pounds), or 1^1/$_2$ dozen very small littlenecks, cleansed (see page 35)

^{1}/$_4$ cup dry fino sherry

2 tablespoons freshly squeezed lemon juice

3 tablespoons minced fresh parsley

Freshly ground pepper

Kosher or sea salt

Heat the oil in a large skillet. Slowly cook the onion, garlic, bay leaf, and chile.

Add the clams and briefly sauté, then pour in the sherry and lemon juice, sprinkle in 2 tablespoons of the parsley, and cook over high heat until the clams open and the sauce is reduced and slightly thickened. Season with pepper and salt, if necessary, sprinkle with the remaining tablespoon of parsley, and serve right away with plenty of good crusty bread for dunking.

CLOCHINAS DE PLAYA AL LIMÓN ✺
STEAMED MUSSELS WITH LEMON AND ONION

Dozens of lively restaurants specializing in paella—some have been here for more than a century—face the Playa de Levante, Valencia's broad, fine-sand beach. Shoulder to shoulder along the gardens and palm-lined beach side promenade, these restaurants all offer similar fare. Among the appetizers are these wonderful mussels with a goodly amount of lemon juice that is softened by slowly sautéed onion.

serves 4 to 6

$1^1/2$ pounds small farm-raised mussels, rinsed and beards removed, or other mussels

Kosher or sea salt

Cornmeal or bread crumbs for sprinkling

3 tablespoons olive oil

1 medium onion, slivered

6 tablespoons freshly squeezed lemon juice

2 tablespoons minced fresh parsley

If your mussels are not farm raised, remove the beards and scrub well. Soak for several hours or overnight in the refrigerator in salted water sprinkled with cornmeal or bread crumbs. Rinse well before using. Heat the oil in a large skillet. Add the onion and sauté for 2 minutes. Cover and cook for about 15 minutes more over low heat, until the onion is tender but not brown.

Add the lemon juice and the mussels, bring to a boil, then cover and cook over medium heat until the mussels have opened. Sprinkle with parsley and serve.

ALBÓNDIGAS EN SALSA DE AZAFRÁN ❧
MINI MEATBALLS IN SAFFRON GARLIC SAUCE

These tiny meatballs, redolent of garlic and saf-fron—added at the last minute for a more pro-nounced flavor—are a surefire hit at any tapas gathering. If you serve more meatballs in each portion, you have a wonderful meal.

serves 4 to 6

$1/2$ pound ground pork

$1/2$ pound ground veal

2 garlic cloves, minced

3 tablespoons minced fresh parsley

1 large egg, lightly beaten

1 slice bread, crusts removed, soaked in water and
   squeezed dry

$1^1/2$ teaspoons plus $1/8$ teaspoon kosher or sea salt

Freshly ground pepper

Flour for dusting

2 tablespoons extra virgin olive oil

2 tablespoons minced onion

$1/4$ teaspoon sweet paprika, preferably Spanish smoked (see
   Pantry, page 14)

$1/2$ cup chicken broth

2 tablespoons dry white wine

$1/8$ teaspoon crumbled thread saffron

Lightly mix together in a bowl the pork, veal, half of the minced garlic, 1 tablespoon of the parsley, the egg, bread, the $1^1/2$ teaspoons salt, and the pepper. Shape into 1-inch balls and dust with flour.

Heat the oil in a shallow casserole and brown the meatballs on all sides. Add the onion and sauté until it is softened. Stir in the paprika, then pour in the broth and wine. Bring to a boil, cover, and simmer for 40 minutes.

Meanwhile, in a mortar or mini processor, mash to a paste the remaining garlic, 1 tablespoon of the remaining parsley, the saffron, and the remaining $1/8$ teaspoon salt. Add to the meatballs and simmer for 5 to 10 minutes more. Sprinkle with the remaining table-spoon parsley and serve.

CHAPTER 2

ENSALADAS
salads

WHENEVER WE FEAST ON SPAIN'S BABY ROAST LAMB—in Posada de la Villa in Madrid or in Figón Zute el Mayor "Tinín" in Sepúlveda, a large bowl of incredibly fresh crisp lettuce with sliced sweet tomatoes invariably arrives with it and is placed at the center of the table. The tomatoes never look like perfect specimens, but they taste far better than any tomatoes I find in New York. The salad arrives unrequested—the common wisdom is that vinegar helps digest the lamb. Be that as it may, there is nothing that tastes better with roast lamb than this simple salad dressed with oil and a mild white wine vinegar that will not overpower the delicacy of the lamb.

It's difficult to convince Americans that it's okay for everyone to partake from the same salad bowl, spearing some lettuce and tomato on their forks every so often as the meal progresses, but that's how it is done in Spain. There are, however, other salads that can be shared as a tapa or served as a first course. If you embellish the basic lettuce and tomato salad with hard-boiled egg wedges, onion, tuna, and olives, it becomes my favorite, *ensalada mixta*.

Roasted red peppers make up another category of well-loved salads, especially in Andalucía, where peppers are sweet beyond compare and the warm climate makes refreshing salads especially appealing. Catalunya has its own regional salads you are not likely to find elsewhere—*empedrat*, for example, with dried cod and white beans, and an escarole salad with a delicious dressing called Xató that incorporates dried sweet red peppers, almonds, and hazelnuts.

ENSALADA MIXTA A LA ESPAÑOLA ❧ SPANISH-STYLE MIXED SALAD

There are typically two kinds of salads on Spanish menus: simple lettuce and tomato or what is popularly known as *ensalada mixta*, a somewhat more embellished version of that basic salad. It is always brought to the table "undressed," and diners season it and drizzle with olive oil and vinegar as they please. To my taste, it is the ideal salad in which all ingredients beautifully complement one another, and my husband, who is not particularly fond of salads, eats this one with gusto. You can vary it as you wish.

serves 4

About 4 cups torn hearts of romaine lettuce

$1/2$ medium onion, preferably Vidalia or other sweet onion, slivered

1 small carrot, scraped and coarsely grated

About 10 sliced pickled beets, cut in halves

2 ripe and flavorful small tomatoes, cut into $1/2$-inch wedges

2 large hard-boiled eggs, sliced

Kosher or sea salt

Freshly ground pepper

$1/4$ cup light-meat tuna in olive oil, preferably Spanish (see Pantry, page 16), in chunks

16 small Spanish green olives with pits, preferably cured, otherwise rinsed of their brine

8 large white asparagus spears, preferably Spanish (see Pantry, page 10)

Extra virgin olive oil

Wine vinegar, preferably mild white wine vinegar (see Pantry, page 18)

Place the lettuce on individual salad plates, scatter on the onion, and cover with the grated carrot. Arrange the beet halves and tomato and egg wedges around the edges of the plates. Sprinkle everything with salt and pepper. Place the tuna at the center of the salad and scatter with the olives. Finish with the asparagus spears, attractively arranged. Dress to taste with oil and vinegar. Serve.

ENSALADA CON SALSA XATÓ ❧
ESCAROLE, TOMATO, ANCHOVY, AND BLACK OLIVE SALAD WITH XATÓ DRESSING

What's old is suddenly new, my friend Cinta Gutiérrez tells me. Xató, a traditional sauce from Catalunya of garlic, nuts, and dried red pepper, is all the rage among Catalan chefs, and competitions are regularly held to award the tastiest versions.

Although Xató is excellent with many dishes, including grilled fish and meats, I think it is one of the best dressings ever to grace a salad—especially when the salad is a mix of escarole, tomatoes, anchovies, and black olives.

serves 4

2 ñoras (dried sweet red peppers; see Pantry, page 14) or

   1 New Mexico–style dried red pepper, cores cut out with

   kitchen shears and seeded

10 blanched almonds

10 shelled hazelnuts

3 garlic cloves, minced

About $1/4$ teaspoon kosher or sea salt

$1/2$ cup fruity extra virgin olive oil

2 tablespoons red or white wine vinegar

About 6 cups torn escarole leaves

24 grape or cherry tomatoes, whole or halved

8 good-quality anchovy fillets

16 cured black olives

2 tablespoons minced fresh parsley

Preheat the oven to 450°F. Soak the peppers in hot water for 20 minutes. Meanwhile, place the nuts on an oven tray and roast for about 4 minutes, until the almonds are lightly brown. Cool.

Transfer the nuts to a food processor and grind as fine as possible. Scrape the flesh from the peppers and add to the processor, along with the garlic and salt. Beat well. With the motor running, slowly pour in the olive oil and vinegar. Adjust the salt, if necessary.

On individual salad plates, arrange the escarole, cherry tomatoes, anchovies, and olives. Spoon on the sauce (about 2 tablespoons per portion) and sprinkle with parsley to serve.

*Serpent door knocker,
Albarracín, Teruel*

ENSALADA MORA ❧ MOORISH-STYLE GREEN SALAD WITH CUMIN AND PAPRIKA

Cumin and paprika are two wonderful additions to a salad dressing, an idea that comes from southern Spain. It is excellent on any green or mixed salad. serves 4

$3/4$ teaspoon cumin seeds or ground cumin

1 large garlic clove, minced

$1/2$ teaspoon sweet paprika, preferably Spanish smoked (see Pantry, page 14)

1 tablespoon minced fresh parsley

Kosher or sea salt

4 teaspoons red or white wine vinegar

3 tablespoons plus 1 teaspoon extra virgin olive oil

About 4 cups tender torn romaine or escarole leaves, or mesclun

In a mortar mash the cumin, garlic, paprika, parsley, and $1/8$ teaspoon salt. Whisk in the vinegar and the oil and add salt to taste.

Place the greens in a salad bowl and toss in the dressing to serve.

ENSALADA DE PIMIENTOS CON ATÚN "CAZORLA"
PIMIENTO AND TUNA SALAD, CAZORLA STYLE

I liked this salad so much that I ordered it twice during our brief stay at the secluded Cazorla parador in the midst of the Cazorla mountain reserve in the province of Jaén—a deep green oasis within the arid lands of Andalucía. This is just one of the many refreshing and incredibly appealing salads that Andalusians love so dearly and that I never pass up when in southern Spain. This salad can be served as a first course or an accompaniment to simple grilled or roasted fish or meats.

serves 3 to 4

6 medium red bell peppers

Kosher or sea salt

Freshly ground pepper

3 tablespoons flaked tuna, preferably light or dark meat imported from Spain

1 large hard-boiled egg, coarsely chopped

2 tablespoons olive oil

1 tablespoon red wine vinegar

8 small black cured olives

Preheat the oven to 500°F. Place the peppers in a roasting pan and roast for 45 minutes, turning once. Remove from the oven, cover the pan tightly with foil, and let sit for 15 minutes. Peel, core, and seed the peppers and slice in long narrow strips. Arrange in a single layer on a platter. Season well with salt and pepper.

Sprinkle the tuna and egg over the peppers and drizzle with the oil and vinegar. Taste for salt. Scatter with the olives and let sit for at least 30 minutes at room temperature before serving.

ENSALADA DE PIMIENTOS ESTILO ANDALUZ ❧
RED PEPPER, TOMATO, AND TUNA SALAD, ANDALUSIAN STYLE

This version of Andalusian red pepper salad comes from the Cazorla restaurant in Madrid and is an especially delicious rendition. Although it may seem somewhat similar to the previous recipe (the name of the restaurant leads me to believe that this salad also comes from the town of Cazorla), it includes tomato, white-meat tuna, and mild bright green olives, and it is served in a bowl with lots of liquid from the peppers and tomatoes. More than salad in itself, it is meant as a side dish to Andalusian fried fish and grilled shrimp, to place on your plate with the fish and take more as you please.   serves 4

6 medium-large, deep red bell peppers

$1/2$ pound good-quality white-meat tuna, preferably imported from Spain (see Pantry, page 16)

$1/2$ pound ripe but firm tomatoes, cut into $1/4$-inch slices, then halved

12 mild bright green olives, such as Cerignola

2 tablespoons minced fresh parsley

6 tablespoons fruity extra virgin olive oil

1 tablespoon wine vinegar, preferably mild white wine vinegar (see Pantry, page 16)

$1/2$ teaspoon sugar

Kosher or sea salt

Preheat the oven to 550°F. Place the peppers in a roasting pan and cook until charred, turning once, 30 to 40 minutes. Remove from the oven and place in a deep dish. Cover with foil and let sit for 15 minutes. Peel off the skin, core, and seed the peppers, reserving the juices.

Slice the peppers into $3/4$-inch strips and place in a bowl. Add the tuna, broken into chunks, the tomatoes, olives, and parsley. Fold in the oil, vinegar, sugar, and salt to taste with a rubber spatula. Refrigerate overnight. Serve cold or at room temperature.

ENSALADA DE EL ROCÍO ❧ TOMATO AND PEPPERS SALAD WITH EGG AND HAM

Yet another great red pepper salad that I love, this one from western Andalucía. It has the quintessential taste of Andalucía—sun-ripened tomatoes, green and brilliantly red peppers, hard-boiled egg, air-cured Iberian ham from the mountains of the province of Huelva, and of course celebrated Andalusian extra virgin olive oil. Each bite transports me to sunny southern Spain.

serves 4

3/4 pound plum tomatoes

3/4 pound Italian red frying peppers, or, if unavailable, red bell peppers

3/4 pound Italian green frying peppers

2 large hard-boiled eggs

Kosher or sea salt

1 small onion, slivered

1 large garlic clove, minced

1/4 teaspoon ground cumin

2 teaspoons wine vinegar, preferably mild white wine vinegar (see Pantry, page 18)

1/4 cup extra virgin olive oil

Very thin slices Serrano or prosciutto ham (about 1/4 pound)

Preheat the oven to 500°F. In a roasting pan, arrange the tomatoes and peppers and roast for 20 minutes, turning once. Cool, skin, and chop coarsely. Mix together and transfer to a platter.

Coarsely chop the egg white and finely chop the yolks. Sprinkle the egg over the tomatoes and peppers. Season with salt and scatter on the onion.

In a mortar, mash to a paste the garlic, 1/8 teaspoon salt, and the cumin. Stir in the vinegar and oil and pour over the salad. Arrange the ham slices on top of the salad and serve at room temperature.

Market stand, Valencia

ESPÁRRAGOS A LA RIOJANA ✤
ASPARAGUS SALAD WITH *PIQUILLO* PEPPERS, EGG, AND ANCHOVY

This salad unites La Rioja's young asparagus with its succulent tomatoes and sweet red peppers in a wonderful dressing that also includes anchovies and finely chopped hard-boiled egg. Ideal for asparagus, the dressing is also tasty on a green salad.

serves 4

2 *piquillo* peppers (see Pantry, page 15), or 1 pimiento, chopped

1 ripe and flavorful small tomato, skinned, seeds gently squeezed out

3 anchovy fillets, chopped

1 tablespoon red wine vinegar

1 tablespoon extra virgin olive oil

$1/4$ teaspoon Dijon mustard

Kosher or sea salt

Freshly ground pepper

1 pound trimmed, cooked, and cooled small asparagus spears

1 large hard-boiled egg, finely chopped

1 tablespoon minced fresh parsley

In a food processor, puree the peppers, tomato, anchovies, vinegar, oil, mustard, and salt and pepper to taste.

Arrange the asparagus on salad plates in a fan shape. Spoon about 1 tablespoon of dressing across the asparagus. Sprinkle with the egg and parsley and serve at room temperature.

EMPEDRAT AL ESTILO DE ANTAÑO DE CINTA GUTIÉRREZ ⚘
CINTA'S OLD-FASHIONED COD AND BEAN SALAD

Salting cod as a means of preservation has been a tradition since ancient times, and in fact, it is thought that Spain's Basque fishermen reached the New World before Columbus in their search for fertile fishing grounds. The beginnings of widespread commerce in the Mediterranean have also been attributed to cod. After the church declared meat-free Fridays and pre-Easter fasting, countries or regions without access to the sea relied on salt cod, which can be kept for extended periods, and countries with good supplies took advantage of the commercial possibilities.

This traditional Catalan recipe comes to me from my friend Cinta, who with her parents takes charge of Els Pescadors restaurant. The restaurant, next to the port of L'Escala in Girona, overlooks a glorious expanse of the Mediterranean Sea and naturally concentrates on the magnificent seafood of this coast. "This is a great dish in summer," says Cinta. And indeed, it is wonderfully refreshing and exceptionally tasty. The salt cod will have a mild taste if soaked as directed. In Catalunya, of course, the olive oil of choice is the local varietal, arbequina (see Pantry, page 14).   serves 6

$1/2$ pound boneless, skinless, dried salt cod

Kosher or sea salt

1 cup cooked white beans, freshly made or canned

1 medium onion, slivered

2 plum tomatoes, cut into $1/2$-inch dice

24 small cured black olives

$1/2$ cup extra virgin olive oil

$1/4$ cup red wine vinegar

3 tablespoons minced fresh parsley

Soak the cod in cold water to cover in the refrigerator for 2 to 3 days, changing the water once or twice daily, until desalted to taste. Drain and dry on paper towels. With a thin sharp knife, cut the cod diagonally across the grain into $1/4$-inch slices, as you would slice a flank steak.

Place in a flat-bottomed bowl and add salt to taste and all the other ingredients, using a rubber spatula to blend. Marinate for 2 hours in the refrigerator before serving.

CHAPTER 3

VERDURAS
vegetables

IN THE FALL, WOMEN SIT AT THEIR DOORSTEPS IN THE region of La Rioja roasting red peppers over wood-burning grills, and balconies are festooned with red peppers drying in the brilliant autumn sunlight. In Extremadura thousands of peppers are laid out like a crimson carpet to dry before being pulverized into paprika. Navarra has its *pimientos del piquillo,* the aristocrats of red peppers, as different from ordinary pimientos as common fish roe is from caviar. Exceptionally sweet, gently piquant, brilliantly red, intensely flavorful, firm-textured yet thin and delicate, *piquillos* are strictly artisan products, hand peeled and fire roasted. In Murcia and Valencia, the "Garden of Spain," where a mild climate allows vegetables to grow year-round, peppers become big, picture-perfect specimens. Tiny green *pimientos de Padrón*—generally sweet, but on occasion unexpectedly fiery, quickly fried and sprinkled with sea salt—are a delicacy in Galicia in northwestern Spain. In fact, no vegetable is more emblematic of Spain than the pepper, and Spaniards have been inordinately fond of them ever since Columbus discovered this native American vegetable in the New World, where it had been cultivated for many centuries.

A reader of an article I once wrote in the *New York Times* praising the extraordinary quality of fresh fish in Madrid complained that she was shortchanged in one of the restaurants I recommended: the fish was very expensive, and yet it came to the table without even a potato on the plate. Similarly, I am often asked why Spaniards don't seem to eat any vegetables. True, a vegetable is not likely to appear with a main course, but that is because vegetables stand on their own. They must be ordered independently in a restaurant and are served separately at home.

Vegetables, in fact, are enormously important in the Spanish diet and in home cooking (you need only see the care and artistry with which they are displayed in markets like La Boquería in Barcelona), and since vegetables are generally served as a separate course (or even as a light meal), their preparation tends to be more elaborate than a vegetable thoughtlessly tossed on a plate as garnish. In Spain you will find medleys of vegetables *(pistos),* vegetable casseroles, sometimes called *menestras,* vegetables sautéed with garlic, olive oil, and Serrano ham (a vegetable's perfect counterpoint), baked vegetables, and fried vegetables. Dried legumes, of course, hold a place of honor in Spanish kitchens because they keep for extended periods and are part of so many traditional regional dishes. You will find those recipes in the chapter Soups and One-Pot Meals.

Vegetables have always been seasonal items in Spain, eaten only when they are available locally. Probably one of the reasons greens called *acelgas* or *grelos* (in the family of Swiss chard and collard greens) are so widely popular is that they have an extended growing season. In Spanish households they are a much-loved first course.

Potatoes are in a category of their own (some Spanish cookbooks devote entire chapters just to potatoes), and it is hard to imagine Spanish cooking before potatoes were brought from America. The egg and potato omelet, *tortilla española*, is a national obsession, and *patatas fritas* (obviously not called French fries in Spain) are ubiquitous, served with chops and other plain grilled meats regularly in homes and in traditional restaurants.

Peppers in Plasencia

It is a sight to behold. Thousands upon thousands of long narrow red peppers drying in the bright October sunshine—a veritable carpet of peppers spread out here in front of the headquarters of La Chinata, makers of artisan paprikas, near the city of Plasencia in the region of Extremadura. We are in the lushly green peaceful valley known as La Vera, dotted with villages like Valverde de la Vera and Jarandilla de la Vera that are as poetic as their names. This is an eminently agricultural area, known in particular for its cherries and its red peppers.

We don't know why the peppers before us are laid out in this manner, but our friend and owner of this operation, Cecilio Oliva, explains. "These peppers are destined to become excellent but unremarkable paprika. Get in my car and I'll take you to the pepper fields so you can see the peppers that will become Spain's Rolls-Royce of paprikas—distinctively smoked and bestowed with the Denomination of Origin label, Pimentón de la Vera."

Peppers, native to the New World, were used as a condiment in the Old World—first in Spain and later in such far-flung countries as Hungary and China. The varieties of peppers grown in Extremadura were introduced to the region in 1495, when the Catholic Kings met Columbus in the Guadalupe monastery. He showed them the products he had brought back from this new land, among them, peppers. The monks in Guadalupe cultivated them and in turn introduced the monks at the Yuste monastery in the valley of La Vera to peppers, and it was here that peppers found their ideal environment.

The plants we see in mid-October are laden with brilliantly red peppers, and nearby a group of ramshackle metal structures piques our curiosity. Cecilio stops the car and leads us to one. We soon find out that this is where the smoking process takes place. Cecilio explains that holm oak, so common in

central Spain, provides the heat and smoke to dry the peppers. It is a slow process that lasts about two weeks while the peppers rest on platforms high above the smoldering embers. The smoke combined with the aroma of red peppers is heady. "The peppers have to be hand turned every day," Cecilio says. "This lengthy and painstaking procedure gives the paprika its characteristic color, earthy fragrance, and a taste beyond compare. When the peppers have finished drying, we grind them to a powder in traditional stone mills—a simple and altogether primitive process. We use three different varieties of peppers to achieve sweet, bittersweet, and piquant paprikas."

Most of this smoked paprika is destined to make chorizo, and it is what gives this typically Spanish sausage its robust color and distinctive flavor. But chefs and home cooks alike know how smoked paprika from La Vera gives a flavor lift to so many meat, chicken, and rice dishes. I would not be without it in my kitchen, and every time I reach for it in my cupboard, I recall that unforgettable morning in the fields of La Vera.

ESPINACAS CON MEMBRILLO AL SÉSAMO ❧
SAUTÉED SPINACH WITH QUINCE AND TOASTED SESAME SEEDS

Another exceptional recipe with a Moorish touch given to me by Julia Piñedo, who holds court in her restaurant Posada del Moro in Cazalla de la Sierra. The quince is an ideal match with spinach, and the toasted sesame seeds add a final touch of flavor and texture. Quince, a fruit reminiscent of apple and pear, but never eaten raw (it is much too sour), is available in the fall. It is very popular in Spain as a preserve and especially delicious served with Manchego cheese.

serves 4 to 6

2 teaspoons sesame seeds

2 tablespoons olive oil

1 medium onion, preferably Vidalia or other sweet onion, finely chopped

1 quince (about $1/2$ pound) or Golden Delicious apple, peeled and cut into $3/8$-inch cubes

$1^{1}/2$ pounds spinach, well washed, thick stems removed, and coarsely chopped

Kosher or sea salt

Freshly ground pepper

Preheat the oven to 350°F. Spread the sesame seeds on an oven tray and cook until lightly golden, 5 to 6 minutes.

Heat the oil in a skillet and sauté the onion and quince for 2 minutes. Cover and continue cooking over low heat for 10 minutes more. Add the spinach, season with salt and pepper, cover, and continue cooking slowly, stirring occasionally, until the spinach is done to taste, about 3 minutes. Sprinkle with the sesame seeds and serve.

ESPINACAS A LA CATALANA DE PILAR DEL OLMO ❧
PILAR'S SPINACH SAUTÉED WITH RAISINS AND PINE NUTS

We happened upon El Robost de la Cartoixa restaurant in the hamlet of Scala Dei, where we had come to see the ruins of the Scala Dei monastery and the local winery as part of our visit to the Catalan region of El Priorat, renowned for fine wines. The simple food was expertly prepared from faultless local ingredients and it turned out to be an absolutely superb and memorable meal, beginning with a tapa of eggplant, pimientos, and anchovy (page 28), followed by grilled rabbit with *alioli,* sautéed white beans (page 80), this outstanding spinach, Scala Dei wine, and finishing with pears steeped in wine. We quickly struck up a friendship with owner Pilar del Olmo, a lively woman who is as diminutive as her restaurant, only to discover—not to our surprise—that everything we were eating came from her grandmother's recipes.

In Catalunya, spinach and other greens are often served in combination with raisins and pine nuts, creating a wonderful blend of flavors and textures.

serves 4

2 tablespoons raisins

2 tablespoons pine nuts

Kosher or sea salt

1¾ pounds baby spinach, well washed, stems trimmed

2 tablespoons olive oil

2 whole peeled garlic cloves, lightly crushed

Freshly ground pepper

Soak the raisins and pine nuts in warm water to cover for 1 hour. Drain and dry on paper towels.

Bring a large pot of salted water to a boil, add the spinach, and cook until just tender, about 3 minutes. Transfer to a colander, refresh with cold water, and drain, gently pressing with your hands to extract as much water as possible. Chop coarsely.

Heat the oil in a skillet, add the garlic, and brown lightly, pressing with the back of a wooden spoon to extract its flavor. Sprinkle in the pine nuts and sauté briefly until lightly golden. Stir in the spinach and raisins, season with salt and pepper, and sauté for a minute. Cover and cook very slowly for about 5 minutes. Let sit covered for 10 minutes more. Reheat before serving.

JUDÍAS VERDES AL AJILLO CON VINAGRE ❧
GREEN BEANS WITH GARLIC AND VINEGAR

Since vegetables in Spain typically are served on their own as a first course, such ingredients as garlic, chopped hard-boiled egg, and fried or toasted bread cubes are common additions. They transform plain vegetables into dishes that can become light meals. Instead of frying the bread cubes you can brush them with oil and toast them in a 350°F oven until golden, turning once, but the fried cubes are crunchier and use no more oil than those made in the oven. **serves 6**

Kosher or sea salt

1 small onion, cut in half

2 fresh parsley sprigs

2 whole peeled garlic cloves plus 2 garlic cloves, thinly sliced

2 tablespoons plus 2 teaspoons olive oil

1 pound green beans, preferably broad flat green beans, ends trimmed

Two $1/2$-inch slices bread cut from a French-style loaf, cubed

2 teaspoons red or white wine vinegar

1 large hard-boiled egg, finely chopped

Bring a pot of salted water to a boil with the onion, parsley, whole garlic, and 1 tablespoon of the olive oil. Add the beans and cook at a high simmer for about 20 minutes, until cooked to taste.

Meanwhile, to fry the bread, heat 2 teaspoons of the olive oil in a small skillet, add the bread, and fry until golden, turning once. Drain on paper towels. Add the remaining tablespoon oil and the sliced garlic to the skillet and sauté until the garlic is golden. Reserve.

When the green beans are done to taste, drain them, discarding the parsley, whole garlic, and onion, and place on a warm serving platter. Pour on the sliced garlic with its oil, sprinkle with salt, and drizzle with the vinegar. Scatter the egg and bread cubes over the beans and serve.

JUDÍAS VERDES CACEREÑAS ✿ SAUTÉED GREEN BEANS, CÁCERES STYLE

In a charming little volume, *Recetas Para Después de Una Guerra*, author Luis Fausto Rodríguez de Sanabria intertwines simple postwar recipes, based on the simplest of ingredients, with stories of life's hardship after the Spanish Civil War. The recipes, naturally, center on cheap and readily available ingredients, like codfish, sardines, tripe, potatoes, and vegetables. These green beans gain flavor from the additions of *panceta, paprika, and vinegar.*

serves 4

Kosher or sea salt

$1^1/2$ pounds broad flat green beans, ends snapped off

2 tablespoons olive oil

$1/4$ cup pancetta cut into $1/4$-inch cubes, or Serrano ham or prosciutto with some fat

$1/4$ teaspoon sweet paprika, preferably Spanish smoked (see Pantry, page 14)

1 teaspoon red or white wine vinegar

Bring a large pot of salted water to a boil. Add the beans, return to a boil, then cook at a high simmer for about 20 minutes, until done to taste. Drain.

Heat the oil in a large skillet. Add the pancetta and sauté for a minute, then add the beans and sauté for another 2 minutes. Lower the heat, stir in the paprika and the vinegar, and cook for another minute before serving.

ACHICORIAS SALTEADAS DE FRAY JUAN LUIS BARRERA ⚜
FRAY JUAN'S SAUTÉED CHICORY WITH HAM AND CUMIN

This is the best preparation ever for greens and most especially for chicory, a green often considered the poor cousin of the green vegetable family. But what great flavor chicory has when prepared with cumin, ham, paprika, and crunchy bread bits. Fray Juan, a brother at the Guadalupe monastery in the region of Extremadura and in charge of the monastery's public restaurant, is the master of traditional cooking of Extremadura and has the gift of taking the simplest ingredients and creating splendid dishes.

serves 4

Kosher or sea salt

1 to 1^1/2 pounds washed and trimmed chicory

2 tablespoons olive oil

2 whole peeled garlic cloves

Two ^{1}/2-inch-thick slices bread, cut from a French-style loaf

^{1}/2 teaspoon ground cumin

^{1}/4 cup Spanish Serrano ham or prosciutto sliced ^{1}/8-inch thick, then cut into ^{1}/4-inch dice

^{1}/2 teaspoon paprika, preferably Spanish smoked bittersweet (see Pantry, page 14)

Bring a large pot of salted water to a boil, add the chicory, and cook at a high simmer for about 12 minutes, until tender. Drain in a colander, refresh with cold water, then place between paper towels and gently squeeze out more of the water. Chop coarsely.

In a large skillet, heat the oil, then sauté the garlic and bread until they are golden, turning once. Transfer the garlic and bread to a mortar, leaving the oil in the skillet. When the bread and garlic are cool, add to the mortar ^{1}/4 teaspoon salt and the cumin and mash well.

Reheat the skillet and lightly sauté the ham. Stir in the paprika, the chicory, and the mortar mixture. Sauté for a minute and salt to taste. Serve.

ACELGAS EN REHOGADILLO ❧ CUMIN-SCENTED SAUTÉED GREENS

"This is my mother's recipe and at eighty-three years old, she continues to make it," says Tomás Herranz, owner and chef of El Cenador del Prado in Madrid. "I like it so much that I have incorporated it into my menu as a puree to accompany duck confit." Just one example of how creative chefs take simple dishes from their childhood memories and reinvent them.

These greens, which reappear everywhere in Spain with minor variations, can be a side course or, as is customary in Spain, a first course. With the addition of halved hard-boiled eggs and slices of bread—fried or brushed with olive oil and baked—this could be a light meal.   serves 6

Kosher or sea salt

2 pounds Swiss chard, well washed, thick stems trimmed

3 tablespoons olive oil

1 slice bread, about $^3/_8$ inch thick, cut from a French-style loaf

2 whole peeled garlic cloves

$^1/_2$ teaspoon ground cumin

2 teaspoons red wine vinegar

$^1/_4$ cup finely chopped onion

1 medium tomato, skinned and chopped

3 large hard-boiled eggs, cut in halves, optional

Slices of fried bread (see page 75), optional

Bring a pot of salted water to a boil. Add the Swiss chard and cook until done to taste, 20 to 30 minutes. Refresh in a colander with cold water and drain well, pressing lightly to remove excess water.

Heat the oil in a large skillet. Sauté the bread and garlic until golden. Remove to a mortar, leaving the oil in the skillet, and mash to a paste. Mash in the cumin and vinegar.

Reheat the skillet and slowly sauté the onion until softened. Add the tomato and sauté for 2 minutes more. Stir in the mortar mixture and cook away the vinegar. Add the greens and sauté for a few minutes more. Taste for salt.

Serve, if you wish, with halved hard-boiled eggs and slices of fried bread.

BERENJENA CON MIEL DE JULIA PIÑEDO ⚜
JULIA'S BATTER-COATED FRIED EGGPLANT WITH HONEY, MINT, AND SESAME SEEDS

This recipe comes from talented cook Julia in the Andalusian town of Cazalla de la Sierra, and its Eastern touches of honey and sesame are clearly of Moorish origin. It makes a nice accompaniment to any simple meat.   serves 4

One $1/2$-pound eggplant, peeled and cut into $1/8$-inch
    crosswise slices

$1^1/8$ teaspoons kosher or sea salt

$1^1/2$ tablespoons sesame seeds

$1/3$ cup flour

$1/2$ teaspoon baking powder

$1/2$ cup milk

1 large egg, lightly beaten

Mild olive oil for frying

$1^1/2$ to 2 tablespoons honey

1 tablespoon minced fresh mint leaves

Preheat the oven to 350°F. Soak the eggplant slices in 2 cups water mixed with 1 teaspoon of the salt for 30 minutes. Meanwhile, scatter the sesame seeds on a small oven tray and toast until lightly golden, 5 to 8 minutes. Reserve.

Drain the eggplant and dry well on paper towels. In a small bowl mix together the flour, remaining $1/8$ teaspoon salt, and the baking powder. Whisk in the milk and egg.

Pour the oil in a large skillet to a depth of at least $1/2$ inch (or better still, use a deep-fryer set at 375°F) and heat until it quickly browns a cube of bread. Dip the eggplant slices in the batter, coating well, then place immediately in the hot oil and cook for about 30 seconds on each side, until lightly golden. Drain on paper towels.

Warm the honey in a small saucepan or in a microwave. Drizzle lightly over the eggplant, sprinkle with the sesame seeds and the mint, and serve right away.

JUDÍAS BLANCAS REHOGADAS "SCALA DEI" ⚜ SAUTÉED WHITE BEANS

These slightly crunchy little white beans, boiled then sautéed, from Pilar del Olmo, were part of a perfect Catalan meal she served us at her restaurant in Scala Dei that included grilled rabbit with alioli and Spinach Sautéed with Raisins and Pine Nuts (page 74).　　　　serves 4

½ pound small dried white beans, preferably pea beans
　(See Pantry, page 11)
Kosher or sea salt
4 whole unpeeled garlic cloves
2 fresh parsley sprigs
1 bay leaf
1 small peeled onion
2 tablespoons extra virgin olive oil plus some for drizzling
Freshly ground pepper

Soak the beans overnight at room temperature in water to cover. Drain and rinse.

Combine 3 cups water in a stew pot with salt to taste and all the other ingredients except the oil and pepper. Bring to a boil, cover, and simmer for 1 to 2 hours, depending on the size of the beans, until the beans are tender. Press the garlic with the back of a wooden spoon to extract the flesh. Discard the garlic skin, parsley, bay leaf, and onion. Rinse the beans in cold water and drain well.

Heat the oil in a skillet until very hot. Add the beans and sauté, stirring frequently, until the beans are slightly crunchy. Season with salt and pepper and drizzle with olive oil.

Wheat fields of
Castilla y León

VERDURAS DE LA HUERTA DE LA FAMILIA NÚÑEZ DE PRADO ❧
THE NÚÑEZ DE PRADO FAMILY'S BATTER-FRIED VEGETABLES

The preparation of Núñez de Prado family recipes is often left in the capable hands of the family cook, Sandra Peña—young, fresh-faced, and fair—who has been around restaurants her whole life and carries knowledge of food in her genes.

These vegetables, cut in julienne strips and matchsticks, lightly coated with flour, egg, and milk and fried (of course, in Núñez de Prado olive oil) are irresistible—gloriously crisp and gossamer light. They will disappear in no time. I suggest you make extra.   serves 4

Kosher or sea salt
One $1/4$-pound baby eggplant, peeled, cut into $1/4$-inch
    crosswise slices, then cut into $1/4$-inch matchsticks
$1/4$ cup milk
1 large egg
Flour
Mild olive oil for frying
$1/2$ medium-large red bell pepper, cored and seeded, cut
    lengthwise into $1/4$-inch julienne strips, then crosswise
    into $1 1/2$-inch pieces
$1/2$ medium-large green bell pepper, cored and seeded, cut
    lengthwise into $1/4$-inch julienne strips, then crosswise
    into $1 1/2$-inch pieces
$1/4$ medium onion, slivered
$1/4$ pound zucchini, cut into $1/4$-inch crosswise slices, then cut
    into $1/4$-inch julienne strips

Combine 1 cup water with $1/2$ teaspoon salt in a bowl. Add the eggplant matchsticks and soak for 20 minutes. Drain and dry on paper towels.

In a bowl, beat the milk and egg together with a fork. Place the flour on a piece of wax paper. Pour the oil into a skillet to a depth of at least $1/2$ inch (or better still, use a deep-fryer) and heat to the smoking point (about 375°F).

Place the vegetables in small batches in the milk and egg. Remove with a slotted spoon, draining off the excess liquid. Toss the vegetables in the flour, coating very lightly, and transfer to the hot oil, shaking the pan or fryer basket to spread them out rapidly in the oil. Do not crowd. Fry very briefly, about 2 minutes, until lightly golden. Remove with a slotted spoon or slotted pancake turner and drain on paper towels. Keep warm in a 200°F oven while continuing to fry the remaining vegetables. Sprinkle with salt and serve.

Núñez de Prado
Olive Oil PURE AND NATURAL

It is a glorious May day, and we stand enveloped by thousands of olive trees. Every tree is cloaked in white blossoms, each of which will be transformed into an olive in the coming months. Our good friend Paco Núñez de Prado, whose family has been making fine olive oils for seven generations here in the Cordoban city of Baena, proudly shows us his groves, where olive trees grow in arrow-straight rows as far as the eye can see. We are surprised that in the spaces between the trees, typically so carefully plowed, the ruddy red earth is not exposed but cluttered with weeds. This is strictly an organic operation, and indeed, the Núñez de Prado family continues to produce olive oil as in times past.

Olives of the *picudo* and *picual* varietals are harvested by hand right off the branch and carefully placed in esparto baskets. Any olives that fall to the ground and bruise are unworthy of the family name. Massive conical granite rolling stones, like those used by the Romans over two thousand years ago, crush the olives. The free-running oil that emerges—*la flor*, the best of the best—is then filtered and bottled, pure and natural. Paco tells me that by this method it takes twenty-four pounds of olive paste to make one liter of oil. Every step is completely artisanal—even sealing each numbered bottle with red liquid wax is a manual operation.

We sample Núñez de Prado olive oil at a stupendous lunch in an impressive room filled with niches in which bonsai olive trees are spotlighted. Each and every dish, prepared by the family cook, Sandra Peña, includes olive oil. For tapas we taste almonds fried in olive oil, prawns dipped in homemade olive oil mayonnaise ("prawns are merely an excuse to eat the mayonnaise," says Paco), delectable tiny fried ham and partridge croquettes (page 46), and fried pork and ham rollups. Our main course continues the olive oil theme: thick slices of Iberian pork loin marinated in garlic and olive oil (page 232), accompanied by gossamer-light fried julienne vegetables (page 82). The meal ends with almond cookies made with olive oil and—who would have thought?—delicious olive oil ice cream.

PISTO DE MARÍA TERESA REZUSTA NARRO ⁂
MARÍA TERESA'S VEGETABLE MEDLEY

María Teresa was sitting in the handicraft shop, Jarrete, passing the time with her friend María Pilar, in the magnificent town of Albarracín—preserved in its entirety as a national monument—in the region of Aragón. When María Pilar, whom we have known for many years, suggested that her friend, a former restaurant cook who had retired from pots and pans but maintained her reputation as the village's best cook, give me one of her recipes, María Teresa blushed a deep red, quite overwhelmed by the request. Yet she agreed to have the recipe for her famed pisto ready for me the next morning.

She wrote it out in great detail, and it was indeed an exceptional version of this mixed vegetable dish known all over Spain. María Teresa's recipe, however, has the uncommon additions of tuna, pine nuts, and hard-boiled egg that easily make this dish substantial enough to be a main course. If available, it's best to use frying peppers because they are less fleshy, and jarred or canned tuna from Spain is far superior and much more solid than supermarket brands, so it can be separated into chunks without falling apart.

serves 6 as a first course or 3 as a main course

2 tablespoons olive oil

$1/2$ pound Italian green frying peppers, cut into $1/2$-inch dice

$1/4$ pound Italian red frying peppers, or red bell peppers, cut into $1/2$-inch dice

$3/4$ pound zucchini, cut into $1/2$-inch dice

1 medium onion, preferably Vidalia or other sweet onion, finely chopped

2 garlic cloves, minced

One 1-pound can crushed tomatoes

Kosher or sea salt

Freshly ground pepper

$1/4$ teaspoon sugar

One 5$1/2$-ounce jar or can tuna in olive oil, preferably Spanish (see Pantry, page 16), broken into small chunks

2 large hard-boiled eggs, finely chopped

3 tablespoons pine nuts

4 *piquillo* peppers (see Pantry, page 15), or 2 jarred pimientos, cut into long narrow strips

One 8-ounce can *tomate frito* (see Pantry, page 16), or a can of stewed diced tomatoes

Heat the oil in a large skillet and slowly sauté the green and red peppers until softened, about 8 minutes. Remove to a warm platter. Add the zucchini, sauté for 5 minutes, and remove to the platter. Add the onion and sauté until wilted, then add the garlic and cook for 2 minutes more.

Transfer the onion and garlic to a deep casserole and add the crushed tomatoes, salt and pepper to taste, and sugar. Bring to a boil and cook, uncovered, at a high simmer for 15 minutes.

Add the reserved peppers and zucchini to the casserole, along with the tuna, egg, pine nuts, *piquillos,* and *tomate frito.* Simmer uncovered for 10 minutes. Serve in shallow individual casserole dishes, preferably earthenware.

PISTO ANDALUZ ❧ VEGETABLE MEDLEY, ANDALUSIAN STYLE

Although the vegetable medley that commonly includes onion, peppers, tomato, and zucchini is typically associated with the region of La Mancha, it is in fact found all over Spain. I love this version from La Bobadilla, an ultradeluxe hotel tucked away in the hills of the province of Granada, and an ideal place to relax in luxury. The hotel features a restaurant with refined creative cooking and another with down-to-earth Andalusian fare, which is, of course, the restaurant where I found this home-style *pisto*.

A fine and even dice of the vegetables is important to the lovely, colorful appearance (although not as precise as chopping with a knife, a handheld Zyliss chopper will shorten preparation time). You could leave out the dried sweet red pepper *(ñora)*, but that would deprive the dish of some of its unique depth of flavor. *Pisto* will keep very well refrigerated for several days and is best when served with simple grilled meats, poultry, or game.

serves 4

2 tablespoons olive oil

1 medium onion, preferably Vidalia or other sweet onion, finely chopped

1 garlic clove, minced

2 tablespoons minced Serrano ham or prosciutto, cut from an $1/8$-inch-thick slice

2 red bell peppers ($3/4$ to 1 pound), finely diced

2 green bell peppers ($3/4$ to 1 pound), finely diced

1 small ñora (dried sweet red pepper; see Pantry, page 14) or 1 New Mexico–style dried red pepper, core cut out with kitchen shears and seeded

$3/4$ pound tomatoes, finely chopped

1 small zucchini, finely diced

1 tablespoon dry fino sherry or white wine

1 tablespoon minced fresh parsley

Kosher or sea salt

Freshly ground pepper

$1/4$ teaspoon ground cumin

Heat the oil in a shallow casserole and slowly sauté the onion, garlic, and ham until the onion is softened. Add the red and green peppers and the ñora and continue cooking slowly until the peppers begin to soften. Stir in the tomato, zucchini, sherry, parsley, salt and pepper to taste, and cumin. Cover and simmer for about 30 minutes, until done to taste.

Press the ñora with the back of a wooden spoon to extract its flavor, then discard the skin. Stir and serve.

MENESTRA A LA EXTREMEÑA DE CHARITO DE PABLO ❧
CHARITO'S GREENS AND POTATO CASSEROLE

Charito, an old family friend, as youthful and exuberant as ever and a fine cook to boot, gave me this recipe as we strolled to a favorite Madrid restaurant for dinner. Although she is from Córdoba (and retains her typical Andalusian accent) she has lived in Madrid most of her adult life with weekends and vacations spent at her country house in Extremadura—thus the name of this recipe. With its greens, potato, and egg, it is a good candidate for a light supper. serves 4

Kosher or sea salt

1 pound Swiss chard, well washed, thick stems trimmed

6 romaine lettuce leaves

$1/4$ cup olive oil

1 large baking potato, peeled and sliced into $1/8$-inch
   crosswise slices

1 medium onion, preferably Vidalia or other sweet onion,
   peeled and sliced into thin rings

1 garlic clove, minced

1 tablespoon minced fresh parsley

$1/4$ teaspoon sweet paprika, preferably Spanish smoked (see
   Pantry, page 14)

1 large egg, lightly beaten

Bring a pot of salted water to a boil, add the Swiss chard and lettuce, and cook at a slow boil until the greens are almost tender, about 15 minutes. Reserve $1/3$ cup of the cooking liquid, then drain the greens, pressing to extract as much liquid as possible. Chop coarsely and return to the pot.

Meanwhile, heat the oil in a large skillet. Add the potato slices one at a time so they don't stick together, alternating them with onion slices. Lightly salt each layer. Cook slowly over medium-low heat, lifting and turning the potatoes occasionally until almost tender, about 20 minutes (the potatoes should not brown).

In a mortar or mini processor mash the garlic, parsley, paprika, and $1/8$ teaspoon salt as fine as possible. Add a few drops of the reserved liquid and continue mashing. Stir in the remaining reserved liquid.

With a rubber spatula, gently fold the potatoes and the mortar mixture into the greens. Simmer for about 8 minutes, until the potatoes are tender and the liquid absorbed. Heat the broiler. Transfer the potato mixture to a shallow ovenproof casserole. Pour the beaten egg evenly over the surface and place under the broiler until the top is lightly browned. Serve.

PATATAS AL JEREZ DE FERNANDO HERMOSO ⚓
FERNANDO'S SHERRY-INFUSED BAKED SLICED POTATOES

The seafood that day in May when I was in Restaurante Bigote in Sanlúcar de Barrameda with a group of American gourmets in tow, was as glorious as ever, but what really captivated everyone were Fernando's potatoes. They seemed simple and straightforward enough, but there was something extraordinary about them that eluded us. I should have known; the subtle flavor was none other than manzanilla, the bone-dry sherry made in this town, and the magic ingredient in so much local cooking.

serves 4

$3^{1}/2$ tablespoons olive oil

$1^{1}/2$ pounds white potatoes, peeled and cut into $^{1}/8$-inch slices

Kosher or sea salt

Freshly ground pepper

2 bay leaves, cut in halves

$^{1}/4$ medium-large onion, slivered

3 tablespoons manzanilla or dry fino sherry

2 tablespoons minced fresh parsley

Preheat the oven to 300°F. Coat an 8 x 12-inch roasting pan, preferably nonstick or Pyrex, with $^{1}/2$ tablespoon of the olive oil. Add half of the potatoes in a slightly overlapping layer and sprinkle with salt and pepper. Scatter the bay leaves and onion over the potatoes and cover with another layer of the remaining potatoes, sprinkling again with salt and pepper. Spoon the remaining 3 tablespoons oil over the potatoes. Place in the oven and bake for 30 minutes. Turn the potatoes, cover lightly with foil, and cook for about 20 minutes more, until the potatoes are almost tender.

Increase the oven temperature to 450°F. Sprinkle the sherry over the potatoes, cover again with the foil, and continue baking until the sherry is absorbed and the potatoes tender, about 10 minutes more. Sprinkle with parsley and serve.

PATATAS AL AZAFRÁN ❧ SAUTÉED SAFFRON-SCENTED POTATOES

Saffron lends a golden glow to the onion that is spooned over the potatoes and is a popular way to make potatoes in the Basque Country.

When made in a green sauce, as indicated in the variation below, these potatoes are quaintly known as "widowed" potatoes, because this is not a potato recipe that can become a meal, as so many do in Spanish cooking. These potatoes—in green sauce and with saffron—are meant to be a side course to accompany simple meat, fish, poultry, and game dishes. serves 4

5 tablespoons olive oil

1 medium onion, preferably Vidalia or other sweet onion, slivered

2 tablespoons chicken broth

Scant $1/4$ teaspoon crumbled thread saffron

4 medium baking potatoes, peeled and cut into $1/8$-inch slices

Kosher or sea salt

2 tablespoons minced fresh parsley

Heat 2 tablespoons of the oil in a large skillet. Add the onion and slowly sauté until softened, about 10 minutes. Stir in the broth and saffron, cook for a minute to evaporate some of the liquid, and remove to a dish.

Wipe out the skillet. Heat the remaining 3 tablespoons oil in the skillet and add the potato slices, one at a time so they don't stick together. Sprinkle with salt. Give the potatoes a turn, cover, and cook over low heat until the potatoes are tender, about 20 minutes, lifting and turning occasionally. Spoon on the onions, sprinkle with parsley, and serve.

VARIATION

Omitting the onion, broth, and saffron, cook the potatoes in 3 tablespoons oil as indicated (the potatoes may be cubed instead of sliced). In a mortar mash to a paste 2 tablespoons minced fresh parsley with $1/8$ teaspoon kosher or sea salt and 2 minced garlic cloves. Stir in $1/4$ teaspoon paprika, 2 tablespoons chicken broth, and 1 teaspoon red wine vinegar and pour over the potatoes when they are done.

CHAPTER 4

SOPAS Y POTAJES
soups and one-pot meals

SUMMER IN CÁDIZ: WHAT COULD BE BETTER THAN A visit to Bar Bahía and a glass of owner Salvador Lucero's cooling gazpacho? Winter in Madrid: a hearty chickpea stew *(cocido)* at centuries-old La Bola restaurant hits the spot. But don't look for gazpacho out of season—you are not likely to find it. And don't invite a Madrileño to *cocido* in the sizzling heat of summer—he will look at you aghast. Both gazpacho and *cocido* are dishes that have special appeal in their time and place and according to season.

Perhaps putting such extremely different dishes together in the same chapter may seem unlikely, but they are both soups, in their own fashion. In this chapter we progress from the refreshing typically Spanish gazpachos, both red and white, to garlic, vegetable, and fish soups—even a soup with tiny meatballs—that are appropriate any time of year. It ends with soups based on potatoes, beans, chickpeas, and lentils—ingredients that are ever present in country cooking.

In times past *potajes* were inexpensive nutritious meals, although the price of many of the ingredients today makes them luxury items. Even gazpacho was originally a more substantial soup, heavy on bread and olive oil and easy to increase on demand at little additional cost. The tale is told of disgruntled Andalusian field workers who complained to their foreman, Manuel, of low wages and pathetically small lunches. He, in turn, relayed their grievances to the landowner, who declined to augment their paychecks but agreed to increase their food rations. "Manuel," he commanded, "starting tomorrow, add more water to the gazpacho." All these soups are closely associated with the cooking of *mamá,* and Spaniards adore them to this day.

Every region of Spain has its soul-satisfying soups: in Galicia it is *caldo gallego* with beans and local greens called *grelos;* in Asturias, *fabada,* based on beans and sausage products of the region; in the Basque Country, *marmitako,* a soup made with white tuna (bonito), tomatoes, and potatoes, and in Castilla, *cocido,* made with meats, chickpeas, sausage, and vegetables, the hands-down favorite and the ultimate comfort food.

There is no need to pair a wine with the lighter soups, but bean and potato stews demand full-bodied red wine from any of the bodegas discussed on pages 5 to 7. Add a green salad like Spanish-Style Mixed Salad (page 58) or Moorish-Style Green Salad with Cumin and Paprika (page 61), and you have a complete and most satisfying meal.

AJO BLANCO MALAGUEÑO DE BARTOLOMÉ RODRIGO LUCENA ❧
BARTOLOMÉ'S MÁLAGA-STYLE WHITE GAZPACHO

A gazpacho typical of Málaga that relies on blanched almonds for its pure white color and creamy consistency. Sweet green grapes are the essential counterpoint to the soup's tang of garlic and vinegar. Chef Bartolomé Rodrigo Lucena, a native of Andalucía whose love of cooking began at his mother's side, is today the chef at Málaga's Parador de Gibralfaro, a government-sponsored hotel spectacularly set on a hilltop with extraordinary views of the city's port and the Mediterranean sea. The shrimp that Bartolomé adds to this traditional gazpacho are unorthodox, to be sure, but give a lovely flavor counterpoint.

serves 4

One 6-inch piece cut from firm-textured French-style bread, crusts removed

$1/2$ pound (about $1^1/2$ cups) blanched almonds

2 garlic cloves, coarsely chopped

2 tablespoons sherry vinegar (see Pantry, page 18)

1 teaspoon kosher or sea salt

1 cup mild extra virgin olive oil, preferably Andalusian *hojiblanca* (see Pantry, page 14)

4 cups ice water

16 to 24 skinned seedless green grapes, or 16 small balls of green melon or apple

12 small cooked and shelled shrimp, optional

Soak the bread in water and squeeze dry. Place it in a food processor, add the almonds and garlic, and blend until very smooth. Add the vinegar and salt, and with the motor running, add the oil in a thin stream until fully incorporated. Gradually pour in the water.

Transfer to a covered bowl and chill for several hours or overnight. Before serving, taste for salt and vinegar and adjust if necessary. Serve in small soup bowls and garnish each serving with 4 to 6 grapes or melon or apple balls and 3 shrimp, if using.

GAZPACHO ANDALUZ DE GONZALO CÓRDOBA ✿
GONZALO'S ANDALUSIAN GAZPACHO

The classic Andalusian gazpacho, found with surprisingly few variations all over Andalucía, is the ultimate summer cooler. Preparation requires no stove and it is among the most refreshing drinks imaginable (indeed, in Andalucía gazpacho is often served by the glass, and I like to keep a jar in my refrigerator to pour as I will on steamy summer days).

This version comes from Gonzalo Córdoba, an old friend who is the heart and soul of El Faro—my favorite restaurant in the city of Cádiz—and it is a paradigm of fine gazpacho, using tomatoes ripened under the Andalusian sun, fine sherry vinegar made nearby in Jerez de la Frontera, and Córdoba's superb *hojiblanca* olive oil (see Pantry page OO). Notice that this gazpacho does not include cucumber or onion—ingredients that Gonzalo believes mask the pure tastes and fresh flavors of gazpacho's principal elements. The cumin is optional, but it does lend an intriguing and subtle flavor accent.   serves 6

$2^1/2$ pounds very ripe and flavorful tomatoes, quartered

2 garlic cloves, coarsely chopped

1 medium red bell pepper, coarsely chopped, plus more for optional garnish, finely chopped

One 2-inch bread cube cut from firm-textured French-style loaf, crusts removed

2 tablespoons sherry vinegar (see Pantry, page 18)

2 teaspoons kosher or sea salt

$1/2$ teaspoon ground cumin, optional

1 teaspoon sugar

$1/2$ cup mild extra virgin olive oil, preferably Andalusian *hojiblanca*

In a food processor place half of the tomatoes, the garlic, pepper, bread, vinegar, salt, cumin, if using, and sugar. Blend until no large pieces remain. With the motor running, add the remaining tomatoes, and when well processed, gradually add the oil. Beat until as smooth as possible.

Pass through a food mill or strainer, pressing with the back of a metal soup ladle to extract as much liquid as possible; discard the solids. Chill for several hours or overnight. Taste for salt and vinegar and adjust if necessary. If desired, thin with ice water and pass bowls with a garnish of peppers so that guests can help themselves.

SOPA DE ACEDERAS DE LA MADRE DE MARI CARMEN ❧ SWISS CHARD, BRUSSELS SPROUTS, LETTUCE, AND LEEK SOUP FROM MARI CARMEN'S MOTHER

The mother of our friend Mari Carmen was Swedish by birth but lived her married life in Spain. Mari Carmen has lovingly kept her mother's fragile handwritten notebook that includes her recipes and those of Spanish cooks she employed over the years. I sometimes needed Mari Carmen's help in reading her mother's flowing script, in which one letter blended into the next, but it turns out there were many terrific recipes, such as this soup chockful of green vegetables (the original recipe calls for sorrel leaves—if you can find sorrel, by all means use it, but I have substituted Swiss chard, which is readily available).

I prepared it once as an afterthought, just one hour before I was expecting dinner guests, because it looked so simple. Indeed, it was as easy as it seemed and more delicious than I expected. You could leave out the egg yolks, but they do make a more refined soup and give added flavor. If you include potatoes and slices of bread, as Mari Carmen's mother suggests, this soup becomes a meal.

serves 6

2 tablespoons olive oil

2 cups romaine lettuce hearts, thinly sliced crosswise

2 garlic cloves, minced

6 tablespoons well-washed and finely chopped leek (white part only)

1 teaspoon dried chervil

2 tablespoons minced shallots

4 cups (about $1/2$ pound) trimmed and finely chopped Swiss chard

6 small Brussels sprouts, trimmed and quartered

7 cups chicken broth

Kosher or sea salt

Freshly ground pepper

3 large egg yolks

Peeled and cubed white or red potatoes, pan-fried or boiled, optional

Bread slices, cut from a French-style loaf, optional

In a large deep casserole heat the oil and slowly sauté the lettuce, garlic, leek, chervil, shallots, Swiss chard, and Brussels sprouts for several minutes, stirring occasionally, until the lettuce and Swiss chard have cooked down. Pour in the broth, season with salt and pepper, and bring to a boil. Cover and simmer for 1 hour.

When ready to serve, place the yolks in a cup or small bowl and stir in a few tablespoons of the hot broth. Stir into the soup and warm the soup over low heat. Add the potatoes and bread, if desired, and serve.

SOPA DE JAMÓN DE PILAR MONTEOLIVA ❧ PILAR MONTEOLIVA'S HAM SOUP

Once more, our friend Pilar's mother shows how, from an absolute poverty of ingredients, a delicious, wonderfully flavorful soup is born. Here, as in so many Spanish country soups, cured ham, chopped hard-boiled eggs, dried sweet red peppers (ñoras), and bread play starring roles. The original recipe calls for water, but I have substituted broth to further enrich the soup. **serves 4**

1/4 cup olive oil

Four 3/8-inch slices French-style bread

1/2 cup diced Serrano ham or prosciutto cut from an
    1/8-inch-thick slice, then cut into 1/4-inch pieces

6 cups chicken broth

4 whole peeled garlic cloves

Freshly ground pepper

4 small ñoras (dried sweet red peppers; see Pantry, page 14)
    or 2 New Mexico–style dried red peppers, cores cut out
    with kitchen shears and seeded

Kosher or sea salt

2 large hard-boiled eggs

1 tablespoon minced fresh parsley

In a soup pot, heat the oil and sauté the bread until golden on both sides. Drain on paper towels and reserve. Add the ham to the pot and sauté for a minute, then add the broth, garlic, pepper, and the dried red peppers. Bring to a boil, taste for salt, cover, and simmer for 30 minutes.

Transfer the garlic and dried red peppers to a mortar and mash to a paste, discarding the pepper skin. Mash in the egg yolks, adding a little broth to facilitate the mashing, then add the mortar mixture to the broth. Finely chop the egg whites.

To serve the soup, divide among soup bowls, sprinkle with the egg white and parsley, and float the reserved bread on top.

Galician oxen

CALDO DEL BIERZO DE CÁNDIDA ACEBO ✣
CÁNDIDA'S VEGETABLE SOUP FROM EL BIERZO

The tiny village of Compludo, where the family of Cándida lives, is in the fertile valley of El Bierzo in the Castilian province of León. El Bierzo is famous for its fine wines and the outstanding quality of its vegetables, which in Cándida's recipe contribute to a beautifully flavored soup—good by the cup or as a light meal. The beef is used only to enhance the broth—it is not part of the finished soup, for it would change the character of the soup entirely.

serves 6

$1/2$ pound beef stew meat in 1 piece

1 ham bone or ham hock

1 small chorizo (about 2 ounces)

Kosher or sea salt

Freshly ground pepper

3 cups coarsely chopped Swiss chard leaves

$1/2$ pound very small new potatoes, not more than $1 1/2$ inches in diameter, or larger potatoes cut into $3/4$-inch dice

$1/4$ pound fresh or frozen baby fava beans or limas

1 tablespoon extra virgin olive oil

In a soup pot, bring 7 cups water to a boil. Add the beef, the ham bone, chorizo, and salt and pepper to taste and return to a boil. Cover and simmer for $1 1/4$ hours.

Add the Swiss chard, potatoes, beans, and oil. Taste for salt. Simmer for 45 minutes more. Discard the bone and the meat. Cut the chorizo into $1/4$-inch slices and return to the soup.

A Country Lunch in Compludo MEMORIES ARE MADE OF THIS

Intrigued by a reference Luis finds to a seventh-century iron forge—still in operation, no less—we veer off the road we are following along the celebrated Way
of Saint James in a sparsely inhabited mountainous area of the province of
León. Cautiously we follow a tortuous road of hairpin turns deep into an idyllic
valley, where the sound of rushing water fills the air and stunning mountains
rise all around us. The forge we find there is indeed fascinating, and we stop to
marvel at the resourcefulness of our forefathers. The caretaker shows us how
this ingenious system relies on water power to lift a massive tree trunk and
lower a hammerhead onto molten iron. We are completely absorbed in the
demonstration and explanation and lose track of the hour. Suddenly we realize
it is past lunchtime, and we are terribly hungry. Our prospects of finding a
place to eat in these remote surroundings are slim. By good fortune, we see a
hand-painted sign that reads BAR with an arrow indicating the way. We follow it
and happen upon the tiny forgotten village of Compludo. Its streets are un-
paved, the wooden balconies of the slate-roofed houses overflow with flowers,
and chickens roam and peck wherever they please.

The bar, Bodegón, is heaven sent, and we happily feast on simple village
fare—potato omelet, garden-fresh salad, crusty country bread, and homemade
chorizo and lamb chops, both grilled over an open fire—a most perfect meal.
We finish with a magnificent homemade apple yogurt cake. We quickly become
fast friends with owners José María, his wife, María, and sister Cándida. Their
mother, father, and nonagenarian grandfather, who has just returned from
tending the fields, join us.

Since then we have returned to Compludo whenever possible to visit our
friends and to once more enjoy splendid country food amid these bucolic surroundings.

SOPA CASTELLANA DEL SIGLO XV DE CÁNDIDO LÓPEZ ❧
CÁNDIDO'S CASTILIAN GARLIC SOUP

It has been said that Mesón de Cándido in Segovia is even more emblematic of the city than its spectacular two-thousand-year-old Roman aqueduct, which, despite being constructed without mortar, has withstood the centuries. Mesón de Cándido, in the shadows of the aqueduct, was established by the legendary Cándido López in a location where a tavern had stood for centuries. Visited by just about every celebrity and dignitary in the world (autographed photos attest to that), Mesón de Cándido, today in the hands of Cándido's children and grandchildren, remains as evocative and utterly charming as ever.

Cándido's wonderful recipe for this earthy Castilian soup has its roots in past centuries and depends on paprika for its flavor, although the original version from the fifteenth century could not have used paprika, since it is native to America and had not yet been introduced to Spain.

serves 4

5 tablespoons olive oil

4 garlic cloves, thinly sliced

Four $1/2$-inch slices good-quality country bread, cut from a small round loaf

3 ounces Serrano or prosciutto ham, cut into $1/8$-inch slices and chopped

1 tablespoon paprika, preferably Spanish smoked bittersweet (see Pantry, page 14)

4 cups homemade or canned low-salt beef broth

Kosher or sea salt

Freshly ground pepper

$1/2$ teaspoon ground cumin

Pinch of crumbled thread saffron

4 large eggs

Preheat the oven to 450°F. In a shallow casserole, heat the oil, then add the garlic and cook over moderate heat until it begins to sizzle. Add the bread and sauté slowly, turning once, until golden. Stir in the ham, cook for a minute, then sprinkle in the paprika. Pour in the broth and bring to a boil. Season with salt, pepper, cumin, and saffron.

Transfer to individual ovenproof flat-bottomed bowls, preferably earthenware *cazuelas*. Break one egg at a time into a cup and slide an egg into each bowl. Transfer to the oven and bake for about 4 minutes, until the eggs are just set.

SOPA DE ALBONDIGUILLAS Y ALCACHOFAS DE CARMEN PASTOR ✦
CARMEN PASTOR'S MEATBALL AND ARTICHOKE SOUP

The little pork meatballs with a touch of cinnamon and pine nuts in this unusual soup from Carmen Pastor—mother of our good friend Mari Carmen—make an exceptionally tasty contribution to a wonderful soup. Coincidentally, another friend, Reme Domínguez, once gave me a similar recipe for meatballs from her mother, who, like Mari Carmen's mother, lived in the Valencia region (those meatballs were part of a wonderful paella I included in my book *¡Delicioso! The Regional Cooking of Spain*). Bread is the thickening agent in this soup, as is so often the case with traditional Spanish soups. **serves 4**

3 tablespoons bread crumbs

4 cups plus 2 tablespoons chicken broth, preferably homemade

1 pound lean ground pork or a mixture of ground pork and veal

2 tablespoons finely chopped pine nuts

1 slice bacon, finely chopped

1 tablespoon minced fresh parsley

$1/8$ teaspoon cinnamon

1 garlic clove, minced

1 large egg, separated

Kosher or sea salt

Freshly ground pepper

3 tablespoons olive oil

$1/4$ medium onion, finely chopped

$1/2$ teaspoon sweet paprika, preferably Spanish smoked (see Pantry, page 14)

4 to 6 artichoke hearts, fresh or frozen, quartered

1 slice good-quality sandwich bread, crusts removed

In a medium bowl, soak the bread crumbs in the 2 tablespoons chicken broth. Add the pork, pine nuts, bacon, parsley, cinnamon, garlic, egg yolk, $1 1/4$ teaspoons salt, and the pepper to taste and mix well with your hands. Shape into meatballs not larger than $3/4$ inch.

In another bowl, whisk the egg white with a fork until foamy. Heat 2 tablespoons of the oil in a shallow casserole. Dip the meatballs in the egg white, then sauté in the hot oil until barely cooked through. Remove to a warm platter and wipe out the casserole.

Heat the remaining tablespoon oil in the casserole and slowly sauté the onion until softened. Stir in the paprika, then add the 4 cups broth, the artichokes, and the meatballs. Simmer uncovered for 15 minutes.

Break up the bread slice and combine in a small bowl with 4 tablespoons broth taken from the casserole. Whisk until smooth. Stir into the soup, taste for salt, and serve.

Door knocker,
Almagro, Ciudad Real

SOPA DE PESCADO CON PIMENTÓN DE PILAR MONTEOLIVA ✺
PILAR MONTEOLIVA'S FISH SOUP WITH DRIED RED PEPPERS

A tasty soup from the personal recipe collection of Pilar Monteoliva, mother of our dear friend Pilar Vico. Although it is made with a minimum of ingredients, cumin and dried red peppers make the soup special. Pimentón usually translates as paprika, but here it refers to the dried peppers commonly used in home cooking in southeastern Spain.

makes 4 small servings

2 1/2 cups Fish Broth (page 159) or clam juice preferably enhanced with thyme, bay leaf, parsley, celery, onion, and saffron and strained

1/2 pound sea bass, grouper, or snapper fillets

1/2 pound whole plum tomatoes

2 ñoras (dried sweet red peppers; see Pantry, page 14) or 1 New Mexico–style dried red pepper, cores cut out with kitchen shears and seeded

Kosher or sea salt

2 garlic cloves, minced

1/4 teaspoon ground cumin

Freshly ground pepper

4 teaspoons olive oil

In a soup pot combine 1 cup water, the broth, fish, tomatoes (left whole), ñoras, and salt to taste. Bring to a boil, cover, and simmer for 30 minutes. Remove the fish to a warm platter and cut into 1/2-inch cubes. Transfer the ñoras to a mortar and mash to a paste. Add the garlic, cumin, and pepper to taste and continue to mash. Mash in the oil, then gently mash in the tomatoes, discarding the skin. Return the mortar mixture and the fish to the broth. Taste for salt and reheat before serving.

CREMA DE CANGREJOS DE CÁNDIDO LÓPEZ ⚜
CÁNDIDO'S CREAMY CRAYFISH SOUP

Legendary chef Cándido López spent his life in Segovia in his centuries-old restaurant, delighting generations of Segovianos as well as other Spaniards and visitors from all over the world. You might wonder why crab soup is a traditional dish in a restaurant on the central plains of Spain. Simply because the crabs are river crabs (crayfish), and they are very much a part of local cooking. If you can find fresh crayfish, by all means use them. Otherwise a small lobster is an excellent substitute.

At Mesón de Cándido the soup is thickened with cream, but the original recipe from a housewife in Segovia used egg yolks, which I think give a richer flavor and a lovely color. Although of humble origins, *crema de cangrejos* can be used as part of a most elegant meal.

Purchase your lobster or crayfish alive, then have your fishmonger kill it, leaving it whole, not split. Cook the same day. The directions for the crayfish are the same as for the lobster, except the crayfish tails are left whole and the heads and claws need not be cut up.

serves 4

1^1/4 to 1^1/2 pounds freshly killed lobster, or 2 to 2^1/2 dozen crayfish

3 tablespoons unsalted butter

1 tablespoon olive oil

^{1}/2 medium-large carrot, scraped and chopped

^{1}/4 medium onion, chopped

1 bay leaf

1 tablespoon minced fresh parsley

^{1}/4 pound tomato, chopped

2 tablespoons brandy

1 cup Fish Broth (page 159) or clam juice preferably enhanced with thyme, bay leaf , parsley, celery, onion, and saffron and strained

^{1}/2 cup dry white wine

^{1}/8 teaspoon sweet paprika, preferably Spanish smoked (see Pantry, page 14)

^{1}/8 teaspoon crumbled thread saffron

1^1/2 teaspoons fresh thyme, or ^{1}/4 teaspoon dried

Freshly ground pepper

Kosher or sea salt

2 large egg yolks, or 2 tablespoons heavy cream

Leaving the shell on, cut the tail from the lobster and divide into 3 rings. Open the head and transfer the green matter (tomalley) to a mortar. Cut the head into 4 pieces. Divide each large claw into 2 pieces and lightly crush for easy removal of the meat. Leave the small claws whole. When cutting the lobster, reserve as much of the liquid that collects as possible.

Heat 1 tablespoon of the butter and the oil in a soup pot and sauté the carrot, onion, and bay leaf until the onion is softened. Stir in the parsley and tomato and sauté for 3 minutes more. Add all of the lobster pieces and sauté over high heat, turning once, for 5 minutes. Staying well away, add the brandy and ignite. When the flames die, stir in the fish broth and wine. Bring to a boil, cover, and simmer for 10 minutes.

Remove the lobster pieces to a platter. Shell the tail and large claws and cut the meat into $^1\!/_2$-inch pieces and reserve. Reserve the shells and the small claws. Add the head to the mortar with the tomalley and lightly mash. Return the head and tomalley to the pot, along with all of the lobster shells and the small claws. Stir in the paprika, then add $3^3\!/_4$ cups water, the saffron, thyme, pepper, and salt if necessary. Bring to a boil, cover, and simmer for 45 minutes. Strain and return the broth to the pot.

Place the yolks in a small bowl, stir in some of the hot liquid, then add to the pot. Stir in the remaining 2 tablespoons butter and the reserved lobster meat. Heat gently and serve.

SOPA DE PESCADO DE JUAN MARI ARZAK ✌ JUAN MARI'S FISH SOUP

Juan Mari Arzak, undisputed father and master of new wave Spanish cooking, provided me with the recipe for this intensely flavorful fish soup, which he learned to make from his mother. In the Basque Country the fish of choice for soup is scorpion fish, a hideous creature that appears to be wearing a coat of armor. It is sometimes available in American markets, but other firm-fleshed fish can be used.

If you let the soup sit for a while, preferably overnight in the refrigerator, it will gain immensely in taste. Canned vegetable broth and/or bottled clam juice is fine in lieu of homemade fish broth, since the fish and vegetables in the soup will strengthen and enhance the broth. In addition, the cooked shrimp are mashed to a paste and the fish flaked, further intensifying the flavor. If you prefer the soup to have bits of seafood, add more shrimp in the last minute of cooking.　serves 4 to 6

$1\frac{1}{2}$ pounds cleaned fish, such as scorpion fish, halibut, scrod, or monkfish, with skin and any bone

$\frac{1}{4}$ cup olive oil

1 medium onion, cut lengthwise into $\frac{1}{2}$-inch julienne slices

2 medium leeks, trimmed and well cleaned, cut into 2-inch lengths, then into $\frac{1}{2}$-inch julienne slices

2 medium carrots, trimmed and scraped, cut into 2-inch lengths, then into $\frac{1}{2}$-inch julienne slices

4 fresh parsley sprigs

2 bay leaves

4 fresh thyme sprigs, or $\frac{1}{2}$ teaspoon dried

4 whole unpeeled garlic cloves

1 large fish head, such as cod or monkfish, cut into several pieces, optional

30 to 40 small shrimp in their shells

16 to 24 shelled medium shrimp, optional

3 tablespoons brandy

8 cups Fish Broth (page 159; double the recipe), vegetable broth, or clam juice, or in combination

Kosher or sea salt

Freshly ground pepper

Cut the fish into several pieces. Heat the oil in a soup pot. Add the onion, leeks, carrots, parsley, bay leaves, thyme, and garlic and sauté until the onion is wilted. Add the fish, fish head, if using, any fish scraps, and the unshelled shrimp and sauté for a minute. Pour in the brandy and, staying well away, ignite. Before the flames die, cover to extinguish. Add the fish broth, bring to a boil, and cook at a high simmer for 10 minutes. Transfer the fish and the shrimp to a warm platter and reserve. Remove any skin and bones from the fish and shell the shrimp. Return the fish scraps and the shrimp shells to the pot. Bring the fish broth to a boil, then cook at a high simmer, uncovered, for another 15 minutes, to reduce and thicken the broth. Strain, pressing with the back of a metal soup ladle to extract as much liquid from the solid pieces as possible, and return the liquid to the pot. Discard the solids.

In a food processor, finely chop the reserved shrimp and then, with the motor running, add 2 tablespoons or more of the fish broth and continue to chop until the shrimp are mashed to a paste. Return the shrimp to the soup pot, stir, then strain, again pressing with the back of a soup ladle to extract as much liquid from the solid pieces as possible. Return the broth to the pot.

Flake the reserved fish and stir into the pot. Also add the shelled shrimp, if using. Season with salt and pepper, bring to a boil, then remove from the heat. Cover and let sit for a few hours or overnight in the refrigerator. Heat and serve.

SOPA DE PATATAS CON GAMBAS Y HUEVO DE PILAR MONTEOLIVA ❧
PILAR MONTEOLIVA'S POTATO, EGG, AND SHRIMP SOUP

Another fine recipe from the quaint handwritten cookbook of the mother of our friend Pilar Vico, who must have been quite fond of soups judging from the quantity of soup recipes she transcribed to her small tome. This is a lovely, slightly thickened, well-seasoned broth scattered with diced potatoes, shrimp, and hard-boiled egg. The soup gains in flavor if left to sit for at least 30 minutes before serving. serves 4 in cup-size portions

Kosher or sea alt

1 cup Fish Broth (page 159) or clam juice

$^1/_4$ pound small shrimp in their shells

$^1/_2$ pound small new potatoes, peeled

1 medium tomato, cut in half, seeds gently squeezed out

$^1/_2$ medium onion, chopped

$^1/_4$ pound Italian green frying peppers, chopped

2 whole peeled garlic cloves

2 fresh parsley sprigs

$1^1/_2$ teaspoons fresh thyme, or $^1/_4$ teaspoon dried

$1^1/_2$ teaspoons chopped fresh rosemary, or $^1/_4$ teaspoon dried

$^1/_8$ teaspoon crumbled thread saffron

1 tablespoon olive oil

2 large hard-boiled eggs, coarsely chopped

Bring 3 cups salted water and the fish broth to a boil in a soup pot. Add the shrimp and cook very briefly, until just opaque. Remove the shrimp, leaving the liquid in the pot. Shell the shrimp and reserve and return the shells to the pot. Add the potatoes, tomato, onion, peppers, garlic, parsley, thyme, rosemary, saffron, and oil and bring to a boil. Cover and simmer for 30 minutes, or until the potatoes are tender. Remove and reserve the potatoes.

Strain the soup broth, pressing with the back of a metal soup ladle to extract as much liquid as possible. Return the broth to the pot. Cut the potatoes into $^1/_2$-inch pieces or, with a melon scoop, cut round pieces of a similar size. Add to the pot along with the reserved shrimp and half the eggs. Taste for salt and simmer for 5 minutes. Cover and let sit for 30 minutes.

Reheat and serve in small soup bowls, sprinkled with the remaining egg.

SOPA DE LENTEJAS DE CÁNDIDA ACEBO ❧ CÁNDIDA'S LENTIL SOUP

What makes this lentil soup from our friend Cán-
dida different and delicious is the fine chopping
of all its ingredients. Instead of the traditional
Spanish versions with chunks of ham and
chorizo, here everything blends together, giving
great flavor to each and every spoonful.

American lentils do not need soaking, but if
you use the outstanding lentils from Spain you
will have to treat them like any other dried bean
and soak them overnight.   serves 4 to 6

1 pound lentils, preferably Spanish (see Pantry, page 10)

Kosher or sea salt

Freshly ground pepper

1 medium onion, cut in half

4 whole unpeeled garlic cloves

2 fresh parsley sprigs

2 bay leaves

$^{1}/_{2}$ cup peeled red potatoes cut into $^{1}/_{4}$-inch dice

2 medium onions, finely chopped

1 large carrot, scraped and cut into $^{1}/_{4}$-inch dice

2 ounces Serrano ham or prosciutto, cut into $^{1}/_{4}$-inch dice

$^{1}/_{2}$ cup skinned chorizo (see Pantry, page 16), cut into
$^{1}/_{4}$-inch dice

2 teaspoons red or white wine vinegar

If your lentils are Spanish, soak overnight in cold water
to cover. Drain and rinse. Place the lentils in a pot with
6 cups water, salt and pepper to taste, the halved
onion, garlic, parsley sprigs, and bay leaves. Bring to a
boil, cover, and simmer for 1 hour.

Add the potatoes, chopped onions, carrot, ham,
chorizo, vinegar, and salt to taste. Cover and continue
simmering for 30 minutes more, or until the lentils are
tender. Remove the garlic cloves from the pot and
squeeze the garlic flesh into the soup, discarding the
skin along with the bay leaves and parsley sprigs, and
serve.

PATATAS GUISADAS CON COSTILLAS DE ANTONIA ROLLÓN ❧
ANTONIA'S STEWED POTATOES WITH PORK RIBS

On a recent trip to the Toro wine region in western Castilla, with a group of American gourmets in tow, we visited Bodegas Fariña and lunched at the winery on down-to-earth Castilian fare prepared by Antonia Rollón from nearby Fresno. "All my life I watched my mother and grandmother cook, and I learned just by looking," explained cheerful, soft-spoken Antonia, who looked quite chic with her short, red-tinted, slicked-back hair.

Although this potato stew was disarmingly simple—a poor man's dish that was little more than potatoes, it elicited raves from my sophisticated travelers, who insisted on knowing how it was prepared. I distributed the recipe to everyone, and I am told that this dish is now a favorite in households from Greenwich, Connecticut, to Kansas City, Missouri. Spanish bittersweet smoked paprika is the key ingredient that transforms an otherwise ordinary dish into something memorable.

The pork ribs need to be in small pieces but can be difficult to hack—better to leave that job to your butcher. The recipe calls for breaking the potatoes with the point of a knife rather than cutting them into cubes. Strange as it may seem, this technique really does make a difference in texture and taste.

Serve with plenty of good crusty bread.

serves 4

Marinade

1¼ teaspoons bittersweet Spanish smoked paprika or other
imported paprika (see Pantry, page 14)

⅛ teaspoon hot Spanish smoked paprika (see Pantry, page
14) or cayenne

4 garlic cloves, minced

1 small onion, coarsely chopped

3 tablespoons minced fresh parsley

3 tablespoons extra virgin olive oil

¾ teaspoon ground cumin

½ teaspoon dried oregano

1 large bay leaf

Kosher or sea salt

Freshly ground pepper

1¾ pounds pork baby back ribs, hacked apart lengthwise
into 1½-inch-wide pieces, then hacked crosswise into
2-inch lengths

2 tablespoons olive oil

3½ pounds Idaho potatoes, peeled

¾ teaspoon, (or to taste) bittersweet Spanish smoked
paprika (see Pantry, page 14) or other imported paprika

Hot Spanish smoked paprika (see Pantry, page 14) or cayenne

Ground cumin

Kosher or sea salt

Combine the marinade ingredients in a large bowl. Add the ribs, coating them well with the marinade. Cover and marinate for 1 hour at room temperature, or for several hours (or overnight) in the refrigerator.

Heat the oil in a large shallow casserole. Add the ribs with their marinade and slowly sauté, turning once, until the meat loses its color. Pour in 4½ cups water, bring to a boil, cover, and simmer for 1½ hours.

Break the potatoes into irregular 1½- to 2-inch pieces by inserting the point of a paring knife into the potatoes, then twisting the knife until the pieces break off. Add the potatoes, the bittersweet paprika, and hot paprika, cumin, and salt to taste. Cover and cook for another 15 minutes, or until the potatoes are just tender. Serve in shallow soup bowls and provide plenty of good crusty bread.

ALUBIAS ROJAS DEL GOIERRI DE JUAN MARI ARZAK ❧
JUAN MARI'S BASQUE RED BEAN STEW

It is no small accomplishment for a restaurant outside France to receive three coveted Michelin stars, and yet for more than a decade, Arzak has done just that. Even so, for Juan Mari and daughter Elena, who are the restaurant's creative team, praise from their clients means much more than all the accolades of the press.

Like so many great chefs, Juan Mari learned to cook from his mother, who ran a successful restaurant in the Basque city of San Sebastián. But Juan Mari applied new concepts to the rich Basque culinary heritage, creating what became known as "New Basque Cuisine." Nevertheless, Juan Mari's cooking continues to be based on wonderful local produce, and he is ever mindful of the exceptional cooking of his mother, Francisca. In fact, his elegant, cozy restaurant continues to be in the very same place where it began in 1897. "My restaurant is still here by the road outside of San Sebastián in the house my grandparents built as a tavern and where I was born," Juan Mari says with pride.

This exceptional dish of red beans with chorizo and black sausage comes from his mother, and because the meat products are precooked, the fat is greatly reduced. Bean stews in the Basque Country are typically accompanied by long, skinny hot Basque peppers called *guindillas vascas.*

serves 4

1 pound dried deep red beans, preferably Spanish caparrones (see Pantry, page 10)

Kosher or sea salt

4 tablespoons olive oil

1 medium onion, cut in half

1/4 pound sweet semicured cooking chorizo (see Pantry, page 16)

1/4 pound black sausage with onion (*morcilla*; see Pantry, page 16)

1/4 pound salt pork

2 medium green bell peppers

3 garlic cloves, minced

Guindillas vascas (Basque hot peppers; see Pantry, page 15), optional

Soak the beans overnight in cold water to cover. Drain, then combine in a stew pot with 6 cups water, salt to taste, 2 tablespoons of the oil, and half of the onion. Bring to a boil, cover, and simmer until the beans are tender, about 2 hours.

Meanwhile, prick the chorizo and black sausage with a fork and place in a skillet with the salt pork. Cover with water and simmer for 20 minutes. Cut the sausages into 1-inch pieces and the salt pork into 1-inch chunks and reserve.

Finely chop the remaining onion half. In a skillet heat the remaining 2 tablespoons oil and slowly sauté the green peppers, onion, and garlic for 10 minutes. Cover and continue cooking slowly for another 15 minutes.

Add the sausages, salt pork, and the onion mixture to the beans, taste for salt, and serve accompanied by Basque hot peppers, if possible.

HABICHUELAS CON PERDIZ DE RAFAELA ORTIZ GÓMEZ ✀
RAFAELA'S BEAN AND PARTRIDGE STEW

The tiny town of Zuheros is the epitome of an Andalusian village—spotless streets and whitewashed houses, many with coats of arms emblazoned over their doorways. A riot of color spills forth from flower planters lining village streets, and orange bougainvillea grow exuberantly. From the town heights the panorama is spectacular—endless rows of olive trees stretch out below in the valley of the Bailón River. A rocky crag looms over the town square and is the dramatic backdrop for the ruins of a tiny ninth-century Arab castle—in its turn built over Roman remains.

We stayed at the family-owned and -operated Hotel Zuhayra, simple and immaculately kept in every detail, and dined in the hotel's restaurant. There we made the acquaintance of Rafaela Ortiz Gómez, in charge of the kitchen and from a family who has been living in Zuheros for generations, raising sheep and goats, although her grandfather, because of his exceptional skill in setting broken bones, was the town's *curandero.* Rafaela turned out to be a fine cook and gave me this excellent recipe for a stew of white beans, potatoes, and partridge (quail works just as well), made extra special by the flavor imparted by the dried sweet red peppers (*ñoras*) that are commonly used in the cooking of Zuheros.

serves 4

1 pound dried white beans, such as Spanish fava beans (see Pantry, page 10), or navy beans

3 tablespoons olive oil

1 medium onion, finely chopped

2 small Italian green frying peppers, finely chopped

4 garlic cloves, minced

2 small ñoras (dried sweet red pepper; see Pantry, page 14) or 1 New Mexico–style dried red pepper, cores cut out with kitchen shears and seeded

1 medium ripe and flavorful tomato, finely chopped

Kosher or sea salt

Freshly ground pepper

2 partridge or 4 quail, quartered

1/2 cup dry white wine

3/4 cup chicken broth

1 large bay leaf

1/2 pound very small new potatoes, not more than 1 1/2 inches in diameter, peeled

(continued)

*Arab castle,
Zuheros, Córdoba*

Soak the beans overnight at room temperature in cold water to cover. Drain. In a stew pot, heat 2 tablespoons of the oil and sauté the onion, green peppers, garlic, and the dried red peppers until the onion and peppers are softened. Stir in the tomato and cook for 2 minutes. Add the beans, about 6 cups water, and salt and pepper to taste. Bring to a boil, cover, and simmer for 2 hours.

Meanwhile, sprinkle the partridge or quail with salt. In a shallow casserole, heat the remaining tablespoon oil, add the partridge or quail, and lightly brown, turning once. Stir in the wine, broth, bay leaf, and salt and pepper to taste. Bring to a boil, cover, and simmer for 30 minutes.

Fish out the *ñoras* from the bean pot, scrape off the flesh, and return it to the pot, discarding the skin. Add the potatoes and simmer for 10 minutes. Add the partridge or quail and its cooking liquid, cover, and simmer until the potatoes and beans are tender. Serve in shallow soup bowls, preferably flat-bottomed earthenware.

Manchego Cheese Canapés
with Olives and *Piquillo* Peppers,
page 26

Clams with Ham and
Artichoke Hearts, page 35

Luisa Osborne's Shrimp Pancakes,
page 43

Pimiento and Tuna Salad,
Cazorla Style, page 62

Bartolomé's Málaga-style
White Gazpacho, page 92

Isabel's Vegetable Paella, page 132

Pasta, Rabbit, and Green Bean Stew
from Aurora's Family, page 146

Grandmother's Bread Bits with Peppers, Chorizo, and Sun-Dried Tomatoes, page 150

POTAJE DE GARBANZOS Y CHOCOS ❧ CHICKPEA AND CUTTLEFISH STEW

A favorite dish in western Andalucía, this delicious and simple-to-prepare stew brings together chickpeas and cuttlefish (sepia), which are a wonderful match. Although the texture of cuttlefish works better than finer-fleshed squid, you can substitute squid if cuttlefish is not available

serves 4

1 pound dried chickpeas, preferably Spanish

1 pound cleaned cuttlefish, or large squid

1 whole unpeeled head garlic, loose skin removed

2 tablespoons olive oil

4 fresh parsley sprigs

$1^1/2$ teaspoons sweet paprika, preferably Spanish smoked
   (see Pantry, page 14)

1 medium tomato, finely chopped

1 small whole peeled onion

One 1-inch piece medium-hot dried red chile pepper,
   preferably Spanish *guindilla* or *guajillo* (see Pantry, page
   14), cored and seeded

2 bay leaves

About $3/4$ pound very small new potatoes, not more than
   $1^1/2$ inches in diameter, peeled

Kosher or sea salt

Soak the chickpeas overnight at room temperature in cold water to cover. Drain.

Separate the cuttlefish tentacles into individual tentacles (for squid, cut the tentacles in half crosswise). Cut the body into $1/2$-inch lengthwise strips, then crosswise into $1^1/2$-inch pieces.

Combine in a deep stew pot the chickpeas, 5 cups water, the garlic, oil, parsley, 1 teaspoon of the paprika, the tomato, onion, chile, and bay leaves. Bring to a boil, cover, and simmer for $1^1/2$ hours.

Add the cuttlefish and potatoes, season with salt, and continue cooking for another 30 minutes, or until the chickpeas, potatoes, and cuttlefish are tender. Squeeze the garlic flesh into the stew and discard the skin. Stir in the remaining $1/2$ teaspoon paprika. Cover and let sit for 15 minutes before serving, reheating if necessary.

COCIDO GALLEGO CON BOLOS DE OLLA DE DIGNA PRIETO ✢
DIGNA'S GALICIAN CHICKPEA STEW WITH *BOLOS*

Although little known outside of Spain, chickpea stew is perhaps the most emblematic and best-loved dish in Spanish cooking, and every region of the country has its version. It is a direct descendant of the Sephardic stew *adafina*, albeit with later additions of pork products. Spaniards get teary-eyed and wax poetic over *cocido*, for it is a comfort food without equal, and everyone, be they Catalan, Galician, Castilian, or Andalusian, has fond memories of the *cocidos* of their youth. It has been praised in poetry and glorified in song ("you are my nourishment and my pleasure/you are purest glory/and I am madly in love with you"), and although in times past it was an everyday dish, today it has evolved into a special-occasion meal.

Perhaps most famous is Madrid's *cocido madrileño*, but this version from my friend Digna in Galicia is equally satisfying, incorporating typical Galician ingredients like *grelos* (a green similar to Swiss chard) and corn and rye flour (the secret to the region's wonderfully dense and moist breads). Digna's recipe, written in an utterly charming stream-of-consciousness style ("Oh, by the way, I forgot to mention that you need to add . . .") and in an impossibly difficult script, proved to be as on target as other recipes she gave me.

Although *cocido* must simmer for hours, it needs little attention until served. It is presented in several courses: first the flavorful broth, then platters with vegetables—the stars of which are the chickpeas—and an array of meats. Many *cocido* fans consider *bolos*—quenelle-like dumplings, also called *pelotas*—an essential part of their beloved stew. The chickpeas should be cooked in a cheesecloth or cotton net sack for easy removal from the broth, and it's a good idea to cool and refrigerate the cooked meats overnight, as indicated in the recipe, to remove the fat that rises to the surface.   serves 6 to 8

1 pound dried chickpeas, preferably Spanish (see Pantry, page 10)

$1/2$ pound meaty slab bacon in 1 piece

2 beef bones

Kosher or sea salt

Freshly ground pepper

$3/4$ pound smoked ham hock

3 chicken thighs, skin and fat removed

2 pounds beef soup meat

4 fresh parsley sprigs

1 small onion, peeled

1 large leek, well washed

4 whole peeled garlic cloves

$1/8$ teaspoon crumbled thread saffron

1 pound white potatoes, about $2^{1}/2$ inches in diameter, peeled

$3/4$ pound semicured cooking chorizo (see Pantry, page 16)

Bolos

2 tablespoons olive oil

1 large onion, finely chopped

3 garlic cloves, minced

3 teaspoons minced fresh mint

$4^{1}/2$ tablespoons cornmeal

$4^{1}/2$ tablespoons rye flour (available in health food stores)

2 tablespoons lightly beaten egg

Kosher or sea salt

Freshly ground pepper

$1^{3}/4$ pounds Swiss chard, trimmed and coarsely chopped

1 cup cooked very fine pasta, such as angel hair

Soak the chickpeas overnight at room temperature in cold water to cover. Drain and loosely enclose in a cheesecloth or cotton net sack.

Combine in a very large soup pot the chickpeas in the sack, 18 cups water, the bacon, beef bones, and salt and pepper to taste. Bring to a boil, cover, and simmer for 30 minutes. Add the ham hock, chicken, beef, parsley, onion, leek, and garlic. Bring to a boil, skim off the foam, cover, and simmer for $2^{1}/2$ hours. If you wish, cool and refrigerate overnight, then remove the fat that rises to the surface.

Remove 4 cups broth from the soup pot to a smaller pot. Add the saffron, potatoes, and chorizo, cover, and simmer for 40 minutes, continuing to simmer the large pot as well.

To make the *bolos,* heat the oil in a large skillet and sauté the onion, garlic, and mint for a minute, then cover and cook very slowly for about 20 minutes, until the onion is softened. Transfer to a bowl and add the cornmeal, rye flour, egg, $^1/_4$ cup broth from the large pot, and salt and pepper to taste. Fish out the bacon from the large pot. Finely chop enough of the bacon to measure 9 tablespoons and add to the bowl. Return the remaining piece of bacon to the large pot.

Work with your hands to combine the ingredients in the bowl. Form the mixture into sausage shapes, about 2 inches long and 1 inch wide. Add the Swiss chard and the *bolos* to the small pot with the potatoes and chorizo. Simmer for 20 minutes more. Remove both pots from the heat and let sit for 30 minutes.

To serve, remove the meats and vegetables from the pots. Strain the broth from both pots into one pot. Taste for salt and stir in the cooked pasta. Discard the bones and the skin and fat from the ham hock, and cut the ham, beef, bacon, and chicken into serving pieces. Cut the chorizo in halves or thirds and the potatoes in halves. Coarsely chop the leek. On one large microwave-safe platter place the chickpeas and the chorizo. On another large microwave-safe platter arrange the meats, potatoes, leeks, *bolos,* and Swiss chard. Drizzle with some broth to keep moist.

Serve the soup, then present the two platters as a second course. If necessary, heat the platters briefly in a microwave oven before bringing to the table.

POTAJE DE JUDÍAS DE PILAR MONTEOLIVA ❧ PILAR MONTEOLIVA'S BEAN STEW

Of all the delicious Spanish bean stews I have eaten over the decades, this one from the mother of my friend Pilar has a depth of flavor like no other. I attribute it to the addition of saffron and ñoras—the dried sweet red peppers that contribute great taste to so much of Spain's family cooking.   serves 4 to 6

1 pound large dried kidney beans, preferably Spanish
    judiones (see Pantry, page 10)

2 tablespoons olive oil

1 medium onion, preferably Vidalia or other sweet onion,
    coarsely chopped

1 whole unpeeled head garlic, loose skin removed

4 small ñoras (dried sweet red peppers; see Pantry, page 14)
    or 2 New Mexico–style dried red peppers, cores cut out
    with kitchen shears and seeded

1 medium tomato, chopped

3 sprigs fresh parsley

1 tablespoon fresh thyme, or $1/2$ teaspoon dried

8 peppercorns

Scant $1/4$ teaspoon crumbled thread saffron

1 large bay leaf

Kosher or sea salt

$1/4$ pound sweet semicured cooking chorizo (see Pantry,
    page 16)

$1/4$ pound Serrano ham or prosciutto, cut in 1 thick piece
    from the narrow end

$1/4$-pound piece slab bacon or salt pork, optional

Soak the beans overnight at room temperature in cold water to cover. Drain. In a stew pot, heat the oil and sauté the onion, garlic, and ñoras until the onion is softened. Add the tomato, parsley, thyme, peppercorns, saffron, and bay leaf and sauté for a minute or two. Add 7 cups water, salt to taste, chorizo, ham, and slab bacon, if using. Bring to a boil, cover, and simmer for 2 to $2^{1}/2$ hours, until the beans are tender and the liquid slightly thickened.

Fish out the dried peppers, garlic, chorizo, ham, and bacon, if used. Scrape off the flesh of the peppers and add to the stew, discarding the skin. Squeeze the garlic flesh into the stew and discard the skin. Cut the chorizo into thick slices and the ham and bacon into chunks and return to the pot. Reheat, if necessary, and serve.

GARBANZOS A LA ZAMORANA ❧ CHICKPEA STEW, ZAMORA STYLE

Some of the most traditional dishes from the province of Zamora in northern Spain call for fairly large amounts of paprika—three exceptional examples are Stewed Potatoes with Pork Ribs (page 110), Rice with Pork and Paprika, Zamora Style (page 142), and this chickpea stew, which we sampled in Zamora's lovely Renaissance parador. With its strong punch of paprika, this is one of my favorites, especially when I want a simple chickpea stew rather than the more elaborate cocido (page 118). Once again, results will be far superior if Spanish smoked paprika is used.   serves 4 to 6

1 pound dried chickpeas, preferably Spanish (see Pantry, page 10)

1 pound lean pork, cut into $3/4$-inch cubes

Marinade (page 111)

Kosher or sea salt

One $1/4$-pound chunk Serrano ham or prosciutto, cut from the narrow end

4 teaspoons paprika, preferably Spanish smoked bittersweet (see Pantry, page 14)

1 medium onion, cut in half

1 medium tomato, chopped

Soak the chickpeas overnight at room temperature in cold water to cover. Marinate the pork as indicated on page 111.

Drain the chickpeas, then combine them in a large stew pot with 7 cups water, salt to taste, and all the other ingredients, including the pork and its marinade. Bring to a boil, cover, and simmer for about 2 hours, until the chickpeas are almost done. Uncover, increase the heat, and boil for 15 to 30 minutes, until the chickpeas are tender (there should be some liquid, but the stew should not be soupy). Taste for salt. Cover and let sit for 10 minutes before serving.

Storks in Acederas, Badajoz

CHAPTER 5

ARROCES Y PASTAS
rice and pasta dishes

WHEN AMERICANS SPEAK ABOUT A SPANISH RICE DISH they mean just one thing: paella, an eye-catching and festive dish that when made in America invariably consists of chicken, shellfish, and vegetables, cooked in a wide flat paella pan. True, it is a spectacular creation and a great party dish, but in Valencia, paella's homeland, where rice is grown in the marshy delta land between the Júcar and the Turia rivers, there are many other kinds of rice dishes, and indeed, the practice of mixing meats and shellfish in the same paella is frowned upon.

If you are looking for classic paellas, you might consult my book *Paella! Spectacular Rice Dishes from Spain*. What you will find in this chapter are more unusual and sometimes quite homey rice dishes, many with far fewer ingredients than better-known paellas and sometimes made in earthenware *cazuelas* rather than paella pans. After all, paella began as a peasant dish, prepared and eaten by workers in the fields of Valencia, and seafood was not originally among its ingredients. Nevertheless, there are several paellas here that are great company dishes, among my favorites, the Egg-Crusted Salt Cod and Potato Paella (page 137) and Isabel's Vegetable Paella (page 132). All the paella recipes in this chapter can be doubled, if de-sired, and cooked in a 17- to 18-inch paella pan to serve 6 to 8.

But not all Spanish rice dishes come from the Valencia region. Rice is also grown in Catalunya and is a popular dish there. In the Basque Country several dishes rely on rice, like *arroz con almejas* (Rice with Clams, page 139). And although rice is rarely served in Spain as a side course, the Basque dish *chipirones en su tinta* (stuffed baby squid in ink sauce) is always served with plain white rice. Even in the Castilian heartland there are occasional rice dishes, but they are much heartier, like one of my favorites from Zamora (page 142), based entirely on pork products.

I never considered pasta a subject worthy of consideration in Spanish cooking. Only in Catalunya, as far as I knew, did pasta figure into regional cooking in more important ways than as a soup noodle (historically Catalunya—and Barcelona in particular—had close ties to the Spanish territories of Naples and Sicily in the fifteenth and sixteenth centuries). *Canelones*, cooked Spanish style, and *Rossejat de Fideus* (crisped pasta with shrimp) are two very typical Catalan dishes. The only other dish I was aware of in which pasta was a principal player was a paella made with pasta called *fideuá*. Recently, however, I discovered *andrajos*—

pasta stews with meat, fish, or rabbit from the province of Jaén in Andalucía, and suddenly pasta took on new importance. Recipes for *andrajos* came to me coincidentally from two different sources—one from the mother of a chef in the city of Málaga and another from the family of our friend Aurora in the province of Jaén. These recipes represent two prime examples of traditional cooking that Spaniards outside of that region don't even know exists. One other category in this chapter are *migas,* traditional and very popular bread-based dishes.

Red wines are best with the pasta dishes in this chapter, and because of the complexity of ingredients in a paella—even when it is based on fish—red wine or, better still, a fruity chilled rosé *(rosado)* from Navarra is ideal. The rosés of Navarra are far from being innocuous pink wines; these are wines of great character and depth, made from the native Garnacha grape, and in the Valencia region they are the wines of choice with paella.

Tapas are typically served before a paella meal, and a green salad, like Spanish-Style Mixed Salad (page 58), is a refreshing companion to any of the rice dishes.

ARROZ AL HORNO ❧ BAKED RICE

This rice is not a meal in itself, like the other rice recipes in this chapter, but it is a great accompaniment to many fish, poultry, and meat dishes and takes well to sauces.

serves 4

2 tablespoons olive oil or butter

2 tablespoons minced onion

1 cup Valencian short-grain rice (see Pantry, page 15), or Arborio

1 cup chicken broth

2 tablespoons minced fresh parsley

1 1/2 teaspoons fresh thyme, or 1/4 teaspoon dried

A few strands of saffron, crumbled

Kosher or sea salt

Preheat the oven to 400°F. Heat the oil in a deep casserole, then add the onion and cook until the onion is softened. Stir in the rice, coating it with the oil. Pour in the chicken broth and 1 cup water, stir in the parsley, thyme, saffron, and salt to taste, and bring to a boil. Remove from the flame, cover, and transfer to the oven. Cook for 15 minutes, remove from the oven, and let sit, covered, for 5 to 10 minutes before serving.

ARROZ DEL JUEVES DE LA MADRE DE RAMÓN SAN MARTÍN ⚛
THURSDAY'S RICE WITH MUSSELS FROM RAMÓN'S MOTHER

New York restaurateur Ramón San Martín recalls his childhood in Valencia and his parents' struggle to feed their children with very limited means. "My father was paid on Saturdays, so by Thursday there was not much left for food. In Valencia rice was a staple that was eaten every day, and there was nothing cheaper than a paella made with mussels. Saturday's Rice (page 130), on the other hand, was much more festive."

Thursday's Rice, to my taste, is every bit as good as other Valencian rice dishes, and once more shows how simple fresh ingredients can produce excellent results. If you use cultured mussels, the overnight soaking is probably not necessary, since they will not be sandy. And if the mussels are not cultured, you will probably need fewer because they tend to be larger.

serves 4

60 very small mussels (about 1^1/2 pounds)

Kosher or sea salt

Cornmeal or bread crumbs for sprinkling

1 cup bottled clam juice

Freshly ground pepper

3 tablespoons minced fresh parsley

4 garlic cloves, minced

^{1}/4 cup olive oil

1 small onion, finely chopped

1^1/2 teaspoons paprika, preferably Spanish smoked bittersweet (see Pantry, page 14)

1^1/2 cups Valencian short-grain rice (see Pantry, page 15), or Arborio

2 tablespoons freshly squeezed lemon juice

Rinse the mussels and remove the beards. If the mussels are not cultured, place them in a bowl of salted water to cover. Sprinkle cornmeal or bread crumbs over them and refrigerate for several hours or overnight to cleanse them.

In a large pot, combine 3 cups water with the clam juice, salt and pepper to taste, and 20 of the mussels. Bring to a boil, cover, and simmer for about 30 minutes. Meanwhile, in a mortar mash to a paste 2 tablespoons of the parsley, half of the minced garlic, and $1/8$ teaspoon salt.

Remove the cooked mussels from their shells, finely chop, and reserve. Measure the cooking broth to 3 cups, cover the pot, and keep warm over the lowest heat. Preheat the oven to 400°F for a gas oven, 450°F for an electric one.

Heat the oil in a paella pan measuring 13 inches at its widest point (or a shallow casserole of a similar size) and slowly sauté the remaining garlic and the onion. Stir in the paprika and the rice and sauté for 3 minutes so that the rice absorbs the oil. Pour in the reserved broth and the lemon juice, bring to a boil, and boil for 5 minutes. Add the reserved chopped mussels, the mortar mixture, and the remaining mussels in their shells and boil for about 5 minutes more, until the rice is no longer soupy but sufficient liquid remains to continue cooking the rice.

Transfer to the oven and cook, uncovered, for 10 to 12 minutes in a gas oven, 15 to 20 minutes in an electric one, until the rice is almost al dente. Remove to a warm spot, cover with foil, and let sit for about 5 minutes, until the rice is cooked to taste. Sprinkle with the remaining tablespoon parsley and serve.

ARROZ DEL SÁBADO DE LA MADRE DE RAMÓN SAN MARTÍN ❧
SATURDAY'S RICE WITH SHRIMP AND CHORIZO FROM RAMÓN'S MOTHER

"Saturday was my dad's pay day," explains Ramón San Martín, who grew up in Valencia, *"and this allowed my mother, Julia, to indulge in a little luxury for that day's meal. Before going to market she would sauté vegetables with the ham and sausage for the paella and separately cook the rice, removing it from the heat before it was completely done. In the market she looked for what was most appealing and reasonably priced, which often was shrimp. When she returned home, she combined the sautéed ingredients with the rice and the shrimp, and the meal was on the table in minutes."*

I have enhanced the liquid in which the rice cooks with the shrimp shells and some clam juice, but Ramón's mother, in the interest of frugality, saved the shells to flavor another day's rice.

serves 4

1/2 pound medium shrimp in their shells

2 cups Fish Broth (page 159) or clam juice preferably enhanced with thyme, bay leaf, parsley, celery, onion, and saffron and strained

Kosher or sea salt

Freshly ground pepper

1 bay leaf

4 tablespoons olive oil

1 1/2 cups Valencian short-grain rice (see Pantry, page 15), or Arborio

1 medium onion, finely chopped

1/2 pound Italian green frying peppers, finely chopped

1 small chorizo (about 2 ounces), cut into 1/8-inch slices

1/4 pound Serrano ham or prosciutto, cut into slices 1/4 inch thick, then into 1/2-inch dice

1 medium tomato, finely chopped

1 teaspoon paprika, preferably Spanish smoked bittersweet (see Pantry, page 14)

Preheat the oven to 400°F for a gas oven, 450°F for an electric one. Shell the shrimp and cut into thirds. Combine the shells with the fish broth, 3 cups water, salt and pepper to taste, and the bay leaf. Bring to a boil and simmer for 30 minutes, uncovered. Strain and measure to 4 cups (if there is more, boil down).

Heat 2 tablespoons of the oil in a deep pot. Add the rice and sauté for a minute, then pour in the broth. Season with salt and pepper, bring to a boil, cover, and transfer to the oven for about 12 minutes, until the rice is almost al dente. Keep covered and let sit.

Meanwhile, heat the remaining 2 tablespoons oil in a large skillet and slowly sauté the onion and peppers until softened. Add the chorizo and ham and sauté for 2 minutes more. Stir in the tomato and salt to taste and cook for another 3 minutes. Add the paprika and shrimp and sauté slowly until the shrimp are just done. Stir the rice into the skillet, mixing to coat well with the pan mixture. Serve when the rice is thoroughly heated.

ARROZ DE VERDURAS DE ISABEL ❧ ISABEL'S VEGETABLE PAELLA

Isabel is still all smiles after a hard day's work tending the fires at L'Establiment on the reed-lined banks of one of the many canals that run through the Valencian rice fields in the little town of El Palmar, a town where each and every restaurant is dedicated to paella. "When I opened the restaurant with my family in 1982, I knew nothing about the restaurant business," she told me, "but I knew how to make very good rice at home, so I just adjusted my recipes to serve more people."

Her all-vegetable paella was one of the best I had ever eaten, and the memory of its taste stayed with me for many weeks. Of course, Isabel attributes its great taste to the garden-fresh vegetables that grow in abundance in Valencia, a region often called the "Garden of Spain," and the wood from orange trees (Valencia's other claim to fame is its orange groves) used to flame the fire and make the *socarrat*—a crisp crust of rice that sticks to the bottom of the paella pan. Nonetheless, when I prepared her paella at home I think the results came quite close to the original.

serves 4

$2^{1}/_{2}$ cups vegetable or chicken broth

Kosher or sea salt

$^{1}/_{8}$ teaspoon crumbled thread saffron

$^{1}/_{4}$ cup olive oil

$^{1}/_{2}$ cup frozen baby lima beans, thawed

8 baby carrots (about 3 ounces), scraped and chopped

8 shiitake mushrooms, brushed clean, stems trimmed, and coarsely chopped

$^{1}/_{4}$ pound green beans, preferably broad flat beans, ends trimmed

2 medium red bell peppers (about $^{1}/_{2}$ pound), cut into $^{1}/_{2}$-inch dice

1 medium zucchini (about 6 ounces), cut into $^{1}/_{2}$-inch cubes

2 garlic cloves, minced

$^{1}/_{2}$ cup chopped whole canned tomatoes

1 teaspoon sweet paprika, preferably Spanish smoked (see Pantry, page 14)

$1^{1}/_{4}$ cups Valencian short-grain rice (see Pantry, page 15), or Arborio

Combine the vegetable broth, salt to taste, and saffron in a pot. Cover and keep warm over low heat. Preheat the oven to 400°F for a gas oven, 450°F for an electric one.

Heat the oil in a paella pan that measures 13 inches across the top. Add the limas, carrots, mushrooms, green beans, peppers, and zucchini and stir-fry over high heat, stirring frequently, for about 10 minutes. Add the garlic and cook for 2 minutes more, then add the tomatoes and paprika and cook over high heat for another minute. Taste for salt (the mixture should be well salted) and pour in the broth. Bring to a boil, add the rice, and boil until the rice is no longer soupy but enough liquid remains to continue cooking the rice, about 10 minutes.

Transfer to the oven and cook, uncovered, until the rice is almost al dente, 10 to 12 minutes in a gas oven, 15 to 20 minutes in an electric one. Remove to a warm spot, cover with foil, and let sit for 5 to 10 minutes, until the rice is cooked to taste. To make the *socarrat* crust, uncover the paella and return to the stove over medium-high heat. Cook without stirring for about 2 minutes, until a crust of rice forms on the bottom of the pan (be careful not to let it burn). Serve, scraping up the crust with the edge of an inverted metal pancake turner.

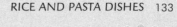

ARROZ CALDOSO CON COLIFLOR Y SEPIA DE LA FAMILIA ROMERO ⚜
THE ROMERO FAMILY'S SOUPY RICE WITH CAULIFLOWER AND CUTTLEFISH

La Playa de Levante is a stretch of beach just outside Valencia where dozens of restaurants specializing in paella stand side by side, among them La Rosa. This outstanding recipe has been passed down through several generations of the Romero family. Their ancestors were fishermen, and their first restaurant was a beachfront lean-to that opened over seventy-five years ago. Today that fragile structure has become a restaurant of substance and is one of the best on the beachfront.

Rice with cauliflower and cuttlefish is an inspired marriage of flavors. Note that this dish is not dry like paella, but slightly fluid (caldoso)—another very popular and traditional way to serve rice in the Valencia region. serves 4 to 6

6 cups Fish Broth (page 159; double the recipe) or clam juice

Scant $^1/_4$ teaspoon crumbled thread saffron

$^1/_4$ cup olive oil

1 pound cleaned cuttlefish or large squid, cut into $^1/_2$-inch dice

Kosher or sea salt

1 pound cauliflower florets

4 large garlic cloves, minced

1 medium onion, coarsely grated

$^1/_2$ pound tomatoes, finely chopped

2 tablespoons minced fresh parsley

1 teaspoon sweet paprika, preferably Spanish smoked (see Pantry, page 14)

2 cups Valencian short-grain rice (see Pantry, page 15), or Arborio

Combine the broth and saffron in a soup pot. Cover and keep warm over a low flame. Preheat the oven to 400°F for a gas oven, 450°F for an electric one. In a shallow casserole about 15 inches across and preferably earthenware, heat the oil and sauté the cuttlefish, sprinkling with salt. Stir in the cauliflower, garlic, and onion and sauté for 5 minutes. Add the tomatoes and parsley, season with salt, and cook for 3 minutes. Turn the heat to low and cook for 10 minutes more.

Stir in the paprika and the rice and sauté until the rice is well coated with the pan mixture. Pour in the broth and boil for 5 to 10 minutes, until the rice is no longer completely soupy. Transfer to the oven and cook for 10 to 12 minutes, uncovered, or until the rice is almost al dente. Remove from the oven, cover, and let sit for 5 minutes, or until the rice is done to taste. Serve.

A Moorish tower, Teruel

Paella in Valencia

PAELLA DE BACALAO CON COSTRA ✤
EGG-CRUSTED SALT COD AND POTATO PAELLA

Bacalao is what gives flavor to this rice dish, but it is not overpowering, even though the cod is only briefly desalted. The rice and potatoes temper the taste of the cod, and what really makes this paella exceptional is its unusual and delicious egg, mayonnaise, and garlic crust. It is one of the mind-boggling 148 kinds of paella made daily at Dársena restaurant in the city of Alicante.

serves 4 to 5

1/4 pound skinned, boneless salt cod

5 tablespoons olive oil

1/2 pound baking potatoes, peeled and cut into 1/8-inch slices, then cut in halves crosswise

1 cup Fish Broth (page 159) or clam juice preferably enhanced with thyme, bay leaf, parsley, celery, onion, and saffron and strained

1/2 cup dry white wine

1/8 teaspoon crumbled thread saffron

1/4 pound Italian green frying peppers, cored, seeded, and finely chopped

3 garlic cloves, minced

1/4 medium onion, finely chopped

1 small tomato, finely chopped

1 tablespoon minced fresh parsley

1 teaspoon paprika, preferably Spanish smoked bittersweet (see Pantry, page 14)

1 1/2 cups Valencian short-grain rice (see Pantry, page 15), or Arborio

Kosher or sea salt

Egg Crust

2 tablespoons mayonnaise

4 large eggs, lightly beaten with a fork

2 garlic cloves, thinly sliced lengthwise

Kosher or sea salt

Rinse the salt cod well to remove as much salt as possible (do not soak to desalt). Dry on paper towels. Preheat the oven to 400°F for a gas oven, 450°F for an electric one. In a paella pan that measures 13 inches across the top (or in a shallow casserole of a similar size), heat the oil and slowly cook the potatoes, turning occasionally, until tender, about 10 minutes. Remove with a slotted pancake turner, letting as much oil as possible fall back into the pan. Drain on paper towels and reserve.

Sauté the cod in the paella pan for about 1 minute on each side. Remove and cut into 1/2-inch strips. Soak in warm water for 30 minutes, changing the water occasionally. Drain, dry on paper towels, and shred. Combine the fish broth, $1\frac{1}{2}$ cups water, the wine, and the saffron in a pot and keep hot over the lowest heat.

Meanwhile, in the paella pan slowly sauté the peppers, garlic, and onion until softened. Add the tomato and parsley and sauté for 3 minutes more. Stir in the paprika, rice, and shredded cod. Pour in the hot broth and salt to taste, and bring to a boil. Continue to boil for about 5 minutes, stirring occasionally, until the rice is no longer soupy but sufficient liquid remains to continue cooking the rice.

Arrange the potatoes over the rice and transfer to the oven. Cook, uncovered, until the rice is almost al dente, 10 to 12 minutes in a gas oven, 15 to 20 in an electric one. Remove from the oven and raise the temperature to 550°F. To make the egg crust, place the mayonnaise in a bowl and gradually whisk in the eggs. Stir in the garlic and salt to taste. Pour over the rice and return to the oven for 5 minutes, or until the egg mixture is lightly browned. Let sit for 5 minutes, uncovered, before serving.

ARROZ CON ALMEJAS CALVETE DE FRANCISCA ARRATIBEL ⚜

FRANCISCA ARRATIBEL'S RICE WITH CLAMS

Juan Mari Arzak is the master and originator of what is called "Nueva Cocina Vasca," or New Basque Cooking, a movement that began some twenty-five years ago and took Basque cooking, which had long been at the forefront in Spain, soaring to new heights. His daughter Elena also succumbed to the call of the kitchen and today works alongside her father at their restaurant, Arzak.

Juan Mari's love for fine food and passion for cooking came by way of his grandparents, who opened a tavern and family-style restaurant just outside of San Sebastián. When his father and mother Francisca took over the business, it became popular as a place to celebrate baptisms, first communions, and weddings (couples would check with "Paquita," as Francisca was called, to find out when she was free before setting their marriage dates). Her cooking, based on traditional Basque fare, acquired fame and encouraged Juan Mari to follow in her footsteps.

This clam and rice dish is a fine example of Paquita's style, based on fresh ingredients, simple preparations, and well-calibrated flavors that need no embellishments.   serves 4

7 cups vegetable broth

$1/4$ cup olive oil

1 green bell pepper, finely chopped

2 large garlic cloves, minced

2 cups Valencian short-grain rice (see Pantry, page 15), or Arborio

$1^1/2$ pounds Manila clams or cockles, scrubbed clean

$1^1/3$ cups minced fresh parsley

Kosher or sea salt

Pour the vegetable broth into a pot, cover, and keep warm over low heat. Heat the oil in an 11-inch shallow casserole, preferably earthenware, and sauté the green pepper until softened. Add the garlic, and when it begins to turn golden, stir in the rice and clams and sauté for 2 minutes. Stir in the parsley.

Pour in the broth, add salt to taste, and cook at a high simmer for 20 to 25 minutes, until the rice is almost done to taste. Remove from the heat, cover lightly with foil, and let sit in a warm spot for 5 to 10 minutes, until the rice is al dente. Serve.

PAELLA DE CONEJO DE JOSEFA ACOSTA ⚜
JOSEFA ACOSTA'S RABBIT PAELLA WITH ARTICHOKES AND GREEN BEANS

Ferran Adrià, the undisputed world master of a revolutionary style of cooking that takes place as much in his laboratory in Barcelona as in the kitchen of his restaurant, El Bulli, near the town of Roses, looks back fondly on the simple dishes of his childhood. "As you can imagine, for me the world's best cook is my mother, Josefa. She certainly had a hard time with me and my brother, Albert, now the restaurant's pastry chef, because we didn't like too many foods. Oddly enough we only became adventurous after we left home. But even now, we always try to set aside a day every week to go home to eat and remember our gastronomic infancy." Among Ferran's favorite dishes is this rabbit paella. "This is how my mother used to make paella, particularly on Sundays," he tells me.

Although paella is generally a quick-cooking dish, in this recipe the rabbit stews first, creating a tasty broth. If you prefer chicken (although I highly recommend the rabbit for an exceptionally delicious paella) it can be substituted. I hope my friend Ferran will forgive the liberty I have taken with his mother's cooking method. Making paella on top of the stove is a tricky operation, especially for those inexperienced in making paella, but finishing the rice in the oven, as I have done here, makes it almost foolproof.   serves 4

One 2$\frac{1}{2}$-pound rabbit or chicken, hacked into 1$\frac{1}{2}$-inch
   pieces
Kosher or sea salt
5 tablespoons olive oil
5 fresh or frozen artichoke hearts, quartered
$\frac{1}{4}$ pound green beans, preferably broad flat beans, ends
   trimmed and cut into 1-inch lengths
$\frac{1}{4}$ pound plum tomato, finely chopped
1$\frac{1}{2}$ teaspoons paprika, preferably Spanish smoked bittersweet (see Pantry, page 14)
3 cups chicken broth
1$\frac{1}{2}$ cups Valencian short-grain rice (see Pantry, page 15), or
   Arborio
$\frac{1}{8}$ teaspoon crumbled thread saffron

Sprinkle the rabbit on both sides with salt. Heat 3 tablespoons of the oil in a paella pan measuring about 13 inches at its widest point. Sauté the rabbit over medium-high heat until brown, turning once. Add the artichokes and green beans and sauté for 2 minutes. Push the rabbit and vegetables to the sides of the paella pan and put the tomato in the center. Cook over high heat for 5 minutes, or until the tomato is reduced and takes on a golden color. Stir in the paprika, then pour in the broth and 1 cup water. Bring to a boil and cook at a high simmer, uncovered, for 20 minutes. Preheat the oven to 400°F for a gas oven, 450°F for an electric one.

Place a large strainer over a bowl and pour in the contents of the paella pan. Measure the liquid to 3 cups and wipe out the pan. Heat the remaining 2 tablespoons oil in the pan, add the rice, and stir until the rice absorbs the oil.

Return the rabbit and vegetables to the pan and pour in the reserved 3 cups broth and the saffron. Adjust the salt, if necessary (it should be well seasoned), and cook at a full boil for 10 minutes, or until the rice is no longer soupy but sufficient liquid remains to continue cooking the rice.

Transfer to the oven and cook, uncovered, for 10 to 12 minutes in a gas oven, 15 to 20 minutes in an electric one, until the rice is almost al dente. Remove to a warm spot, cover with foil, and let sit for about 5 minutes, until the rice is cooked to taste.

Ferran Adrià with his father and mother, Josefa

ARROZ A LA ZAMORANA ❧ RICE WITH PORK AND PAPRIKA, ZAMORA STYLE

Muleteers in the nineteenth century brought rice from the eastern coast of Spain to the northern Castilian province of Zamora, where it became an integral part of traditional cooking. Obviously the rice dishes in this landlocked region do not feature products of the sea, nor the variety of vegetables found in Valencian rice dishes, but a goodly amount of paprika and a variety of pork products create exceptional flavor.   serves 4

$1/8$ teaspoon crumbled thread saffron

8 garlic cloves, minced

3 tablespoons minced fresh parsley

Kosher or sea salt

1 pig's foot, split

2 ounces fatback

1 bay leaf

Freshly ground pepper

2 tablespoons olive oil

$1/4$ pound boneless pork loin, cut into $1/2$-inch dice

1 medium onion, finely chopped

1 medium green bell pepper, finely chopped

$1^1/2$ teaspoons fresh thyme, or $1/4$ teaspoon dried

$1/4$ teaspoon dried oregano

1 small tomato, finely chopped

2 tablespoons Serrano or prosciutto ham cut into $1/4$-inch dice

$1^3/4$ cups Valencian short-grain rice (see Pantry, page 15), or Arborio

$1^1/2$ teaspoons paprika, preferably Spanish smoked bittersweet (see Pantry, page 14)

In a mortar or mini processor mash to a paste the saffron, one-quarter of the minced garlic, 1 tablespoon of the parsley, and $1/8$ teaspoon salt. Set aside.

In a deep pot combine the pig's foot, fatback, 6 cups water, the bay leaf, and salt and pepper to taste. Bring to a boil, cover, and simmer for $1^1/2$ hours. Remove the pig's foot, debone, and finely chop. Cut the fatback into $1/2$-inch dice and reserve. Measure the cooking liquid to $3^1/2$ cups, boiling down if there is more.

Preheat the oven to 400°F for a gas oven, 450°F for an electric one. In a shallow casserole, preferably earthenware, about 15 inches across, heat the oil and sauté the pork loin until it loses its color. Add the onion, the remaining garlic and parsley, the green pepper, thyme, oregano, and ground pepper to taste and sauté until the onion is softened. Mix in the tomato and ham and the reserved pig's foot and cook for 2 minutes. Stir in the rice and sauté until the rice has absorbed some of the oil. Stir in the paprika, then add the reserved broth and boil for 10 minutes, until the rice is no longer soupy but sufficient liquid remains to continue cooking the rice. Add the mortar mixture and stir.

Scatter the fatback over the rice and transfer to the oven. Cook, uncovered, until the rice is almost al dente, about 13 minutes in a gas oven, 15 to 20 minutes in an electric one. Remove to a warm spot, cover with foil, and let sit for 5 to 10 minutes, until the rice is cooked to taste. Bring the casserole to the table and serve.

ANDRAJOS DE ÚBEDA DE LA ABUELA DE BARTOLOMÉ RODRIGO LUCENA ✿
DRIED COD, SHRIMP, AND PASTA STEW FROM BARTOLOMÉ RODRIGO LUCENA'S GRANDMOTHER

Andrajos literally means pieces of old worn-out clothes or rags and refers to the strips of pasta that are part of this dish. A cross between a soup and a stew, this is one of the few truly Spanish pasta preparations. Pasta in Spain is generally relegated to soup noodles, although in Catalunya, which in the sixteenth century had close ties to Italy (in fact, the kingdoms of Naples and Sicily were Spanish possessions), there are several traditional dishes based on pasta (such as the *Canelons de l'Àvia de Pilar del Olmo,* page 148).

The relative blandness of the pasta is a perfect foil for the somewhat strong taste of salt cod. Bartolomé, the slight, shy, soft-spoken chef at the Parador de Málaga, freely admits that his grandmother's version of this dish did not include shrimp. Indeed, in the landlocked Andalusian province of Jaén, a housewife in times past had probably never seen a shrimp in her life, but salt cod was common everywhere. However, Bartolomé understands modern tastes, and his updated version of his grandmother's recipe works beautifully.

serves 4

$1/4$ pound salt cod

3 tablespoons olive oil

8 fresh or frozen artichoke hearts, quartered

1 pound green bell peppers, finely diced

1 medium onion, preferably Vidalia or other sweet onion, finely diced

1 pound tomatoes, finely chopped

$1/4$ teaspoon sweet paprika, preferably Spanish smoked (see Pantry, page 14)

$1/4$ teaspoon hot paprika, preferably Spanish smoked (see Pantry, page 14)

Kosher or sea salt

2 teaspoons sugar

3 cups Fish Broth (page 159), clam juice, or chicken broth

1 large garlic clove, minced

$1/8$ teaspoon crumbled thread saffron

2 fresh mint leaves, minced, or a pinch dried

2 tablespoons dry white wine

10 medium shrimp, shelled and cut into thirds

Pasta

1 cup flour

$1/4$ teaspoon salt

1 tablespoon minced fresh parsley

Soak the cod in cold water to cover in the refrigerator for 2 to 3 days, changing the water once or twice daily, until desalted to taste. Drain and dry on paper towels.

In a medium skillet, heat 1 tablespoon of the oil and slowly sauté the cod for 10 minutes. Cool, shred, and reserve. Wipe out the skillet.

Heat the remaining 2 tablespoons of oil in the skillet and sauté the artichokes, peppers, and onion until the onion and peppers are softened. Add the tomatoes, sweet and hot paprikas, salt to taste, and sugar and sauté for 10 minutes. Stir in the broth, bring to a boil, and simmer for 30 minutes.

Meanwhile, to make the pasta, combine the flour and salt in a bowl, then stir in $1/2$ cup water. Turn out on a work surface and knead to form a smooth elastic dough, adding a little flour if necessary. Roll very thin and cut into twelve $2^1/2$-inch circles. Cut each circle into quarters.

In a mortar or mini processor, mash the garlic, saffron, and mint to a paste. Stir in the wine, then add the mortar mixture to the vegetables and cook for 10 minutes more. Add the cod and shrimp and simmer for another 5 minutes. Scatter in the pasta pieces and continue cooking until the pasta is al dente. The mixture should be soupy (add more broth or water if necessary). Serve in soup bowls, preferably flat-bottomed earthenware, sprinkled with parsley.

TALLARINES DE QUESADA DE LA FAMILIA DE AURORA SÁNCHEZ ✥
PASTA, RABBIT, AND GREEN BEAN STEW FROM AURORA'S FAMILY

This version of andrajos *that in our friend Aurora's family village of Quesada is called* tallarines *is outstanding, from the rabbit to the mortar mash of dried red pepper (ñora), garlic, and peppercorns. "You can use lasagna pasta to make this," Aurora says, "but it is a bit thick and it's easy enough to make your own."*   serves 4

One 3-pound rabbit, cut into $1^{1}/_{2}$- to 2-inch pieces, bony leg
    tips hacked off and discarded

Kosher or sea salt

2 tablespoons olive oil

2 *ñoras* (dried sweet red peppers; see Pantry, page 14) or
    1 New Mexico–style dried red pepper, cores cut out with
    kitchen shears and seeded

2 garlic cloves, minced

12 peppercorns

$1^{1}/_{2}$ cups plus 2 teaspoons chicken broth

1 small onion, finely chopped

1 small Italian green frying pepper, finely chopped

1 medium tomato, finely chopped

$^{1}/_{2}$ pound green beans, preferably broad flat beans, ends
    trimmed, cut into 1-inch pieces

Homemade pasta (page 144), or 8 pieces pasta for lasagna,
    broken in halves crosswise

Sprinkle the rabbit with salt. Heat the oil in a large shallow casserole and slowly sauté the *ñoras*, turning occasionally, until slightly softened. Transfer to a mortar, leaving the oil in the casserole. Add the garlic, $^{1}/_{2}$ teaspoon salt, and the peppercorns to the mortar and mash as fine as possible. Add the 2 teaspoons chicken broth and continue mashing to a paste, stirring in a little more broth if needed.

Add the onion and green pepper to the casserole and sauté slowly until the vegetables are softened. Stir in the tomato and sauté for 5 minutes more. Add the rabbit and sauté, turning once, until it turns white (it should not brown).

Stir in the remaining $1^{1}/_{2}$ cups chicken broth and the green beans. Salt to taste, cover, and simmer for 20 minutes. Add the pasta, submerging it in the broth, and cook for about 20 minutes more, until it is al dente, adding a little more broth, if necessary, and stirring occasionally (the stew should be slightly soupy). Serve in shallow soup bowls or individual earthenware casseroles.

ANDRAJOS CON CHORIZO ❧ CHORIZO, TOMATO, AND PASTA STEW

Although the tomato and pasta soften the spiciness of chorizo, this is still a hearty dish—heartier than the other two versions that precede it—and like the others, a meal typical of the Andalusian province of Jaén.

serves 4

3 tablespoons olive oil

1 medium onion, finely chopped

4 garlic cloves, minced

1 pound chorizo, skinned and cut into $1/2$-inch dice

$1^1/2$ pounds plum tomatoes, chopped

1 bay leaf

1 tablespoon fresh thyme, or $1/2$ teaspoon dried

$1/2$ cup dry white wine

Kosher or sea salt

Freshly ground pepper

Homemade pasta (page 144), or 8 pieces pasta for lasagna, broken in halves crosswise

In a shallow casserole, heat the oil, then slowly sauté the onion and garlic until the onion is softened. Add the chorizo and sauté for 2 minutes more. Stir in the tomatoes, bay leaf, and thyme and continue cooking for another 5 minutes. Add the wine, $1^1/4$ cups water, and salt and pepper to taste and simmer for 30 minutes.

Meanwhile, make the pasta. Stir the pasta into the tomato mixture and cook very briefly, until the pasta is al dente. The mixture should be soupy (if not, add a little more broth). Serve, preferably in flat-bottomed earthenware bowls.

CANELONS DE L'ÀVIA DE PILAR DEL OLMO
MEAT-FILLED ROLLED PASTA FROM PILAR'S GRANDMOTHER

Lively Pilar del Olmo loves to chat with her clients in her tiny restaurant in the Catalan hamlet of Scala Dei, and generously provided me with many of her grandmother's recipes, almost all of which appear on the menu. Canelones is among the most traditional dishes from Catalunya, and they are, in fact, very popular all over Spain. "I like my canelones simple," says Pilar, "the way my grandmother made them for me when I was a child." Indeed, my husband, Luis, who grew up in Madrid, has equally fond memories of his grandmother Clara's canelones.

Although the word canelon as written in Catalan (in Spanish it is canelone) is of Italian origin (Catalunya and Italy were closely linked in the sixteenth and seventeenth centuries and Barcelona was the port of entry for Italian products and Italian cooking styles), the recipes using these pasta squares are totally Spanish.

Spanish pasta squares are available from mail-order sources (the pasta is much thinner than a cannelloni or manicotti shell), or you can substitute any of the other pasta products listed below. Note that the flour in the meat mixture is toasted, which gives a slightly nutty flavor.

makes 20 *canelons* to serve 4 to 5

1 tablespoon flour
2 tablespoons olive oil
1 pound ground pork
1/2 pound ground chicken, preferably dark meat
1/4 pound ground veal
Kosher or sea salt
Freshly ground pepper
1 large onion, finely chopped
1 garlic clove, minced
1 tablespoon minced fresh parsley
1 cup milk
4 tablespoons aged Manchego cheese or Parmesan
Canelone pasta squares (see Pantry, page 11); homemade pasta (page 144; double the recipe), cut into 4-inch squares; fresh wonton skins; or dried unridged manicotti

White Sauce

5 tablespoons unsalted butter
5 tablespoons flour
2 cups milk
Kosher or sea salt
Freshly ground pepper
1/4 teaspoon ground nutmeg
1 tablespoon grated onion
Bread crumbs for sprinkling
Unsalted butter

In a very small skillet, toast the flour over medium-high heat for 5 to 10 minutes, stirring frequently, until lightly browned.

In a large skillet, heat the oil and sauté the pork, chicken, and veal, breaking up the meats with the edge of a wooden spoon and sprinkling with salt and a generous amount of pepper as they cook, until the meats lose their color. Add the onion, garlic, and parsley and continue cooking until the onion is softened and lightly browned.

Stir in the milk, bring to a boil, then add the toasted flour and 1 tablespoon of the cheese and cook until the mixture is thickened and most of the liquid absorbed. Taste for salt and pepper (it should be well seasoned). Cool slightly. Transfer to a food processor and beat until the mixture has a fine, paste-like consistency.

Meanwhile, boil the pasta in salted water until it is al dente. Refresh with cold water, drain, and dry on paper towels. Place $1^1/2$ to 2 tablespoons filling along one side of each pasta square. Roll and arrange, seam side down, in a greased casserole dish in which the *canelones* fit snugly. Preheat the oven to 450°F.

To make the white sauce, melt the butter in a saucepan. Stir in the flour and cook for a minute or so. Gradually add the milk, then season with salt and pepper to taste, nutmeg, and the grated onion. Cook until thickened and smooth, stirring constantly.

Pour the white sauce over the *canelones*. Sprinkle with the remaining 3 tablespoons cheese and the bread crumbs and dot with butter. Bake for about 10 minutes, until bubbly and lightly browned.

MIGAS CAMPERAS DE LA ABUELA DE JESÚS ❧ GRANDMOTHER'S BREAD BITS WITH PEPPERS, CHORIZO, AND SUN-DRIED TOMATOES

Migas, pieces of bread usually sautéed with sausage and vegetables, is a down-to-earth Spanish country dish based on commonplace ingredients combined in a way that makes them exceptionally tasty and ever so appealing. Jesús, our group's bus driver one year, gave me this recipe from his grandmother, who hails from Herrera del Duque in Extremadura's province of Badajoz, and to this day it remains one of his favorite dishes. "It is a meal for hunters and country folk, eaten from a common dish," he explained while deftly maneuvering his oversized bus along a narrow winding road. "Everyone sits around the table, takes a taste of the meats, some peppers, and plenty of *migas* and repeats as they wish."

The ideal accompaniment to *migas* is Spanish-style fried eggs (page 153), and when the yolks seep into the *migas*, the dish is ambrosia.

serves 4

1 medium, round, firm-textured country bread, crust removed and cut into $1/2$-inch cubes

$1/4$ cup olive oil

8 long, thin medium-hot Italian green peppers, or small sweet Italian frying peppers

Kosher or sea salt

$1/2$ pound sweet semicured cooking chorizo (see Pantry, page 16), half cut into $1/2$-inch cubes, the other half into $1/4$-inch slices

$1/2$ pound pancetta, half cut into $1/2$-inch cubes, the other half into $1/8$-inch slices, then into several pieces

Eight 1-inch-wide strips sun-dried tomatoes

15 to 20 garlic cloves, coarsely chopped

$2^1/2$ teaspoons sweet paprika, preferably Spanish smoked (see Pantry, page 14)

8 fried eggs (page 153), optional

Spread the bread cubes on a cookie tray and allow to dry for several hours. Heat the oil in a large skillet and sauté the peppers over medium heat until lightly browned. Cover and continue cooking until softened. Remove to a warm platter and sprinkle with salt.

Raise the heat and add to the skillet the sliced chorizo, sliced pancetta, and the tomato strips. Sauté for a minute or two and remove to the platter with the reserved peppers. Add the garlic and the cubed chorizo and cubed pancetta to the skillet and sauté for a minute or two. Remove to another warm platter. Turn off the heat, cool the oil slightly, and stir in the paprika. Add $^1/_3$ cup of the bread cubes and 3 tablespoons water and stir to form a paste.

Heat the bread paste in the skillet, add the remaining *migas,* and stir to coat well. Cook over low heat for 20 minutes, stirring frequently, until golden and lightly crisped. Stir in the reserved garlic, cubed chorizo, and cubed pancetta. Cook for a few minutes more and remove from the heat.

If serving with the eggs and from a common dish, fry the eggs as directed and place them over or around the *migas* in the skillet. Briefly warm the platter with the reserved chorizo, pancetta, peppers, and tomato and scatter the meats and vegetables over or around the *migas.* Bring the skillet to the table and place at the center. If serving individually, divide the *migas* among individual dishes and arrange the fried eggs, if using, and the reserved meats and vegetables around or over the *migas* on each plate.

The Incredible Egg, Spanish Style

At Casa Lucio in Madrid, where bigwigs hold court in humble tavern surroundings, the first course comes to the table unrequested. It is assumed that everyone wants to begin with Lucio's celebrated *huevos estrellados*—nothing more than top-quality eggs from free-range hens, fried in olive oil until crisp and placed over a bed of perfectly fried potatoes. Before reaching the table, however, the eggs are "smashed," allowing the yolks to seep into the potatoes. It is a dish I dream about, and no matter how often I visit Casa Lucio, I can hardly wait for that platter of eggs and potatoes to be set before us.

Indeed, fried eggs, more than anything else in Spanish cooking, inspire nostalgia, and they are eaten for breakfast, lunch, or dinner. Whenever my husband, Luis, is overcome with hunger, he tells his fried egg story. "I was at the country house of a friend in the town of Brunete near Madrid with the intention of hunting game birds the following morning. We set out at dawn on a cold damp day in November and walked the fields for hours with no luck at all. When we returned at eleven-thirty in the morning we were chilled to the bone, and I was absolutely ravenous. The caretaker's wife prepared a plate for each of us of several fried eggs buried under a huge mound of fried potatoes, and we devoured it. That, to me, was the best meal of my life." Indeed, to this day, whenever I ask Luis what he would like for dinner on his birthday, he replies without hesitation: "Fried eggs."

So over the years I have made it a habit to pose the following question to everyone I know in Spain, from friends and family to three-star chefs: "When you were a kid and very hungry, what did you ask your mother or grandmother to prepare?" The answer is always the same: "Fried eggs," and I realized that eating fried eggs—not omelets or scrambled eggs, just fried eggs—was a full-fledged Spanish phenomenon, worthy of a sociological investigation. I don't know why fried eggs took on such importance, but the roots must go back centuries (consider the seventeenth-century Velázquez painting, *An Old Woman Fry-*

ing an Egg). Mind you, the fried eggs everyone in Spain has in mind are not the rubbery griddle-fried eggs we are accustomed to, but Spanish style, fried in a generous amount of olive oil and emerging with a tender crunchy white and a soft silky yolk.

Everyone, of course, adds a personal touch: some like their eggs with *piquillo* peppers, or with sautéed chorizo or Serrano ham. One friend of ours likes a pinch of saffron in the frying oil, another a crushed garlic clove. Always audacious Ferran Adrià of El Bulli likes to fry the egg whites and yolks separately, to achieve the perfect point of doneness for each. He calls his recipe "Fried Eggs to Dream About." Gonzalo Córdoba in Cádiz must have his eggs with fried onions, and Fernando Hermoso in Sanlúcar de Barrameda insists on eggs gathered from the free-range hens that roam El Coto Doñana, a wildlife preserve across the Guadalquivir River.

Here is the basic recipe:

HUEVOS FRITOS A LA ESPAÑOLA
SPANISH-STYLE FRIED EGGS
serves 1

1 to 2 large eggs
Mild olive oil for frying
Kosher or sea salt

Crack an egg into a cup. Pour the oil to a depth of $1/4$ inch in a 9-inch skillet and heat to the smoking point. Slide 1 egg into the oil. Working quickly, fold in the rough edges with a wooden spoon, and with a large metal spoon scoop up some of the pan oil and pour it over the egg. Repeat rapidly several times until the egg puffs slightly and becomes crisp around the edges but the yolk remains soft. Remove with a metal slotted pancake turner and rest briefly over paper towels to drain. Sprinkle with salt. Repeat, if serving 2 eggs. Repeat once more—if you are really hungry.

CHAPTER 6

PESCADOS Y MARISCOS
fish and shellfish

SPANIARDS ARE EVER SO FUSSY ABOUT THEIR FISH, AND Spain has formidable quantities of the freshest seafood in a dazzling variety not likely to be found elsewhere in the world. Fish is indeed a passion, and Spaniards—especially those living along the country's long Mediterranean and Atlantic coasts, as well as the people of Madrid, who will eat nothing but the best—are undoubtedly among the world's most discriminating fish eaters; they demand quality, and no price can thwart their desire.

Spain's fish markets are a sight to behold. Glistening fresh fish with clear eyes—often still twitching—and lovingly displayed. You will find hake, bass, tuna, turbot, squid, cuttlefish, langoustine, bonito, red mullet, and many others—up to sixty varieties can be found in a single market like the one in San Sebastián. By lunch hour, the stalls are picked clean and hosed down until the next day's deliveries.

As far as preparation is concerned, Spaniards generally reject elaborate sauces and seasonings; fish cookery must be as straightforward as possible. Vegetables and potatoes are frowned upon as unnecessary frills unworthy of sharing the dinner plate with a magnificent piece of fish. Indeed, the most dyed-in-the-wool consider even a squirt of lemon to be an act of treason. Nevertheless, in this chapter you will find some wonderful fish recipes, like turbot with mushrooms from the Basque Country, monkfish in sherry sauce from Andalucía, and hake with peas in saffron sauce from Madrid.

Spain has had a longtime love affair with *merluza*—European hake of exquisitely delicate flesh, as esteemed in the Basque Country as it is in Madrid. The Spanish taste for *merluza* is reflected in the unusual number of recipes for this fish you will find in this chapter, for which you can substitute scrod if hake is not available. Salt cod, despite its reputation as survival food, is a sentimental favorite that everyone in Spain remembers from childhood, and in skilled hands it can be sublime. Of course, there is freshwater fish as well. Sports fishermen flock to Spain to angle for salmon and trout in the magnificent rushing rivers of northern Spain, and there are several recipes in this chapter for these game fish.

You will notice that there are few recipes for shellfish in this chapter, and the reason is twofold. Although shellfish is found in astonishing variety—in Galicia alone there are forty kinds, from *percebes* (goose barnacles) to sea urchins and spider crabs—shellfish is more likely to be a first course or tapa, and the most popular ways to prepare it as a main course are grilled and boiled, no recipe required. In Catalunya grilled fish or shellfish might be accompanied by incomparable *romesco* sauce (page 162), and elsewhere perhaps by a good mayonnaise or vinaigrette. But otherwise seafood is left plain and simple so its fresh briny taste shines through.

Shellfish is often accompanied in Spain by a chilled dry fino sherry—a perfect match—or a fine white wine like Albariño. But when it comes to fish, depending on the preparation and the kind of fish, a light red may be appropriate, as I think it is for the Sautéed Turbot with Mushrooms (page 164) and the Honey-Coated Fried Tuna (page 169).

CALAMARES AL HORNO DE RUPERTO BLANCO ⚜
RUPERTO'S BAKED STUFFED SQUID IN ALMOND SAUCE

The Guadalquivir River cuts through the heart of Sevilla before emptying into the Atlantic at San-lúcar de Barrameda, and Sevilla was the port of entry for boats returning from the New World with treasure troves and new food products. Seafood is supreme here, but curiously, our irre-pressible friend Ruperto in his bar, Casa Ruperto, serves nothing from the sea. His tapas, which have achieved fame in Sevilla, include wonderful fried almonds, mini marinated meat skewers, and magnificent marinated quail. Don't as-sume, however, that fish is not on the menu in Ruperto's home. It most definitely is, and among the dishes that Ruperto and his wife, Josefa, pre-pare is this one, which I love.

Ruperto's exceptionally tasty dish would be dif-ficult to surpass. The squid is stuffed with a mix-ture of its tentacles, garlic, and parsley, then baked in a wine sauce with toasted almonds, and it is another fine example of Ruperto's innate good taste. Small new boiled potatoes and Pimiento and Tuna Salad, Cazorla Style (page 62) could be served with this dish. **serves 4**

1^1/2 pounds cleaned squid with tentacles, the bodies not more than 3 inches long

4 tablespoons minced fresh parsley

2 garlic cloves, minced

Kosher or sea salt

2 tablespoons olive oil

12 blanched almonds

Two ^{1}/4-inch bread slices, cut from a French-style loaf

^{3}/4 cup plus 2 tablespoons dry white wine

1 medium onion, slivered

^{1}/2 cup Fish Broth (page 159) or clam juice

Freshly ground pepper

1^1/2 teaspoons fresh thyme, or ^{1}/4 teaspoon dried

1 bay leaf

Boiled small new potatoes

Finely chop the squid tentacles and combine in a small bowl with 2 tablespoons of the parsley, half of the minced garlic, and ^{1}/2 teaspoon salt. Stuff the squid with this mixture and reserve.

In a shallow casserole, heat the oil and brown the almonds and bread slices until golden. Remove to a mortar. Mash the almonds, bread, the remaining 2 tablespoons parsley, and $^1/8$ teaspoon salt as fine as possible. Add the 2 tablespoons wine and continue mashing to a paste.

Add the onion, remaining garlic, and a little more oil, if necessary, to the casserole and slowly sauté until the onion is softened.

Preheat the oven to 350°F. Add the mortar mixture to the casserole and stir in the remaining $^3/4$ cup wine, the fish broth, salt and pepper to taste, thyme, and bay leaf and cook for a minute. Add the stuffed squid and bake for 45 minutes, basting the squid occasionally.

Serve the squid with the potatoes, ladling some of the sauce on each portion.

CALDO DE PESCADO FISH BROTH

This recipe makes about 4 cups, which may be more than you need for any one recipe, but it is always good to keep some in the refrigerator or freezer. **makes 4 cups**

1 cup clam juice

1 bay leaf

$^1/_4$ teaspoon dried thyme

Kosher or sea salt

6 peppercorns

1 medium onion, cut in half

1 small leek, well washed

1 small carrot, scraped

2 fresh parsley sprigs

1 small whiting (about $^3/_4$ pound), cleaned

$^1/_2$ dozen mussels, rinsed and debearded

Combine all the ingredients with 4 cups water in a large pot. Bring to a boil, cover, and simmer for 1 hour. Strain.

PULPO ENCEBOLLADO DE DIGNA PRIETO ❧
DIGNA'S OCTOPUS WITH PAPRIKA IN SIMMERED ONIONS

Another great dish from my trusty fount of fine Galician recipes, Digna Prieto. In Galicia octopus is enormously popular, served at just about every tapas bar and at country festivals where it is boiled in steaming metal drums. It is typically presented on a wooden dish drizzled with oil and sprinkled with paprika.

If you have never cooked octopus before, don't despair. It is quite simple to do, despite the unusual ritual of dunking it several times in boiling water—a method used to tenderize and give shape to the octopus. And cooking it with a generous amount of simmered onions and Spanish smoked paprika produces wonderful succulence and outstanding flavor. Small boiled new potatoes would typically be served with this dish, and a green salad would also go well.   serves 4

Two 1-pound cleaned octopus

2 tablespoons olive oil

4 garlic cloves, thinly sliced

2 medium onions, preferably Vidalia or other sweet onion, finely chopped

2 teaspoons sweet paprika, preferably Spanish smoked (see Pantry, page 14)

Kosher or sea salt

Hot paprika, preferably Spanish smoked (see Pantry, page 14)

Bring a large pot of water to a boil. Dunk the octopus in the boiling water for a few seconds, remove, and repeat two more times, leaving the octopus out of the water for a minute between dunkings. Cover and simmer for 1 hour. Drain and cool. Snip off the ends of the tentacles with kitchen shears, discard the sac-like mouth, then cut the octopus into 1-inch pieces. Dry the pot.

Heat the oil and slowly sauté the garlic and onions for a few minutes. Cover and simmer slowly until the onions are softened but not browned, about 20 minutes more. Stir in the sweet paprika, octopus, and salt to taste. Raise the heat to medium-low, cover, and continue cooking for 10 minutes more. Serve, sprinkled with the hot paprika.

BESUGO A LA ESPALDA DE IRENE ESPAÑA ❧
IRENE'S PORGY WITH GARLIC AND VINEGAR SAUCE

Spaniards generally like their fish with little enhancement so that freshness is the dominant factor. In this recipe from our good friend Irene—the heart and soul of Casa Irene—just a little vinegar, garlic, and dried chile are enough to make this dish special. And although Irene lives tucked away in the little village of Artiés in the Catalan Pyrenees, the Mediterranean Sea is not very far away, and same-day fresh fish is easy to come by.

Serve with Sautéed Saffron-Scented Potatoes (page 89) and a green salad.   serves 4

$^1/_4$ cup plus 1 tablespoon olive oil

Two 1$^3/_4$-pound porgies or red snapper, cleaned, heads on

Kosher or sea salt

Freshly ground pepper

4 garlic cloves, thinly sliced

Two 1-inch pieces medium-hot dried red chile pepper, such as Spanish *guindilla* or *guajillo* (see Pantry, page 14)

2 tablespoons red wine vinegar

2 tablespoons minced fresh parsley

Preheat the oven to 450°F. Place the 1 tablespoon oil in an ovenproof dish in which the fish just fits and turn the fish in the oil. Sprinkle with salt and pepper and let sit for 10 minutes.

Meanwhile, in a small skillet, heat the remaining $^1/_4$ cup oil and slowly cook the garlic and chile until the garlic begins to sizzle but is not yet browned. Add the vinegar and cook it away. Reserve.

Place the fish in the oven for 15 to 20 minutes, until a meat thermometer registers 145°F when placed in the thickest part of the fish. Remove from the oven and fillet, leaving the skin on, or if you prefer, removing it. Reheat the garlic sauce and spoon over each fillet. Sprinkle with parsley and serve.

A Calçotada to Remember

How could anyone traveling with us that spring in Catalunya ever forget our introduction to *romesco* sauce and a prized onion called *calçot?* Organized by our friend Armando Béjar in a charming *masía,* as country houses in Catalan are called, on the outskirts of Barcelona, our experience begins with tapas in the *rebost,* a rustic cellar redolent of the earthy scents of sausage, cheese, and olives. Then the ritual of the *calçotada,* or "leek bash," begins. It is a merry event that takes place all over Catalunya from late January to early spring, but especially in the town of Valls in the Catalan province of Tarragona, when these long-stemmed, white onions, resprouted under mounded earth to keep them white and tender, are ready to eat.

For our *calçotada,* we don bibs and gloves, as custom dictates, and progress to the patio, where heavy iron grills are heating and mountains of leeks await the hot coals. As they are placed on the grill, smoke billows forth, and when they are well charred, we take them one by one in our fingers, slip off the outer leaves, and dip the *calçots* in bowls of Catalunya's unique *romesco* sauce, a delectable blend of garlic, tomato, dried red peppers, olive oil, almonds, and hazelnuts. Holding the *calçots* aloft, we pop them into our expectant mouths, an untidy process to be sure, and instantly understand the reason for the gloves and bibs. The rhythm is infectious and the *calçots* addictive.

The rest of the meal is anticlimactic and altogether incidental. The *calçotada* stole the show.

SALSA ROMESCO DE CINTA GUTIÉRREZ ✧
CINTA'S SLOW-COOKED *ROMESCO* SAUCE

"Romesco sauce," explains our friend Cinta, "is associated with Tarragona, but we all do it in Catalunya, and everyone has his own technique, even if

the ingredients are always more or less the same." This *romesco*, for example, roasts the garlic and tomato while other versions leave them raw and then cooks them for hours with the oil, vinegar, and *ñoras*, producing a rich complex flavor. *Romesco* is common in Catalunya as a complement to grilled fish and shellfish (it is especially good with lobster and shrimp), as a salad dressing, and as a dip for grilled *calçots*. You can also spread it on toasted bread rounds.

makes 1 cup

32 whole peeled garlic cloves

¹/2 pound plum tomatoes

1 cup olive oil

5 tablespoons red wine vinegar

2 *ñoras* (dried sweet red peppers; see Pantry, page 14) or 4 New Mexico–style dried
   red peppers, cores cut out with kitchen shears and seeded

24 blanched almonds

24 shelled hazelnuts

1 teaspoon kosher or sea salt

Preheat the oven to 350°F. Place the garlic and tomatoes in a roasting pan and roast until the garlic is lightly browned, about 30 minutes. Transfer the garlic and tomatoes to a saucepan and add the oil, vinegar, and *ñoras*. Place over the lowest heat for 4 to 5 hours, uncovered.

Meanwhile, raise the oven temperature to 450°F. Place the almonds and hazelnuts on a cookie tray and toast for about 4 minutes, until the almonds are lightly brown. Cool and mash in a mortar or processor. When the garlic and tomato mixture has finished cooking, add the mashed nuts and the salt and continue cooking for 1 hour more. Cool slightly, then transfer to a processor and blend until as smooth as possible. Pass through a strainer, pressing with the back of a metal soup ladle to extract as much liquid as possible. *Romesco* sauce can be stored for several days in the refrigerator, but bring to room temperature before serving.

RODABALLO CON HONGOS DE LA MADRE DE JUAN MARI ARZAK ❧ SAUTÉED TURBOT WITH MUSHROOMS, GARLIC, AND SCALLION FROM JUAN MARI'S MOTHER

Mushrooms are the perfect flavor complement to the fish in this most elegant dish, which can be prepared in minutes. It comes from the mother of celebrated chef Juan Mari Arzak. You could serve it with Moorish-Style Green Salad with Cumin and Paprika (page 61). serves 4

4 turbot or halibut steaks, about 1 inch thick

Kosher or sea salt

$1/4$ cup plus 2 tablespoons olive oil

5 tablespoons unsalted butter

4 garlic cloves, minced

2 tablespoons minced leek or scallion (white part only)

1 pound mushrooms, such as brown, oyster, or shiitake, brushed clean, stems trimmed, mushrooms cut into $1/8$-inch lengthwise slices

2 tablespoons minced fresh parsley

Sprinkle the fish with salt and let sit for 10 minutes. In a skillet slowly heat the oil, butter, garlic, and leek until the garlic just begins to sizzle. Add the mushrooms and salt to taste, and sauté over medium heat, adding more oil if necessary, until the mushrooms have softened.

Grease a stovetop griddle and heat to the smoking point. Sauté the fish until done, turning once, about 4 minutes to a side. Spoon the mushrooms over the fish. Sprinkle with parsley and serve.

ESCABECHE DE RAPE A LA ANTIGUA ❧ MONKFISH IN SPICED *ESCABECHE*

Five centuries ago spices were all the rage, and they were often used in combination with vinegar—in part to mask the taste of less than fresh fish and meats and also as a food preservative.

To modern tastes, however, seasonings in dishes from centuries past were often grossly overused—although not in this sixteenth-century recipe in which ginger, coriander, cumin, and saffron lend subtle flavor. Escabeche in Spanish cooking generally refers to a spiced vinegar and wine combination in which the fish first cooks, then marinates. It is still very popular in Spain, especially during the summer months.

Monkfish is ideal for this recipe, but other firm-textured fish, like tuna or halibut, also work well. Small boiled and cooled new potatoes can be served with this dish and also benefit from being drizzled with some of the marinade. serves 4

2 pounds monkfish, tuna, or halibut, in 1-inch-thick steaks

Kosher or sea salt

Freshly ground pepper

2 tablespoons olive oil

$1/2$ pound onions, slivered

1 medium-large carrot, scraped and cut into $1/4$-inch crosswise slices

$1/2$ cup red or white wine vinegar

1 cup dry white wine

One quarter-size slice fresh ginger, peeled and crushed with the back of a wooden spoon

8 peppercorns

6 coriander seeds

$1/2$ teaspoon ground cumin

Scant $1/8$ teaspoon crumbled thread saffron

1 whole peeled garlic clove

1 bay leaf

Sprinkle the fish with salt and pepper. Heat the oil in a shallow casserole and sauté the fish until done, 7 to 8 minutes, turning once. Remove to a warm platter.

Add the onion and carrot to the casserole and sauté for a minute, then cover and cook very slowly until softened, about 10 minutes. Add the vinegar, wine, ginger, peppercorns, coriander seeds, cumin, saffron, garlic, and bay leaf. Bring to a boil and cook at a high simmer for about 15 minutes. Cool.

Return the fish to the casserole, cover, and marinate in the refrigerator at least overnight and up to 2 days, turning the fish and spooning the marinade over it occasionally. Serve cold or at room temperature with the marinade and vegetables over and around the fish.

Gaudi's Casa
Batlló, Barcelona

RAPE AL PAN FRITO DE FERNANDO HERMOSO ❧
FERNANDO'S MONKFISH IN SHERRY SAUCE

"My son was weaned on fish," declares Fernando Hermoso, chef and co-owner with his brother Paco of Restaurante Bigote in Sanlúcar de Barrameda, a delightful white-washed Andalusian town where life revolves around its waterfront at the mouth of the Guadalquivir River. Fernando's son, who inherited his father's cherubic face and today expertly directs the dining room, looks none the worse for wear, considering his unorthodox upbringing. And in this southwestern corner of Andalucía, where seafood is the mainstay of the local diet and truly a passion of its people, Fernando's assertion is totally believable.

This simple but wonderful fish preparation has the distinctive taste of Sanlúcar because of the local dry manzanilla sherry in which the fish simmers. Serve with a green vegetable, like Cumin-Scented Sautéed Greens (page 78).

serves 4

1 large ñora (dried sweet red pepper; see Pantry, page 14) or 1 New Mexico–style dried red pepper, core cut out with kitchen shears and seeded

2 pounds monkfish or other firm-textured fish steaks such as swordfish or halibut, about 1 inch thick

Kosher or sea salt

3 tablespoons olive oil

Two 1/2-inch slices bread, cut from a French-style loaf

1 small onion, finely chopped

6 whole peeled garlic cloves

2 tablespoons minced fresh parsley

3/4 cup manzanilla or dry fino sherry

2 teaspoons sweet paprika, preferably Spanish smoked (see Pantry, page 14)

Soak the ñora in warm water to cover for 10 minutes. Drain and cut in half. Sprinkle the fish on both sides with salt and let sit at room temperature.

Heat 1 tablespoon of the oil in a deep pot in which the fish will fit in one layer. Fry the bread until lightly browned, cool, and transfer to a mortar. Add to the pot the onion, garlic, parsley, and ñora and cook until the onion is softened. Add to the mortar and mash the mixture as fine as possible (I don't recommend doing this in a food processor because it would change the color and the character of the sauce). Add 2 tablespoons of the sherry and continue to mash. Mix in the paprika, salt to taste, and the remaining sherry.

Add the remaining 2 tablespoons oil to the pot and arrange the fish on top. Pour the mortar mixture over the fish, bring to a boil, and cover and simmer for 15 minutes, or until the fish is just cooked.

LUBINA A LA NARANJA DE IRENE ESPAÑA ❧
IRENE'S STRIPED BASS IN ORANGE CREAM SAUCE

A winning rendition of striped bass, in Irene's delicate style, made with cream and flavored with julienned orange peel and orange juice. Serve with Baked Rice (page 127) and a green vegetable.

serves 4

Zest of $^1/_2$ orange, orange part only, julienned

$^1/_2$ cup freshly squeezed orange juice

About 3 cups Fish Broth (page 159) or clam juice preferably
   enhanced with thyme, bay leaf, parsley, celery, onion, and
   saffron and strained

$^1/_2$ cup heavy cream

Kosher or sea salt

Freshly ground pepper

1$^1/_2$ tablespoons unsalted butter

4 striped bass fillets with skin, about $^1/_2$ pound each

Heat about 1 cup water in a small saucepan, add the orange zest, and blanch for 5 minutes. Drain and cut into julienne strips.

In the saucepan combine the orange juice, $^1/_2$ cup of the broth, the cream, and salt and pepper to taste and boil down to half. Stir in the butter and the orange julienne strips. Reserve.

Pour the remaining 2$^1/_2$ cups broth into a large skillet and bring to a boil. Add the fish, cover, and simmer for about 4 minutes for every half inch of thickness. Remove the fish and transfer to 4 dinner plates. Reheat the sauce and spoon over the fish. Serve.

ATÚN FRITO CON MIEL ❧ HONEY-COATED FRIED TUNA

"La Cocina familiar antigua" is a wonderful compendium of recipes from home cooks all over Andalucía, and there I found this recipe with Moorish sweet and savory overtones, adapted from a recipe contributed by Jesús García. Pairing tuna with honey turns out to be an unexpectedly delicious match. And if the fish is cut into 1-inch cubes instead of steaks, you have a wonderful tapa. *Pilar's Spinach Sautéed with Raisins and Pine Nuts (page 74) complements the slight sweetness of the fish.*

serves 4

2 pounds fresh tuna, cut into $3/4$- to 1-inch steaks

Kosher or sea salt

2 large eggs

$1/2$ teaspoon dried parsley flakes

Mild olive oil for frying

Honey

Flour for dusting

Sprinkle the tuna on both sides with salt and let sit for 10 minutes. In a dish, beat together with a fork the eggs and parsley.

Pour oil into a skillet to a depth of $1/8$ inch and heat. Spread a light coating of honey on each side of the tuna steaks, dust with flour, then coat with the egg mixture and transfer directly to the skillet. Cook over medium-high heat, turning once, until the coating is golden and the tuna cooked to taste, 5 to 8 minutes. Serve.

SALMONETES RELLENOS A LA PLANCHA DE MANUEL MARINO ✣
MANUEL'S STUFFED RED MULLET

Our friend Manuel Marino hails from the Galician coastal village of San Ciprián and spent a lifetime in the Spanish merchant marine. He is now retired in New York City, but his heart remains in Galicia, where he spends his summers. This recipe for red mullet fillets with a simple filling of bread crumbs, garlic, onion, parsley, and minced Serrano ham is one that he is particularly fond of. Serve with Fernando's Sherry-Infused Baked Sliced Potatoes (page 88).

serves 4

4 red mullet or red snapper fillets, skin on (about
    1 1/2 pounds)
Kosher or sea salt
4 tablespoons olive oil
1/4 cup minced onion
2 garlic cloves, minced
1/4 cup fresh minced parsley
1/4 cup minced Serrano ham or prosciutto
1/2 teaspoon sweet paprika, preferably Spanish smoked
    (see Pantry, page 14)
1/4 cup dry white wine
1/4 cup bread crumbs
Freshly ground pepper
Lemon wedges

Make several shallow slits in the skin side of the fillets. Sprinkle the fish with salt. In a skillet, heat 2 tablespoons of the oil, then sauté the onion, garlic, parsley, and ham until the onion is softened. Stir in the paprika, add the wine, and boil down to half. Remove from the heat. Stir in the bread crumbs and salt and pepper to taste.

Spread the bread crumb mixture over half of the fillets. Place another fillet on top and secure with kitchen twine. Heat the remaining 2 tablespoons oil in a skillet, add the fish, and slowly brown on each side until done, 8 to 10 minutes for each inch of thickness. Cut each fillet crosswise into two portions. Remove the twine and serve with lemon wedges.

LENGUADO EMPANADO CON PIMIENTOS MORRONES DE JOSÉ MANUEL CARO ❧
JOSÉ MANUEL'S MARINATED PIMIENTO-FILLED FILLET OF SOLE

Our favorite tapas bar in Sevilla is Casa Ruperto, run by José Manuel, nephew of our fine friend and the bar's owner, Ruperto Blanco. The recipes given to me by José Manuel are among the best I received, and I particularly liked this marinated fish filled with peppers, breaded, and fried. The initial marinating in lemon and milk and the addition of pimiento—especially if they are piquillo peppers—make all the difference between ordinary fried fish and this one. Serve with Spanish-Style Mixed Salad (page 58).   serves 4

4 thin fillets of sole or similar fish (about 1$\frac{1}{2}$ pounds)

Kosher or sea salt

Freshly ground pepper

$\frac{1}{2}$ cup freshly squeezed lemon juice

$\frac{1}{4}$ cup milk

2 tablespoons minced fresh parsley

2 garlic cloves, minced

One 6- to 7-ounce jar pimientos, preferably *piquillos* (see
   Pantry, page 15), cut into $\frac{1}{2}$-inch-wide strips

2 large eggs, lightly beaten

About 1 cup bread crumbs, preferably a mixture of dried
   bread crumbs and crumbled Japanese-style panko crumbs

Mild olive oil for frying

Arrange the fish fillets in a single layer in a flat-bottomed bowl or deep dish. Sprinkle on both sides with salt and pepper. In a small bowl combine the lemon juice, milk, parsley, and garlic and pour over the fish. Marinate for a couple of hours at room temperature. Drain and dry the fillets on paper towels.

Place the pimiento strips along half of the length of the fillets. Fold the fillets in half crosswise and secure with toothpicks. Dip in the beaten egg, coat well with bread crumbs, and dry on a wire rack for about 20 minutes.

Pour the oil in a skillet to a depth of $\frac{1}{2}$ inch (or better still, use a deep-fryer set at 365°F) and heat until the oil quickly browns a cube of bread. Fry the fish until golden, turning once, about 3$\frac{1}{2}$ minutes. Drain on paper towels and remove the toothpicks. Serve with tartar sauce if you wish.

MERLUZA RELLENA, DOS SALSAS DE CARMEN SERRANO ⚓
CARMEN'S STUFFED HAKE WITH TWO SAUCES

From our dear friend Carmen Serrano, this fish, stuffed with egg slices and *piquillo* peppers or pimientos, is served at room temperature, accompanied by both mayonnaise and a vinaigrette. It makes a lovely summer meal. Serve with very small boiled and cooled potatoes, which will also benefit from a dab of the mayonnaise and vinaigrette.

serves 4

Vinaigrette

$1/2$ cup extra virgin olive oil

2 tablespoons wine vinegar, preferably white

2 tablespoons chopped cornichon or dill pickle

2 teaspoons nonpareil capers in vinegar, drained

2 tablespoons minced onion

2 tablespoons chopped *piquillo* peppers (see Pantry, page 15) or pimiento

1 tablespoon minced fresh parsley

Kosher or sea salt

Freshly ground pepper

$1^1/2$ pounds hake or scrod steaks, about $3/4$ inch thick

2 large hard-boiled eggs, sliced

4 *piquillo* peppers (see Pantry, page 15), or 2 pimientos, cut into $1/2$-inch strips

Kosher or sea salt

Freshly ground pepper

2 tablespoons clam juice or water

2 tablespoons freshly squeezed lemon juice

2 tablespoons extra virgin olive oil

Mayonnaise, homemade (page 36) or good-quality commercial

To make the vinaigrette, whisk together the oil and vinegar in a bowl. Stir in the remaining ingredients.

Butterfly the fish. Arrange the egg and peppers over one side, sprinkle with salt and pepper, and close. Sprinkle the top of the fish with salt.

Preheat the oven to 400°F. In an ovenproof dish, combine the clam juice, lemon juice, and oil. Arrange the fish in the dish and bake for about 15 minutes, until the fish is just cooked through, basting with the juices occasionally. Remove from the oven and cool.

Slice the fish crosswise into pieces about 1 inch thick. Pass the mayonnaise and vinaigrette separately.

MERLUZA EN SALSA DE FRANCISCA ARRATIBEL ❧
FRANCISCA'S HAKE IN GARLIC SAUCE

Fish in garlic sauce, also called "a la vasca," is found all over the Basque Country and is one of the simplest and most delicious ways to prepare hake or its relative, fresh cod. But I have never found a version as good as this one from the mother of acclaimed chef Juan Mari Arzak. The difference is in the extra burst of flavor and appealing crunch from the fried garlic and parsley that are poured over the fish right before serving. You may accompany this with a green vegetable, like Cumin-Scented Sautéed Greens (page 78).   serves 4

4 hake or scrod steaks, 1 inch thick (about 2 pounds)

Kosher or sea salt

$1/2$ cup extra virgin olive oil

8 garlic cloves, minced

$1/2$ pound Manila clams or cockles, well cleaned (see page 35)

1 tablespoon flour

$1/4$ cup Fish Broth (page 159) or clam juice preferably enhanced with thyme, bay leaf, parsley, celery, onion, and saffron and strained

$1/4$ cup minced fresh parsley

Sprinkle the fish with salt and let sit for a few minutes. In a shallow casserole, preferably earthenware, heat $1/4$ cup of the oil and sauté half of the garlic over medium heat until the garlic is lightly colored. Add the fish and clams and sprinkle the flour over the fish. Gently shake the casserole, adding the fish broth and continuing to shake the pan so that the sauce becomes smooth and slightly thickened. Cover and cook for 3 minutes over medium-low heat.

Turn the fish and continue gently shaking the casserole. Sprinkle the parsley over the fish, shake again, cover, and cook for about 3 minutes more, until the fish is just done.

In a small skillet, heat the remaining $1/4$ cup oil with the remaining garlic, until the garlic begins to color. Spoon the garlic and hot oil over the fish and parsley (the oil will fry the parsley). Shake again and serve.

MERLUZA RELLENA DE JAMÓN Y ACEITUNAS DE LUISA OSBORNE ❧
LUISA OSBORNE'S FISH FILLED WITH HAM AND OLIVES

Another recipe from the files of the Osborne family. It has a moist and tasty filling and is eye-catching with its gratin of mayonnaise and egg white, making it a good company dish. You can cook it ahead, but broil the topping at the last minute. Serve with Red Pepper, Tomato, and Tuna Salad, Andalusian Style (page 63).

serves 4

4 hake or scrod steaks, $3/4$ to 1 inch thick (about $1/2$ pound each)

Kosher or sea salt

12 pitted green olives

$1/4$ cup finely chopped Serrano or prosciutto ham, cut from an $1/8$-inch slice

3 tablespoons olive oil

Flour for dusting

2 large eggs, lightly beaten with a fork

1 small egg white

$3/4$ cup homemade (page 36) or good-quality commercial mayonnaise

Butterfly the fish and sprinkle with salt on all sides. Scatter the olives and ham over one cut side of the fish. Close the fish and heat the oil in a skillet. Dust the fish with flour, then coat with the beaten eggs and transfer directly to the hot oil. Sauté over medium heat until the fish is just done, about 8 minutes, turning once. Transfer to an ovenproof dish.

Preheat an oven broiler. Beat the egg white with an electric beater until stiff but not dry. Fold in the mayonnaise and with a rubber spatula, cover the fish with this mixture. Place under the broiler, about 5 inches from the flame, until browned. Watch carefully—it shouldn't take more than a minute. Serve.

Basque fisherman,
San Sebastián

COLA DE MERLUZA DEL PADRE DE PEDRO SUBIJANA ⚬ HAKE STUFFED WITH SHRIMP, MUSHROOMS, AND CAPERS FROM PEDRO SUBIJANA'S FATHER

"My father was a pastry maker and my grandfather a grand gourmet who loved to go to the finest restaurants," my friend and superb chef Pedro Subijana of Akelaŕe restaurant in San Sebastián told me. 'They were refined and sensitive men who loved food, a love that was reflected in a special glow in their eyes when they were eating well. In my house, Christmas was celebrated with culinary rituals—my father always made this stuffed hake—indeed, my family demanded it—and as a child, my role was as his gofer, assisting him in preparation for this festive dinner."

Although hake—or its relative, scrod—is a mild fish, the filling adds plenty of flavor. Pedro recommends serving it with slices of boiled potatoes alternating with hard-boiled egg slices, a very nice complement.   serves 4

2 pounds hake or scrod, about ³/4 inch thick

Kosher or sea salt

Freshly ground pepper

8 teaspoons freshly squeezed lemon juice

2 tablespoons olive oil plus some for brushing

1 medium onion, finely chopped

1 small garlic clove, minced

6 medium white or brown mushrooms, brushed clean, stems removed and very thinly sliced lengthwise

12 small shrimp, shelled and split lengthwise

2 large hard-boiled eggs, finely chopped, plus 1 large egg, separated

7 tablespoons dry white wine

1 slice good-quality sandwich bread, crusts removed, grated

2 teaspoons nonpareil capers in vinegar, drained

2 tablespoons butter, cut into small pieces

3 tablespoons chicken broth

2 tablespoons minced fresh parsley

Butterfly the fish and season inside with salt, pepper, and 4 teaspoons of the lemon juice. Heat the oil in a skillet and slowly sauté the onion and garlic until the onion is softened. Add the mushrooms and shrimp and sauté over medium heat for 2 minutes. Stir in the chopped eggs and 4 tablespoons of the wine. Sprinkle with the bread and capers.

Preheat the oven to 450°F. Beat the egg white with an electric beater until stiff, then beat in the yolk. Stir into the pan mixture and season well with salt. Spread the mixture on one side of the butterflied fish and cover with the top portion. Tie with kitchen twine and cover the cut edge with foil.

Place the fish in a greased baking dish and brush the fish with oil. Add the butter, the remaining 3 table-spoons white wine, and the chicken broth to the baking dish. Bake for 15 to 20 minutes, until the fish is just done. Remove from the oven and sprinkle with the remaining 4 teaspoons lemon juice.

Divide into 4 portions, spooning on the pan juices and sprinkling with parsley. If accompanying with sliced potatoes and eggs, spoon the juices over them as well, and sprinkle with parsley.

MERLUZA CON GUISANTES EN AMARILLO DE ANTONIA BELMAR ❧
ANTONIA'S FISH STEAKS WITH PEAS IN SAFFRON SAUCE

This simple recipe is found in many regions of Spain—I have come across it, for example, in Galicia to the north and to the south in Andalucía—but this first-rate version comes from the mother of our friend Paco Patón, who lived most of her life in Madrid. Peas lend a winning touch of sweetness to the sauce and, of course, a goodly amount of saffron is key to the flavor of the dish. Serve with Tomato and Peppers Salad with Egg and Ham (page 64). serves 4

2 pounds hake or scrod, 1 inch thick

Kosher or sea salt

3 tablespoons olive oil

6 garlic cloves, minced

1 medium onion, finely chopped

2 bay leaves

$1/2$ cup dry white wine

1 tablespoon flour

$2/3$ cup frozen peas

$1^1/2$ cups Fish Broth (page 159) or clam juice preferably enhanced with thyme, bay leaf, parsley, celery, onion, and saffron and strained

Scant $1/4$ teaspoon crumbled thread saffron

Sprinkle the fish on both sides with salt and let sit at room temperature for 15 minutes. Heat the oil in a skillet and sauté the fish over medium heat until it is cooked through, turning once, 8 to 9 minutes (145°F internal temperature). Leave the oil in the skillet and transfer the fish to a flameproof shallow casserole, preferably Spanish earthenware.

Add to the skillet the garlic, onion, and bay leaves and sauté until the onion is softened. Add the wine and cook over high heat until the wine has cooked away. Reduce the heat and stir in the flour, cook for a minute, then add the peas, broth, and saffron. Simmer for 5 minutes, stirring frequently. Taste for salt, turn off the heat, and let sit for 15 minutes. Pour over the fish and heat briefly before serving.

CAZUELA DE BOQUERONES MEDITERRÁNEOS DE MARUJA CABRERA ❧ MARUJA'S FISH FILLETS LAYERED WITH TOMATOES, CAPERS, BREAD CRUMBS, AND CHEESE

If you can find the fresh anchovies that this recipe calls for (they are sometimes available here) by all means, use them. Otherwise substitute a fairly strong-tasting fish, like bass or trout. This delicious and very attractive dish comes to me by way of Elisa Tello, wife of our cousin Rafael Salgado. She got it from her brother-in-law, who got it from his mother, Maruja Cabrera, a native of Nigüela in the Alpujarra mountains of Granada. She is well known among family and friends for her fine cooking and the ease and speed with which she assembles her dishes. Indeed, this baked fish is ever so simple to put together, and it cooks in no time. Serve with Spanish-Style Mixed Salad (page 58). serves 6

$1/2$ cup grated Manchego or Parmesan cheese

$3/4$ cup dried bread crumbs

2 teaspoons dried oregano

Kosher or sea salt

Freshly ground pepper

2 tablespoons minced capers

2 tablespoons minced fresh parsley

4 garlic cloves, minced

$1/4$ cup olive oil plus some for greasing

$1 1/2$ pounds fresh anchovies, butterflied and boned, or 6 bass or trout fillets, skin on

$1 1/2$ pounds large cherry tomatoes, cut into $1/4$-inch-crosswise slices

6 tablespoons dry white wine

Preheat the oven to 450°F. In a bowl, combine the cheese, bread crumbs, oregano, salt and pepper to taste, capers, parsley, and garlic. Generously grease with olive oil a shallow casserole dish or roasting pan.

If using fresh anchovies, arrange a layer, skin side down, in the casserole. Sprinkle with salt, scatter with some of the tomatoes, and season again with salt. Sprinkle with some of the crumb mixture and continue layering until all the fish and crumbs have been used. If using larger fish fillets, arrange half of the fish, skin side down, in the casserole. Sprinkle with salt, then cover with half of the tomatoes. Season again with salt, then sprinkle half of the crumb mixture over the fish. Cover with the remaining fillets, skin side up, then the remaining tomato and crumb mixture.

Drizzle the wine and oil over the fish and bake for 20 minutes, or until the fish is just done.

TRUCHAS EN ESCABECHE DE IRENE ESPAÑA ⚜
IRENE'S PICKLED TROUT

Irene España has lived her entire life in the tiny bucolic village of Artiés in the Catalan Pyrenees. She does not, however, live isolated from the world. Her splendid restaurant, Casa Irene, is a favorite of the king of Spain when he comes here to ski, and France is just a few miles away, allowing Irene and her son Andrés—now the restaurant's chef—to hone their culinary skills on both sides of the border. Trout from rushing mountain rivers is just one of the fine foods found in the fertile Aràn Valley, where Artiés is located. Irene's recipe for this classic Spanish dish is one of the finest I have ever come across, and it makes a wonderfully refreshing light summer meal, a first course when served in half portions, or if cut into tapa-size pieces, a great appetizer. Serve with sliced boiled potatoes, coating them with the fish marinade.

serves 8 as a first course or tapa, or 4 as a main course

Four $1/2$-pound cleaned trout, heads on or off

Kosher or sea salt

Freshly ground pepper

$3/4$ cup olive oil

Four 2-inch pieces leeks (white part only), well washed

2 medium carrots, scraped and cut into 2-inch pieces, then into julienne strips

4 garlic cloves, slivered

Four 2-inch pieces celery, cut into julienne strips

$1/2$ medium-large onion, slivered

$1/2$ teaspoon paprika, preferably Spanish smoked bittersweet (see Pantry, page 14)

2 bay leaves

1 tablespoon fresh thyme, or $1/2$ teaspoon dried

$1/2$ teaspoon dried oregano

$3/4$ cup dry white wine

$3/4$ cup wine vinegar, preferably white

Sprinkle the trout with salt and pepper and let sit for 10 minutes. Heat the oil in a shallow casserole and sauté the leeks, carrots, garlic, celery, and onion over low heat until the vegetables are softened, about 8 minutes.

Stir in the paprika, bay leaves, thyme, oregano, and salt and pepper to taste. Add the trout and cook over medium-low heat for 7 to 10 minutes, turning once. Add the wine and vinegar, bring to a full boil, and boil for a minute. Turn off the heat, cool, then refrigerate for several days, turning the trout occasionally.

Serve either a whole trout per person as a main course or a fillet as a first course, leaving the skin on. Spoon the vegetables and some marinade over each portion.

PESCADO EN SALSA DE SOBREHUSO DE FERNANDO HERMOSO ❧
FERNANDO'S FISH STEAKS IN GARLIC, VINEGAR, AND TOASTED FLOUR SAUCE

Cheery Fernando, a lifelong resident of seaside Sanlúcar de Barrameda in the province of Cádiz, concentrates in his family restaurant Bigote on the marvelous produce of land and sea found in the environs of Sanlúcar. When he cooks with wine it is invariably the local bone-dry sherry called manzanilla; his extraordinary fish is from local waters; and his recipes those cooked here in Sanlúcar for generations.

"Sobrehuso" or "leftover" refers to the portion of the fishermen's catch that was not deemed marketable and therefore prepared on board for the crew along with other staples readily at hand in the boat's galley. The toasted flour gives the silky sauce its color and distinctive flavor, and it is perfect for a mild white fish. Serve with Fernando's Sherry-Infused Baked Sliced Potatoes (page 88).

serves 4

4 fish steaks, about 1 inch thick, such as fresh cod, monkfish, swordfish, or halibut

Kosher or sea salt

2 tablespoons flour

2 tablespoons olive oil

3 garlic cloves, coarsely chopped

1 bay leaf

1 1/4 cups Fish Broth (page 159) or clam juice preferably enhanced with thyme, bay leaf, parsley, celery, onion, and saffron and strained

2 tablespoons wine vinegar, preferably white

Sprinkle the fish on both sides with salt and let sit at room temperature. Place the flour in a small heavy skillet over medium heat and toast, stirring constantly, until lightly browned, about 5 minutes.

In a large skillet, heat the oil and slowly sauté the garlic with the bay leaf until the garlic just begins to color. Stir in the toasted flour, then add the fish broth, vinegar, and salt to taste and simmer, stirring constantly, until slightly thickened. Add the fish, cover, and cook for about 10 minutes, until just cooked through. Remove the fish to a warm platter. If the sauce has thinned, boil it down briefly. Serve, spooning the sauce over the fish.

PESCADO A LA PARRILLA CON SALSA DE ANCHOA DE RUPERTO BLANCO ❧
GRILLED FISH WITH RUPERTO'S ANCHOVY CAPER SAUCE

Ruperto's anchovy sauce lights up everything we dab it on—salads, boiled potatoes, and especially plain grilled fish. Its forceful flavor works beautifully with any food that is mild in flavor. It will keep in the refrigerator for weeks.   serves 4

2 pounds fish steaks, such as monkfish, turbot, or swordfish, about 1 inch thick

Kosher or sea salt

Anchovy Caper Sauce

2 tablespoons minced fresh parsley

4 teaspoons minced scallions (white part only)

2 tablespoons minced celery

2 garlic cloves, minced

2 tablespoons capers

4 large anchovy fillets, chopped

$1/4$ teaspoon dried oregano

$1^1/2$ teaspoons fresh thyme, minced, or $1/4$ teaspoon dried

2 tablespoons extra virgin olive oil

$1^1/2$ tablespoons red wine vinegar

Kosher or sea salt

Freshly ground pepper

Sprinkle the fish with salt and let sit at room temperature. To make the anchovy caper sauce, mash to a paste in a mortar the parsley, scallions, celery, garlic, capers, anchovies, oregano, and thyme. Stir in the oil, vinegar, and salt and pepper to taste.

Grease a stovetop grill and heat until very hot. Grill the fish, turning once, until just cooked through, 8 to 10 minutes. Spoon the anchovy caper sauce over the fish.

Galician peasant

PESCADO AL HORNO DE DIGNA PRIETO ❧
FISH BAKED WITH POTATOES, ONIONS, SAFFRON, AND PAPRIKA

Another outstanding recipe from Digna in El Grove on the Galician coast. It uses the typical ingredients for cooking fish Galician style: potatoes, saffron, paprika, and onion. In the words of Digna, the potatoes "taste like heaven." Indeed they do (the large amount of onion in combination with saffron and paprika is key), and the potatoes are a magnificent accompaniment to this simply baked fish. Serve, if you wish, with a green salad.   serves 4

$1^1/_2$ to 2 pounds fish fillets, such as striped bass, turbot, or
    grouper, skin on

Kosher or sea salt

$^1/_2$ cup freshly squeezed lemon juice

5 tablespoons olive oil

1 pound baking potatoes, peeled and cut into $^1/_8$-inch slices

2 cups very finely chopped onions, preferably Vidalia or other
    sweet onion

Scant $^1/_4$ teaspoon crumbled thread saffron

$^1/_2$ teaspoon sweet paprika, preferably Spanish smoked (see
    Pantry, page 14)

2 tablespoons minced fresh parsley

Sprinkle the fish fillets with salt and arrange in a flat-bottomed bowl or pie plate. Pour on the lemon juice and let sit.

In a shallow ovenproof casserole, heat 3 tablespoons of the oil, add the potatoes in layers, and sprinkle each layer with salt. Turn the potatoes to coat with the oil and sauté over medium heat for 2 minutes. Stir in the onions, $^1/_8$ teaspoon of the saffron, and $^1/_4$ teaspoon of the paprika and sauté for 2 minutes more. Cover and cook over medium-low heat until the potatoes are almost tender, 15 to 20 minutes, lifting and turning the potatoes occasionally.

Preheat the oven to 375°F. Drain the fish and arrange over the potatoes. Drizzle the remaining 2 tablespoons oil over the fish and sprinkle with salt and the remaining $^1/_8$ teaspoon saffron and $^1/_4$ teaspoon paprika. Bake for about 15 minutes, until the fish is just cooked through. You can bring the casserole to the table, or transfer the fish to dinner plates and arrange the potatoes around and over the fish. Sprinkle with the parsley and serve.

SUQUET DE PESCADO DE LA FAMILIA GUTIÉRREZ ✣
THE GUTIÉRREZ FAMILY'S CATALAN FISH AND POTATOES WITH *ALIOLI*

It is all but impossible for anything served with *alioli* not to taste sublime, and this Catalan fish stew is no exception. "This is a dish that was popularized by fishermen and their families," explains my friend Cinta Gutiérrez, who lives in L'Escala and works in the family restaurant Els Pescadors, "and it was eaten—and is still enjoyed—mainly in the area of L'Empurdà and especially in L'Escala." Made from the fish rejected for market, like the lowly *pescadilla* (small hake), *gallo* (a low-quality flounder), *jurel* (horse mackerel), and most surprisingly, monkfish—today a highly prized fish—this dish is the Catalan counterpart of Andalucía's *Pescado en Salsa de Sobrehuso* (page 182). It's so simple to prepare with so few ingredients (it's done in about 20 minutes), but the taste is exceptional and the potatoes are extraordinary.

If you don't wish to make your own *alioli* (although it couldn't be easier to do) and cannot find bottled (see Sources), improvise by combining ³/4 cup mayonnaise with 4 mashed garlic cloves, 2 teaspoons freshly squeezed lemon juice, and 2 teaspoons extra virgin olive oil. Serve with a green salad.   serves 4

Alioli

5 garlic cloves, minced

¹/2 teaspoon kosher or sea salt

1 teaspoon freshly squeezed lemon juice

1¹/2 tablespoons lightly beaten large egg

1 cup mild olive oil

1 pound monkfish, about 1 inch thick

1 pound turbot or other firm-fleshed fish such as halibut, about 1 inch thick

Kosher or sea salt

3 tablespoons olive oil

4 garlic cloves, thinly sliced

1 pound fresh plum tomatoes, skinned and chopped

1¹/4 pounds white potatoes, peeled and cut into ¹/2-inch cubes

3 cups Fish Broth (page 159), or clam juice enhanced with thyme, bay leaf, parsley, celery, onion, and saffron and strained

2 tablespoons minced fresh parsley

To make the *alioli,* mash the garlic and salt to a paste in a mortar. Mash in the lemon juice, then stir in the egg. Using a rubber spatula, transfer the mortar mixture to a food processor. With the motor running, add the oil in a thin steady stream, pausing to scrape down the sides with a rubber spatula if necessary, and beat until thickened and emulsified.

Sprinkle the fish with salt and let sit at room temperature. Heat the oil in a shallow casserole, and sauté the garlic until it begins to color. Add the tomatoes and potatoes and sauté for 2 minutes. Pour in the fish broth, bring to a boil, and boil for 10 minutes. Add the monkfish and turbot and boil for 10 minutes more, adding some water if the liquid cooks away and seasoning with salt.

Remove the fish to a warm platter. Remove the potatoes with a slotted spoon and coarsely mash with a fork. Arrange the fish and potatoes on dinner dishes. Add a little water if necessary to the remaining sauce so that there is enough to pour over each fish portion. Sprinkle the fish and potatoes with parsley and serve with *alioli.*

CHAPTER 7

AVES Y CAZA
poultry and game

RARELY DO YOU FIND CHICKEN ON A RESTAURANT menu in Spain, even in simple establishments. An exception is legendary Casa Lucio, an old tavern near the historic Plaza Mayor in Madrid, and here I always order garlic chicken (pollo al ajillo). The quality of the chicken is without equal—free range to be sure—and it tastes like chicken is meant to taste but rarely does. You are not, however, likely to find anything beyond garlic or roasted chicken in restaurants—certainly nothing like the fascinating and most unusual recipes I discovered when compiling this chapter. There is chicken in sherry sauce and in sweet-sour sauce, chicken with cilantro, with pine nuts, and even with truffles.

Rabbit, quail, and partridge, on the other hand, are another story entirely. Spain is known around the world as a hunter's paradise—for small game like rabbit, partridge, pheasant, and quail, as well as deer, bear, wild boar, and wild goat. When we drive through Spain's dry scrub bush landscape at dusk, the land is alive with scurrying rabbits and quail and partridge that hop, skip, and flap their wings to get out of our path. These are much more likely to be featured than chicken when you dine out, and they are prepared much as they would be in home kitchens. In Catalunya, for example, look for home-style partridge with stuffed cabbage leaves; in Castilla partridge or quail braised in wine with onions, garlic, and carrots, and in every region, wonderful rabbit stews.

In the United States, it is no longer difficult to find quality rabbit and game birds in butcher shops, high-end food shops, and sometimes even in supermarkets. They are likely to be frozen, but if well conserved, almost as good as fresh. Rabbit and game birds are much leaner than chicken and free from problems of mass production. Rabbit really is another "white meat" and well worth trying in some of the different preparations you will find in this chapter and in the Rice and Pasta Dishes and Soups and One-Pot Meals chapters. I think you will agree that quail, for example, braised with onions is a superb, easy-to-prepare meal. I also love quail simply grilled, then brushed with a mortar mash of garlic, parsley, and olive oil.

Pairing wines with poultry and game can be a challenge, but I much prefer young red wines or even reservas with chicken and rabbit, and for game birds an elegant reserva red is unquestionably the right wine.

POLLO DE CORRAL DE CÁNDIDA ACEBO ✤
CÁNDIDA'S STEWED CHICKEN WITH POTATOES

In the remote hamlet of Compludo in the province of León, our good friend Cándida grew up, and although she now lives in a nearby town, her father and ninety-eight-year-old grandfather still live here, and Cándida returns weekends to take charge of the small family bar—the only establishment in town. Chickens wander the streets at will—free range in its truest sense—and villagers naturally cook with ingredients readily at hand. Compludo is in the fertile region of El Bierzo, famed for its fruits and vegetables. Thus, I am not at all surprised that this chicken recipe Cándida gave me makes use of the village chickens and locally grown onions, carrots, peppers, and potatoes. The sauce is exceptional and the potatoes out of this world. All that is needed to complete this meal is a green salad.

serves 4

One 3- to 3^1/2-pound chicken

Kosher or sea salt

Freshly ground pepper

2 garlic cloves, chopped

2 tablespoons minced fresh parsley

^{1}/2 teaspoon sweet paprika, preferably Spanish smoked (see Pantry, page 14)

1^1/4 cups dry red wine

6 tablespoons olive oil

1 medium onion, preferably Vidalia or other sweet onion, finely chopped

^{1}/2 cup finely chopped carrots

1 medium red bell pepper, finely chopped

1 large baking potato, peeled and cut into ^{1}/2-inch cubes

Cut the chicken into small serving pieces, first detaching the wings and legs, then, with kitchen shears, cutting the breast into 4 pieces and each thigh in half crosswise. Sprinkle with salt and pepper.

In a mortar, mash to a paste the garlic, parsley, and $1/8$ teaspoon salt. Mash in the paprika, then stir in the wine and reserve.

Heat 3 tablespoons of the oil in a shallow casserole or skillet and sauté the chicken until browned on both sides. Add the onion, carrots, and bell pepper and sauté until the vegetables are softened. Stir in the mortar mixture and cook slowly for 30 minutes.

Meanwhile, in a large skillet heat the remaining 3 tablespoons oil. Add the potatoes in a single layer, sprinkle with salt, and sauté for 2 minutes, turning with a metal spatula to prevent sticking. Cover and cook over medium-low heat until tender, about 10 minutes, turning with the spatula occasionally. Drain the oil, add the potatoes to the chicken, and continue cooking for 5 minutes more. Serve.

POLLO AL AGRAZ CON PIÑONES ⚜
LEMON CHICKEN WITH GINGER AND PINE NUTS

Carmen Serrano, my friend for over thirty-five years, gave me this excellent recipe for sautéed chicken in a lemon and pine nut sauce. I looked into several Spanish cookbooks from the seventeenth and eighteenth centuries and—wouldn't you know—found several recipes that are practically identical, except the older recipes add ginger, a medieval touch that beautifully accentuates the lemon flavor of the sauce. Baked shortgrain rice (page 127) is a nice accompaniment.

serves 4

2 tablespoons pine nuts

1 garlic clove, minced

2 tablespoons minced fresh parsley

$^1/_8$ teaspoon crumbled thread saffron

Kosher or sea salt

One 3- to 3$^1/_2$-pound chicken

2 tablespoons olive oil

1 medium onion, finely chopped

$^1/_2$ cup chicken broth

2 tablespoons freshly squeezed lemon juice

1 bay leaf

$^1/_2$ teaspoon peeled and grated fresh ginger

Freshly ground pepper

In a mortar or mini processor, mash to a paste the pine nuts, garlic, parsley, saffron, and $^1/_8$ teaspoon salt. Reserve.

Cut the chicken into small serving pieces, first detaching the wings and legs, then, with kitchen shears, cutting the breast into 4 pieces and each thigh in half crosswise. Sprinkle the chicken pieces with salt.

Heat the oil in a shallow casserole and sauté the chicken until it is browned on all sides. Add the onion and sauté until wilted. Pour in the broth and lemon juice, add the bay leaf, ginger, salt and pepper to taste, and bring to a boil. Cover and simmer for 30 minutes. Stir in the mortar mixture and continue cooking for 15 minutes more. Serve.

PULARDA A LA SUPREMA DE TRUFAS DE IRENE ESPAÑA ⚬⚭
IRENE'S BOILED STEWING CHICKEN WITH CREAM AND TRUFFLES

Quick and easy to prepare and simply wonderful, plebeian boiled chicken is made deluxe with a little cream and some truffles that give a haunting flavor. The recipe may not jibe with your notion of Spanish country fare, but in Irene's hometown of Artiés in northern Catalunya, where cows graze and truffles grow, local cooking can be most refined, especially when in the competent hands of our friend Irene. Serve with Baked Rice (page 127), a simple green salad, and perhaps an elegant reserva red wine. serves 5 to 6

One 4$\frac{1}{2}$- to 5-pound chicken, with neck if possible

6 cups chicken broth or water

Kosher or sea salt

10 peppercorns

2 medium carrots, scraped

1 medium leek, trimmed and well washed

4 fresh parsley sprigs

4 fresh thyme sprigs, or $\frac{1}{2}$ teaspoon dried

2 bay leaves

2 tablespoons unsalted butter

2 tablespoons flour

2 tablespoons heavy cream

4 jarred truffles, finely chopped, plus 2 teaspoons truffle juice

Place the chicken in a deep pot and add the broth, salt to taste, peppercorns, carrots, leek, parsley, thyme, and bay leaves. Bring to a boil, skim off the foam, cover, and simmer for 1$\frac{1}{2}$ hours. Transfer the chicken to a warm platter and cut into serving pieces, discarding the wing tips and the chicken skin. Remove the rib and wing bones.

Strain the broth into a bowl and measure to 2$\frac{1}{4}$ cups (if there is more, boil down). Return the chicken to the pot and pour in $\frac{1}{4}$ cup of the reserved broth. Keep warm.

In a saucepan, melt the butter. Add the flour and cook for a minute, stirring constantly. Stir in the cream, then gradually add the remaining 2 cups broth, the truffles, and truffle juice. Cook, stirring constantly, until smooth and thickened. Serve the chicken and spoon on the sauce.

POLLO DEL DÍA ANTERIOR ❧ YESTERDAY'S CHICKEN

Reme Domínguez and Ximo Boix, the dynamic duo who devote their lives completely to their restaurant Tasca del Puerto in Castellón de la Plana, are a whirlwind of energy, enthusiasm, and creativity—and yet family recipes are always part of their repertoire. This chicken recipe was taught to Reme by her mother, who in turn learned it from her mother. The chicken cooks, then marinates in oil, garlic, bay leaf, and vinegar (known as an *escabeche* sauce) and can be served at room temperature or reheated.

"It can be kept in the refrigerator for several days," explains Reme, "and is most appropriate for busy people, since it can be prepared when you have a free moment and eaten when there is no time to cook." Obviously even decades ago a housewife's time was at a premium. I prefer this chicken at room temperature, served with a salad and little new potatoes, peeled, boiled, and cooled.

serves 4

One 3- to 3^1/2-pound chicken

2 medium onions, cut in halves crosswise

3 bay leaves

Kosher or sea salt

3 large eggs

^{1}/4 cup olive oil

Flour for dusting

5 whole peeled garlic cloves, lightly crushed

3 tablespoons red or white wine vinegar

Cut the chicken into small serving pieces, first detaching the wings and legs, then, with kitchen shears, cutting the breast into 6 pieces and each thigh in half crosswise. Place the chicken in a deep pot with the onions, 1 bay leaf, and salt to taste and just barely cover with water. Bring to a boil, cover, and simmer for 45 minutes. Remove the chicken to a platter and chill the broth to remove the fat.

Beat the eggs in a wide bowl or deep dish. Heat the oil in a shallow casserole and dust the chicken with flour. Coat with the eggs and place directly in the hot oil. Fry over medium-high heat, turning to brown all over. Add the garlic, remaining 2 bay leaves, and vinegar and cook until the garlic is golden.

Reheat the broth and strain over the chicken in the casserole. Bring to a boil and simmer for 2 minutes. Cool and chill for several hours or up to several days. Serve at room temperature or reheated.

La Alberca, Salamanca

POLLO ASADO AL COÑAC ⚶ BRAISED CHICKEN IN BRANDY SAUCE

The unusual technique of covering the stew pot with an inverted cover recurs repeatedly in family recipes I have found from Andalusian and Basque cooking, and it clearly helps to retain the small amount of liquid—in essence, just the brandy—in which the chicken is braised. This and a good amount of garlic produce a moist, tender, and unusually tasty chicken. Serve with a green vegetable like Fray Juan's Sautéed Chicory with Ham and Cumin (page 77).   serves 4

One 3- to 3^1/2-pound chicken

Kosher or sea salt

6 garlic cloves, minced

^{1}/2 teaspoon dried oregano

2 tablespoons minced fresh parsley

2 tablespoons olive oil

1 small onion, cut into thin slices

2 bay leaves

^{1}/4 cup brandy

Cut the chicken into small serving pieces, first detaching the wings and legs, then, with kitchen shears, cutting the breast into 4 pieces and each thigh in half crosswise. Sprinkle with salt.

In a mortar mash to a paste two-thirds of the garlic with the oregano, parsley, and ^{1}/8 teaspoon salt and reserve. In a deep casserole or Dutch oven, heat the oil and brown the chicken all over. Stir in the onion, the remaining garlic, and the bay leaves. Sauté for a minute or so, then add the brandy. Ignite, staying well away. When the flames die, stir in the mortar mixture and cover the casserole with an inverted lid or a shallow soup bowl (it should fit snugly). Fill the lid with a few tablespoons of water and simmer the chicken for about 30 minutes more, adding a little water from the lid if necessary. Serve.

POLLO A LA UVA BLANCA CON CILANTRO ❧
CHICKEN WITH WHITE WINE, GRAPE JUICE, AND CILANTRO

This great chicken preparation from Andalucía has a silky sauce with a hint of sweetness and a punch of cilantro. It includes both white wine and white grape juice (white grapes are commonly grown in western Andalucía to make sherry) and the cilantro lends a Moorish touch to the dish. Serve with Baked Rice (page 127).

serves 4

One 3- to 3^1/2-pound chicken

Kosher or sea salt

Freshly ground pepper

3 tablespoons olive oil

1 small-medium onion, slivered

^{3}/4 cup dry white wine

^{1}/4 cup plus 2 tablespoons white grape juice

6 tablespoons minced fresh cilantro

Cut the chicken into small serving pieces, detaching the wings and legs. With kitchen shears, divide the breast into 4 pieces and each thigh in half crosswise. Sprinkle with salt and pepper.

In a shallow casserole, heat the oil and sauté the chicken until golden all over. Add the onion and sauté until wilted. Stir in the wine, grape juice, and 3 tablespoons of the cilantro, then bring to a boil, cover, and simmer for 45 minutes.

Remove the chicken to a warm platter. Boil down the sauce until it is reduced and slightly thickened. Serve, sprinkled with the remaining 3 tablespoons cilantro.

GUISO CALDOSO DE ALDEA ANTIGUO ❧ CHICKEN AND SPARERIB STEW

Another magnificent dish from our friend Digna Prieto, a veritable ball of energy despite her advanced years. This, she tells me, is an old village recipe from Galicia, and it filled my kitchen with the wonderful aromas that greet you at lunchtime in little villages all over Spain. The additions of saffron and cumin give the stew a haunting flavor. A green salad is all you need to complete this meal.   serves 5 to 6

2 tablespoons olive oil

1 pound pork spareribs or baby back ribs, hacked into 2-inch pieces, fat trimmed

Kosher or sea salt

Freshly ground pepper

$3/4$ cup chicken broth

One 3- to $3^{1}/2$-pound chicken

About $1/4$ pound pancetta, cut into $3/4$-inch slices, then into $3/4$-inch cubes

1 medium carrot, peeled and finely chopped

4 garlic cloves, minced

1 medium onion, finely chopped

4 tablespoons minced fresh parsley

$1/2$ pound small new potatoes, about 2 inches in diameter, peeled and cut in halves

$1/2$ cup fresh or frozen peas

$1/4$ teaspoon cumin, preferably freshly ground

$1/8$ teaspoon crumbled thread saffron

In a shallow casserole, heat 1 tablespoon of the oil and sauté the pork ribs until browned, sprinkling with salt and pepper as they cook. Stir in the broth and $^1/3$ cup water. Bring to a boil, cover, and simmer for 1 hour (this can be done in advance). Meanwhile, cut the chicken into small serving pieces. Detach the wings and legs, hack off the bony ends of the legs, cut off and discard the wing tips, and divide each wing into 2 parts. With kitchen shears, divide the breast and each thigh into 4 pieces. Sprinkle with salt and let sit at room temperature.

Remove the ribs to a warm platter and measure the broth to $1^1/2$ cups, adding water if there is less. Skim off the fat that rises to the surface. Reserve the ribs and broth and wipe out the casserole. Heat the remaining tablespoon oil in the casserole and brown the chicken and pancetta, turning once. Add the carrot, garlic, onion, and parsley and sauté until the vegetables are softened.

Add the reserved ribs and broth and the potatoes to the casserole. Bring to a boil, cover, and simmer for 25 minutes. Stir in the peas, cumin, saffron, and salt and pepper to taste. Cover and continue cooking for 15 minutes more. Serve.

Digna Prieto as a young woman

POLLO A LA BUENA MUJER ⚜ THE GOOD WOMAN'S CHICKEN

This chicken, with its delicious, slightly sweet sauce of orange juice, orange segments, mushrooms, brandy, and a hint of saffron, comes from the Andalusian province of Almería, and it is not the first time I have come across this curious title in Spanish chicken recipes (it also exists in French cooking as *bonne femme*). The only common thread I can find is that they are all slowly simmered. Baked Rice (page 127) is a nice accompaniment.

serves 4

One 3- to 3^1/2-pound chicken

Kosher or sea salt

Freshly ground pepper

2 tablespoons olive oil

3 garlic cloves, minced

1 small onion, chopped

^{1}/3 pound brown mushrooms, stems trimmed, mushrooms cut into ^{1}/4-inch crosswise slices

3 tablespoons brandy

5 tablespoons freshly squeezed orange juice

1 small orange, peeled and divided into segments

^{1}/3 cup chicken broth

^{1}/8 teaspoon crumbled thread saffron

Cut the chicken into small serving pieces, first detaching the wings and legs, then, with kitchen shears, cutting the breast into 4 pieces and each thigh in half crosswise. Sprinkle with salt and pepper. Heat the oil in a shallow casserole and brown the chicken all over. Add the garlic, onion, and mushrooms and sauté until the onion is softened. Stir in the brandy, orange juice, orange segments, broth, and saffron. Bring to a boil, cover, and simmer for 45 minutes. Taste for salt and pepper. Serve.

POLLO A LA SEVILLANA ❧ CHICKEN WITH HAM, OLIVES, AND SHERRY

The tantalizing earthy flavor of this chicken is a result of the Andalusian blend of ham, olives, and sherry. In southern Spain, dry fino sherry is naturally poured to accompany such tapas as olives and Spanish ham so it is not suprising that sherry also contributes to a wonderful sauce for chicken that brings to life the flavors of Andalucía and is commonly referred to as "Sevilla Style." Serve with Baked Rice (page 127) and a simple green salad. serves 4

One 3- to 3^1/2-pound chicken

Kosher or sea salt

^{1}/2 cup pitted and sliced green Spanish olives

^{1}/2 cup dry white wine

3 tablespoons olive oil

^{1}/2 medium onion, preferably Vidalia or other sweet onion, chopped

2 garlic cloves, minced

^{1}/4 cup diced Serrano or prosciutto ham

1 teaspoon flour

6 tablespoons dry fino sherry

^{1}/2 cup chicken broth

Freshly ground pepper

1 tablespoon fresh thyme, or ^{1}/2 teaspoon dried

Cut the chicken into small serving pieces, first detaching the wings and legs, then, with kitchen shears, cutting the breast into 4 pieces and each thigh in half crosswise. Sprinkle with salt and let sit at room temperature.

In a small saucepan, combine the olives and wine. Bring to a boil and simmer for 5 minutes. Drain and reserve the olives. In a shallow casserole, heat the oil and brown the chicken all over. Lower the heat, add the onion and garlic, and slowly sauté for 5 minutes. Scatter in the ham, cook for a minute, then stir in the flour. Add the sherry, broth, salt and pepper to taste, and thyme. Cover and simmer for 40 minutes. Add the reserved olives and simmer for 2 minutes more. Serve.

POLLO AL AJILLO ❧ CHICKEN IN GARLIC AND WINE SAUCE

This is a slightly more elaborate version of a typical Spanish garlic sauce. It has a richer, more complex flavor, in part because the garlic and parsley are mashed. The variations on *pollo al ajillo* are endless, but no matter which recipe is used, it is a dish that never fails to please. The sauce works equally well with rabbit. Thinly sliced baking potatoes, roasted with olive oil, and perhaps *piquillo* peppers, cut in strips and lightly sautéed, would nicely complement the chicken.

serves 4

One 3- to $3^1/2$-pound chicken

Kosher or sea salt

3 tablespoons olive oil

16 garlic cloves, coarsely chopped

2 bay leaves

2 tablespoons brandy

$1/2$ cup dry white wine

Scant $1/4$ teaspoon crumbled thread saffron

4 peppercorns

4 tablespoons minced fresh parsley

Cut the chicken into small serving pieces, first detaching the wings and legs, then, with kitchen shears, cutting the breast into 4 pieces and each thigh in half crosswise. Sprinkle with salt and let sit for 10 minutes. Heat the oil in a shallow casserole, add the chicken, and sauté until browned, turning once. Turn off the heat, add half of the garlic and the bay leaves, and let the garlic sizzle in the pan. Reheat the pan; when hot, add the brandy and, standing well back, ignite. When the flame dies, pour in the wine, bring to a boil, cover, and simmer for about 35 minutes.

Meanwhile, in a mortar, mash to a paste the remaining garlic, the saffron, $1/8$ teaspoon salt, the peppercorns, and 2 tablespoons of the parsley. Stir into the casserole, cover, and continue cooking for 15 minutes more. Sprinkle with the remaining parsley and serve.

POLLO AL JEREZ ❧ CHICKEN IN DRY FINO SHERRY SAUCE

A simple succulent chicken with the unique taste of dry fino sherry. It is a dish from southwestern Spain, where sherry is produced. Serve with a green vegetable like Sautéed Spinach with Quince and Toasted Sesame Seeds (page 73).   serves 4

One 3- to 3½-pound chicken

Kosher or sea salt

2 tablespoons olive oil

3 whole peeled garlic cloves, lightly crushed

Scant ⅛ teaspoon crumbled thread saffron

¼ cup chicken broth

⅓ cup dry fino sherry

Cut the chicken into small serving pieces, first detaching the wings and legs, then, with kitchen shears, cutting the breast into 4 pieces and each thigh in half crosswise. Sprinkle with salt.

Heat the oil in a shallow casserole and sauté the garlic until lightly browned, turning once and pressing with the back of a wooden spoon to extract its flavor. Remove the garlic to a mortar and mash with ⅛ teaspoon salt and the saffron. Mash in a little of the broth, then stir in the rest.

Reheat the oil in the casserole, add the chicken, and brown, turning once. Stir in the sherry and the mortar mixture. Bring to a boil, cover, and cook at a high simmer for about 35 minutes. Serve.

FILETES DE POLLO AL ALIOLI DE CHALO PELÁEZ ∻
CHALO'S BREADED CHICKEN CUTLETS WITH *ALIOLI*

Another one of the simple creations of our good friend Chalo. Under the crisp crumb coating is a thin layer of alioli that gives a great added touch of flavor. A variety of dishes go well with this chicken, like Fernando's Sherry-Infused Baked Sliced Potatoes (page 88) and Asparagus Salad with Piquillo Peppers, Egg, and Anchovy (page 66). serves 4

2 large eggs

$^1/_2$ teaspoon dried parsley flakes

1 tablespoon grated cheese, such as Manchego or Parmesan

8 chicken cutlets ($^3/_4$ to 1 pound), sliced very thin

3 tablespoons *alioli*, homemade (page 186) or bottled (see Sources, page 293)

1 cup bread crumbs, preferably a mix of dried bread crumbs and crumbled Japanese-style panko crumbs

Mild olive oil for frying

Kosher or sea salt

In a dish or shallow bowl, beat together the eggs, parsley, and cheese with a fork. Brush the cutlets on both sides with *alioli* (about 1 teaspoon on each side). Dip the cutlets in the egg mixture, then coat with the crumbs, patting lightly so they adhere well. Dry on a wire rack for about 20 minutes.

Pour oil to a depth of $^1/_8$ inch in a large skillet, heat to the smoking point, and reduce the heat to medium-high. Add as many cutlets as will comfortably fit and fry until lightly golden, turning once. Drain on paper towels, sprinkle with salt, and serve right away, or keep warm briefly in a 200°F oven.

HIGADILLOS DE POLLO AL JEREZ ⚜
CHICKEN LIVERS IN SHERRY AND ONION SAUCE

Slow-cooked onion and a touch of dry sherry give great flavor to these sautéed chicken livers, which come from Spain's Sherry Triangle in southwestern Spain and are served over fried bread. A vegetable like Green Beans with Garlic and Vinegar (page 75) goes well with this dish.

serves 4

4 tablespoons olive oil

4 slices good-quality sandwich bread, cut diagonally into triangles

2 medium onions, preferably Vidalia or other sweet onion, slivered

2 pounds chicken livers, picked over

Kosher or sea salt

Freshly ground pepper

6 tablespoons dry fino sherry

2 tablespoons minced fresh parsley

$1^1/2$ teaspoons fresh thyme, or $^1/4$ teaspoon dried

1 bay leaf, crumbled

Heat 2 tablespoons of the oil in a skillet. Add the bread and fry until golden, turning once. Remove the bread and drain on paper towels.

Add the onion to the pan and sauté for 2 minutes, adding a little more oil if necessary. Cover and cook slowly for about 20 minutes, until tender but not browned. Remove and reserve the onion and wipe out the pan.

Heat the remaining 2 tablespoons oil to the smoking point. Add the livers and quickly brown, sprinkling with salt and pepper (the livers should not be cooked through). Deglaze the pan with the sherry and cook down to half. Stir in the reserved onions, the parsley, thyme, and bay leaf, and cook for a minute to blend flavors. Serve over the fried toast.

Castle of Belmonte, Cuenca

PAVO GUISADO AL ESTILO DE FAÍN ✌ TURKEY "FRICASSEE" FAÍN

Faín, the tranquil Andalusian country estate of our friend Soledad Gil, is today a small hotel, set amid olive groves and filled with family mementos. The family cook prepares guest meals, and this turkey "fricassee," or stew, is among my very favorites, made with the free-range turkeys that are raised here.

Because turkey bones are almost impossible to hack, I advise having a butcher hack or saw the turkey parts into a manageable size. The sauce is extraordinarily delicious, and once more it is dried sweet red pepper (ñora) that makes all the difference. Serve with Sautéed Saffron-Scented Potatoes (page 89) and a green salad. serves 4

3 to 3 1/2 pounds turkey parts, such as wings, drumsticks, and/or thighs, hacked or sawed into 2-inch pieces, wing tips and bony ends of the wings and/or drumsticks discarded

Kosher or sea salt

2 tablespoons olive oil

1 medium-large onion, preferably Vidalia or other sweet onion, slivered

2 garlic cloves, minced

1 small ñora (dried sweet red pepper; see Pantry, page 14) or 1/2 New Mexico–style dried red pepper, core cut out with kitchen shears and seeded

1 medium tomato (about 1/4 pound), chopped

1 tablespoon minced fresh parsley

3/4 cup chicken broth

1/2 cup dry white wine

Scant 1/8 teaspoon crumbled thread saffron

Freshly ground pepper

1/4 teaspoon ground cumin

Sprinkle the turkey pieces with salt on both sides. In a large shallow casserole, heat the oil and sauté the turkey until browned on all sides. Add the onion, garlic, and ñora, and slowly sauté until the onion is softened. Stir in the tomato and parsley and sauté for about 2 minutes. Add the broth, wine, saffron, a generous amount of pepper, and cumin. Cover and simmer for 1 1/4 hours. Serve, spooning the sauce over the turkey.

CONEJO A LA ZAMORANA ⚜ RABBIT STEW, ZAMORA STYLE

Zamora is a city with a wealth of Romanesque churches, seignorial houses, and a most unusual domed Byzantine-style cathedral. Its parador was once, in fact, the fifteenth-century palace of the counts of Alba y Aliste. I found this exceptional rabbit stew on the regional menu at the parador. The rabbit was fork tender, and its carrot- and herb-scented sauce, flavored with smoked paprika, an essential ingredient in this part of Castilla, was aromatic and light. Serve with very small boiled new potatoes and a green salad.

serves 4

One 3-pound rabbit, cut into small serving pieces

Kosher or sea salt

3 tablespoons olive oil

1 medium onion, preferably Vidalia or other sweet onion, finely chopped

3 garlic cloves, minced

2 medium carrots, peeled, trimmed, and finely chopped

1/2 teaspoon sweet paprika, preferably Spanish smoked (see Pantry, page 14)

3/4 cup dry white wine

1/4 cup plus 2 tablespoons chicken broth

2 tablespoons minced fresh parsley

4 fresh thyme sprigs

4 fresh rosemary sprigs

1/2 teaspoon dried oregano

1 bay leaf

Freshly ground pepper

Sprinkle the rabbit well with salt. Heat the oil in a shallow casserole and brown the rabbit, turning once. Add the onion, garlic, and carrots, lower the heat, and cook for 5 minutes. Stir in the paprika, then add the wine, broth, parsley, thyme, rosemary, oregano, bay leaf, and salt and pepper to taste. Bring to a boil, cover, and simmer for 45 minutes. Serve.

CONEJO CON AJONJOLÍ ⚜

SAUTÉED RABBIT, BATTER FRIED WITH SESAME SEEDS

This singular rabbit dish, which also works well with skinless chicken, has been adapted from a recipe in an outstanding compendium of recipes gathered from home cooks all over the region of Andalucía entitled La Cocina Familiar Antigua. The recipe, from the province of Córdoba, where hunting is an age-old tradition in the mountains of the Sierra Morena, calls for sautéeing the rabbit, dipping it in a batter, coating it with sesame seeds, and frying to create a surprisingly light and delicious coating. Since the rabbit is prepared simply, you might serve a mixed vegetable dish like María Teresa's Vegetable Medley (page 84) or Charito's Greens and Potato Casserole (page 87).   serves 4

2 tablespoons olive oil

One 2³/4- to 3-pound rabbit, cut into 8 pieces

2 whole peeled garlic cloves, lightly crushed

1 small onion, cut into rings

Kosher or sea salt

Freshly ground pepper

1¹/2 cups chicken broth

1 cup sesame seeds

2 large eggs, separated

Mild olive oil for frying

About ¹/2 cup flour

In a shallow casserole, heat the oil and sauté the rabbit until browned, turning once. Add the garlic, onion, and salt and pepper to taste, and sauté until the onion is softened. Pour in the broth, bring to a boil, cover, and simmer for 30 minutes. Drain the rabbit and dry on paper towels (the broth will not be used, but it makes a delicious soup). Wipe out the pan.

Spread the sesame seeds on wax paper. Beat the egg whites with an electric mixer in a bowl until they form soft peaks. Fold in the yolks and season with salt and pepper. Pour oil into the pain to a depth of ¹/2 inch and heat until the oil rapidly browns a cube of bread. Dust the rabbit pieces with flour, then dip in the egg and coat with the sesame seeds.

Transfer the rabbit to the hot oil and fry quickly until just golden. Sprinkle with salt and serve.

CODORNICES EN HOJA DE PARRA DE LUISA OSBORNE ❧
LUISA OSBORNE'S BRAISED QUAIL IN GRAPE LEAVES

Usually dishes with grape leaves are associated with Greek cooking, but grape leaves are, of course, common in all Mediterranean countries and traditionally were put to good use. In this recipe from Luisa Osborne, a member of the Osborne sherry family, the quail is wrapped in grape leaves and covered with pancetta, both of which help to keep the quail succulent and give it great flavor as well. Serve with thinly sliced baking potatoes roasted in olive oil and Moorish-Style Green Salad with Cumin and Paprika (page 61).

serves 4

8 grape leaves, packed in brine

8 quail, necks trimmed

8 thin slices pancetta or bacon

2 tablespoons olive oil

6 tablespoons finely chopped onion

2 tablespoons brandy

$1^{1}/4$ cups chicken broth

Kosher or sea salt

Separate the grape leaves and place them in boiling water for 3 minutes, in several batches if necessary. Drain on paper towels.

Fold the wing tips of the quail under the breast and push the legs up toward the breast. Fit a grape leaf over and around each quail, pressing lightly so that the leaf adheres. Place a slice of pancetta over each breast and tie the quail lengthwise and crosswise with kitchen twine, as if they were packages.

Heat the oil in a shallow casserole and sauté the onion until it is softened. Stir in the brandy and cook it away. Add the quail and sauté breast side down for 5 minutes. Turn the breasts up and add the broth and salt to taste. Cook over medium-high heat, covered, until cooked, about 25 minutes. Check occasionally and add more broth or water if necessary. Place on a platter and remove the twine, leaving the leaf and pancetta over the quail. Serve with the sauce.

CODORNICES ESTOFADAS DE MI ABUELA JOSEFA ☙
GRANDMA JOSEFA'S BRAISED QUAIL

This simple but outstanding recipe comes by way of my dear friend Carmen Serrano, who in turn received it from the mother of one of her good friends. The slight sweetness of the incredibly good sauce is a result of a large amount of onion (the sauce has little else—there is no liquid except for whatever the onion in the tightly closed stew pot produces). I was at first perplexed by the cooking method—the stew pot is covered with a dish filled with water and onion slices—but I soon realized the logic behind it. The dish acts somewhat like a pressure cooker, holding in the steam, and the water and onion in the plate can be used if the stew needs additional liquid.

I like to serve the quail with Sautéed Saffron-Scented Potatoes (page 89). serves 4

8 quail, split in halves

Kosher or sea salt

2 tablespoons olive oil

2 medium onions, preferably Vidalia or other sweet onion, cut into eighths, plus a few onion slices

3 whole peeled garlic cloves, cut crosswise in halves

3 fresh parsley sprigs

1 bay leaf

Freshly ground pepper

Sprinkle the quail on both sides with salt. Coat a large deep pot with 1 tablespoon of the oil and arrange the quail in the pot, skin side down. Scatter in the onion wedges and garlic, then drizzle with the remaining tablespoon oil. Sauté over medium-high heat until the quail begin to brown. Leave the quail skin side down and add the parsley, bay leaf, and pepper to taste. Cover the pot with a deep plate or shallow soup bowl that fits tightly over the pot. Add a few tablespoons water and a few slices of onion to the covering plate.

Cook over low heat for 30 to 40 minutes, until the onion is tender, removing the plate occasionally to stir and add water from the plate if necessary.

PERDICES CON COLES DE IRENE ESPAÑA ❧
IRENE'S PARTRIDGE WITH STUFFED CABBAGE LEAVES

*A delicious sauce and a most interesting classic
Catalan dish of partridge and pork-stuffed cabbage tied into small packets. The recipe also
sometimes appears without the meat filling, but
I think this version from my friend Irene is far
more interesting. It works equally well with other
game birds like quail, which is easier to find here.
The typically Catalan picada, in this case, of garlic, parsley, and saffron, gives an additional
burst of flavor to the sauce. Serve with a green
salad.* serves 4

12 cabbage leaves

2 to 4 partridge or 8 quail, split in halves

Kosher or sea salt

Freshly ground pepper

Cabbage Stuffing

2 tablespoons dried bread crumbs

2 teaspoons milk

1 pound ground pork

1 teaspoon kosher or sea salt

Freshly ground pepper

1/4 cup finely chopped Serrano ham or prosciutto

1 large egg, lightly beaten

2 tablespoons minced fresh parsley

2 garlic cloves, minced

1 1/2 teaspoons fresh thyme, or 1/4 teaspoon dried

1/4 teaspoon dried oregano

4 tablespoons olive oil

flour

1 small onion, finely chopped

1/2 cup finely chopped leek (white part only)

1 medium carrot, scraped and finely chopped

1/4 cup finely chopped celery

2 garlic cloves, minced

1 medium tomato, finely chopped

2 tablespoons minced fresh parsley

2 bay leaves

1/2 teaspoon dried oregano

1 1/4 cups dry white wine

Picada

2 garlic cloves, chopped

2 tablespoons minced fresh parsley

Scant 1/4 teaspoon crumbled thread saffron

1/4 teaspoon kosher or sea salt

Bring a large pot of water to a boil. Add 2 cabbage leaves and boil for 2 minutes. Remove and drain. Repeat for the remaining leaves.

Sprinkle the partridge with salt and pepper and let sit. In a bowl combine the stuffing ingredients, lightly mixing with your hands. Place 2 tablespoons of the stuffing in the center of each cabbage leaf. Fold in two sides of the leaves, then fold over the other two sides, forming 2- to $2^1/2$-inch rectangles. Tie, as you would a package, with kitchen twine.

Heat 2 tablespoons of the oil in a large shallow casserole and brown the partridge, turning once. Remove to a warm platter. Dust the stuffed cabbage with flour, add to the casserole, and brown on both sides. Remove to the platter. Add the remaining 2 tablespoons oil to the casserole and sauté the onion, leek, carrot, celery, and garlic until the vegetables are softened. Add the tomato, parsley, bay leaves, oregano, and salt and pepper to taste and sauté for 2 minutes more. Sprinkle in 2 teaspoons flour, then stir in the wine. Cover and simmer for 15 minutes. Return the cabbage and partridge to the casserole, cover, and simmer for 30 minutes more, turning the cabbage and partridge once.

Meanwhile, to make the *picada*, mash to a paste all of the *picada* ingredients. Remove the partridge and the cabbage from the casserole, then pass the vegetables through a food mill or a mesh strainer, pressing with the back of a metal soup ladle to extract as much liquid from the remaining solid pieces as possible. Discard the solids. Return the strained liquid to the casserole and stir in the picada. Add the partridge and cabbage and reheat. Remove the string from the cabbage and serve.

CHAPTER 8

CARNES
meats

SPAIN IS THE MOST MOUNTAINOUS COUNTRY IN Europe save for Switzerland, and in the damp green north that means plentiful grazing land for cattle and dairy cows. The central plains, on the other hand, take pride in their baby lamb, and in the arid south, *cabrito*—baby goat—is favored. Pigs, of course, do not require open spaces—except for the Iberian pig that is free range—and are raised all over the country. Wherever you go in Spain, pork, ham, and pork sausage products are plentiful and popular, in particular, chorizo spiced with garlic and paprika, *morcilla* (black sausage), and the star of them all, *jamón ibérico*—cured ham from the native Iberian pig. (See sidebar page 13).

But why, I wondered, are pork loin and thinly cut *filetes de ternera* (young beef cutlets) always present in home kitchens and rarely eaten when dining out? The reason may be one of tradition. Historically, roasted meats, like baby lamb and suckling pig, were the privilege only of nobility and today are still considered feasts for special occasions. Besides, homes did not have ovens—although on festive days, village bakeries would allow townsfolk to use their bread ovens to roast meats. Home cooking relied on stovetop preparations, and perhaps that's why Spaniards to this day thrive on

filetes. During one summer I spent in Madrid as a student, I lived with a family who ate nothing else, day in and day out. Indeed, breaded *ternera* is always a good simple meal, and wherever Luis and I travel in Spain, when in doubt, we order it. It may not be on the menu, but any restaurant will make it for you. Only in the Galician province of Lugo and Ávila in Castilla, both renowned for the quality of their meats, does beef become something out of the ordinary.

Although all the beef recipes in this chapter originally called for *ternera*, which is somewhere between beef and veal, I sometimes recommend beef or, when I feel veal is more in character, I choose it instead. *Ternera blanca*—white veal as we know it—is now available in Spain and gaining popularity, but it is still a novelty. Strange, isn't it, in a country that prides itself on the extremely young age of its baby lamb and pig? *Filetes,* of course, need no recipe, but I have collected wonderful family recipes for beef stews and meatballs, both great favorites in Spanish households.

As for pork, just about every recipe given to me was for loin of pork. Since pigs tend to be eaten younger in Spain, I found the proper equivalent to be pork tenderloin. You may be surprised to find so many pork loin recipes in this chapter, but all were so exceptional that

I hesitated to eliminate any of them. Pork loin, besides, is lean and excellent for anyone looking to reduce fat in the diet. Spaniards, who have one of the world's highest life expectancies, were onto a good thing well before they knew why. Fewer lamb recipes came my way, but they were delicious, like lamb with lemon and Moorish-style lamb with cinnamon, ginger, prunes, and raisins.

When Spaniards dine out, at least in the Castilian heartland, they demand weeks' old baby lamb and suckling pig, just as the nobility once did. Both are so tender and succulent they can be cut with the edge of a plate. The province of Segovia is the epicenter for these roasts, and thousands of *madrileños* stream into the countryside on weekends to eat wood-roasted lamb and pig cooked in brick-lined ovens in rustic inns. We never pass up an opportunity to join them.

Crisp, full-bodied red wines are appropriate with any of the recipes in this chapter, especially the wines from the Ribera del Duero and Toro regions.

LOMO EN DULCE DE LA MADRE DE PILAR ❧
PORK TENDERLOIN IN SWEET SHERRY SAUCE FROM PILAR'S MOTHER

"My mother was a terrible cook," explained my friend Pilar Vico, who grew up in the provincial capital of Albacete in the region of Castilla–La Mancha. "She preferred to spend her time painting. But when I was nine, my father died, and shortly after that, my widowed great-aunt from Granada moved in with us, and the quality of cooking in our household greatly improved."

Pilar, like her mother, does little cooking, but she did keep her mother's handwritten, meticulously transcribed collection of her great-grandmother's recipes, which have a noticeably Andalusian flair (that branch of the family was from the Andalusian province of Jaén). It is a slim notebook with a mottled brown jacket, its pages worn and yellowed with age, its ink faded to a pale gray. Tucked between two pages was her mother's artistic contribution to the volume—a full-color sketch of a pleased-looking chicken hightailing it out of a bright blue steaming stew pot. Next to the pot a knife lay in wait.

This recipe shows the influence of Andalucía's Moorish heritage in its sweet and savory combination and relies on sherry, the quintessential Andalusian wine. It is extremely simple, quick to make and wonderfully tasty. Serve with Baked Rice (page 127) and a green salad.   serves 4

$1^1/_2$ pounds pork tenderloin

Kosher or sea salt

Freshly ground pepper

Flour for dusting

2 tablespoons olive oil

$^1/_2$ medium onion, slivered

2 bay leaves

2 tablespoons minced fresh parsley

$^1/_3$ cup chicken broth or water

$^1/_2$ cup sweet (cream) sherry

$^1/_4$ teaspoon ground cumin

Preheat the oven to 400°F. Sprinkle the meat all over with salt and pepper, then dust with flour. Heat the oil in a shallow, ovenproof casserole and brown the meat all over. Add the onion and sauté until softened, then add the bay leaves and parsley, cook for a minute, and stir in the broth, sherry, and cumin. Bring to a boil, cover, and bake for 35 minutes. Check to be sure there is enough liquid, adding a little more chicken broth if necessary. To serve, slice the meat at an angle, about $^1/_2$ inch thick, and spoon the sauce over it.

Free-range Iberian pigs,
Aracena mountains, Huelva

CARNE EN SALSA MESÓN POQUEIRA ❧ PORK IN ALMOND SAUCE

High up in the magnificent snow-capped Alpu-jarra mountains of Granada—the refuge of the Moors after they were expelled from their beloved Granada in 1492—Mesón Poqueira, in the lovely little village of Capileira, employs an entire family. The sons wait on tables, the father tends the bar, and Mom takes care of the kitchen. Usually I shy away from sauces at restaurants that are unknown to me, but in this case the pork, in a sauce enriched with almonds (of clear Moorish origin) and spiced with plenty of peppercorns, turned out to be distinctive and delicious. Serve with small boiled new potatoes and Asparagus Salad with *Piquillo* Peppers, Egg, and Anchovy (*page 66*).

serves 4

1 teaspoon peppercorns

2 pounds boneless pork, preferably tenderloin, cut into $3/4$- to 1-inch cubes

Kosher or sea salt

2 to 3 tablespoons olive oil

One $3/8$- to $1/2$-inch bread slice, cut from a French-style loaf

20 blanched almonds

1 ñora (dried sweet red pepper; see Pantry, page 14) or $1/2$ New Mexico–style dried red pepper, core cut out with kitchen shears and seeded

2 whole peeled garlic cloves

2 tablespoons dry white wine

2 tablespoons finely chopped tomato

1 bay leaf

$1/2$ cup chicken broth

In a mortar or mini processor, crack the peppercorns. Remove and reserve. Sprinkle the meat with salt and let sit at room temperature. Heat the oil in a shallow casserole and sauté the bread, almonds, ñora, and garlic. Remove to the mortar as each ingredient turns golden and the ñora when it is slightly softened. Leave the oil in the pan. Mash the mortar ingredients well with $1/8$ teaspoon salt, adding the wine a little at a time to aid the mashing. Reserve.

Reheat the oil and sauté the meat until browned. Reduce the heat, add the tomato and bay leaf, and cook for a minute. Stir in the broth, cover, and simmer for 15 minutes. Add the mortar mixture and the peppercorns and simmer for 15 minutes more, adding more broth or water if necessary. Serve.

LOMO RELLENO DE JOSÉ MANUEL CARO ❧ JOSÉ MANUEL'S STUFFED PORK LOIN

My good friend José Manuel is in charge of Casa Ruperto, one of my favorite tapas bars in Sevilla, but all the exceptional tapas served there are recipes from his uncle Ruperto. From the family recipes that José Manuel gave me, however, it is clear that his branch of the family also knows a thing or two about fine simple eating. I love his recipe for pork loin, stuffed with hard-boiled egg, Serrano ham, and pimientos in a full-flavored sauce. Use Spanish *piquillo* peppers if possible—the difference will be noticeable. Roast potatoes and Sautéed Spinach with Quince and Toasted Sesame Seeds (page 73) are nice complements.

serves 4

One 1½- to 1¾-pound boneless pork loin

Kosher or sea salt

Freshly ground pepper

1 garlic clove, minced

1 tablespoon minced fresh parsley

2 *piquillo* peppers (see Pantry, page 15), or 1 small pimiento,
    cut into long thin strips

1 large hard-boiled egg, thinly sliced crosswise

About 1 ounce Serrano ham or prosciutto, cut from an
    ⅛-inch slice and cut into ⅛-inch matchsticks

2 tablespoons olive oil

Flour for dusting

1 small onion, finely chopped

2 tablespoons finely chopped tomato

2 whole unpeeled garlic cloves

4 peppercorns

½ cup dry white wine

Butterfly the meat and score it inside with a sharp thin knife. Sprinkle with salt, pepper, the minced garlic, and parsley. Arrange the peppers, egg, and ham over one cut side of the meat. Close the meat and tie securely lengthwise and crosswise with kitchen twine.

In a deep pot, heat the oil. Dust the meat with flour and brown on all sides. Add the onion and sauté until translucent, then add the tomato, unpeeled garlic, and peppercorns. Sauté for 2 minutes more. Stir in the wine and salt to taste, cover, and simmer for 50 minutes to 1 hour (about 35 minutes per pound), until the meat's internal temperature reaches 160°F.

Remove the meat to a warm platter and cook down the sauce briefly. Press the garlic cloves with the back of a wooden spoon to extract the garlic flesh and discard the skin. To serve, remove the string, slice the meat about ¾ inch thick, and spoon on the sauce.

SOLOMILLO DE CERDO DE CHALO PELÁEZ ❧
CHALO'S PORK TENDERLOIN WITH STEWED ONIONS

Our dear friend Chalo enjoys tinkering in the kitchen, and this tender, tasty pork, with a hint of mustard and a profusion of sweet onions that simmer for 2 hours, is one of his favorites and now one of mine. If you make the onions in advance the tenderloins will cook in about 35 minutes. Chalo likes to serve the meat with a mustard dipping sauce, but the dish is also excellent without it. Serve with Sautéed Saffron-Scented Potatoes (page 89) and a green salad.   serves 6

2 pork tenderloins ($3/4$ to 1 pound each)

Kosher or sea salt

Freshly ground pepper

2 tablespoons coarse country Dijon mustard

2 tablespoons olive oil

4 medium-large Vidalia or other sweet onions

8 peppercorns

1 tablespoon sugar

Chicken broth

$1/4$ cup finely ground mustard seeds, mixed with
   3 tablespoons water, optional

Sprinkle the tenderloins with salt and pepper, patting the meat so that the salt and pepper adhere. Brush all over with the country mustard.

Heat the oil in a large shallow casserole. Sauté the meat over medium-high heat until well browned all over (it should not be cooked through). Remove to a platter and refrigerate. Add the onions, sauté until slightly softened, then turn the heat to the minimum and cook, uncovered, for 1 hour, stirring occasionally. Add the peppercorns and sugar, cover, and continue stirring and cooking slowly for another hour, adding some chicken broth if the casserole dries out.

Remove meat from the refrigerator and return to the casserole. Cover and cook slowly until just done, about 40 minutes, until the meat's internal temperature reaches 160°F. Slice the meat at an angle, $1/4$ to $3/8$ inch thick, and spoon the onions and the sauce over the meat, adding more chicken broth if necessary so that there will be enough sauce. Serve, if you wish, with the mustard dipping sauce.

"By Royal Decree"

We first made the acquaintance of Cándido López, celebrated owner of Mesón de Cándido in Segovia, when he was already an octogenarian with a lifetime of success behind him. A corpulent man of great presence, he was by then a living legend, every bit as famous as Segovia's two-thousand-year-old Roman aqueduct, which stands next to his restaurant. He would sit, imposing and Buddha-like, at the restaurant's outdoor café, taking in the passing scene.

Mesón de Cándido began centuries ago as a modest tavern serving traveling merchants and muleteers. But when Cándido took charge, he brought his natural talents to bear and made his place into an institution. Today his son Alberto and grandchildren Cándido and Alberto, all good friends of ours, proudly carry on his legacy.

Although the province of Segovia is best known for its roast baby lamb, Cándido, enterprising as he was, had other ideas. He would promote roast suckling pig—not prepared whole on a spit, as was customary, but in individual portions. His piglets were barely three weeks old and of a quality beyond compare—the meat milky white and the golden skin crackling crisp—and he made suckling pig the culinary emblem of Segovia. A master of public relations, he charmed everyone who crossed his path. With this talent, coupled with extraordinary business acuity, he amassed a worldwide clientele that traveled to Segovia exclusively to dine in his charming antique-laden restaurant. As autographed photographs covering the walls attest, just about every world leader of the twentieth century passed through his doors and countless American movie stars, from Grace Kelly to Henry Fonda. No one else in the history of Spanish gastronomy can lay claim to such universal recognition.

Perhaps his greatest gift was to realize, well before it became fashionable, that dining is theater. So he revived a ritual going back to the times of the fifteenth-century Castilian King Enrique IV that he performed time and time again. Suckling pigs were brought from the kitchen with great ceremony, resting on litters that in turn were supported on the shoulders of waiters. Without warning, Cándido would appear, taking center stage to read the royal edict that gave his house permission to roast meats (in centuries past this was the provenance only of royalty). Without further ado, he quartered each pig with the edge of a dinner plate to demonstrate their extraordinary tenderness. Then, with a subtle flick of the wrist, Cándido casually tossed the dish to the tile floor, where it shattered, as diners looked on in awe. After a moment of stunned silence, the room invariably erupted in deafening applause.

In recognition of all he did for the city of Segovia and his lifelong efforts to promote Castilian gastronomy, a statue of Cándido now stands in one of the city's main squares. Raising a plate high over the bronzed suckling pigs before him, he appears totally in command, just as he always was during his long career. A remarkable tribute to a self-made man of humble origins who single-handedly transformed Segovia into a culinary place of pilgrimage.

ESTOFADO DE CERDO AGRIDULCE CON CIRUELAS PASAS DE CONCHA LÓPEZ-VIOTA
❧ CONCHA'S SWEET-SOUR PORK WITH PRUNES

While my tour group strolled through Sevilla's Plaza de España—an elegant expanse surrounded by fifty magnificent ceramic tile benches, each with a scene representing a province of Spain—I stayed behind with our guide Concha López-Viota, a young exuberant Sevillana, who was eager to tell me about some of her favorite family recipes. This one comes from her mother-in-law, and although I initially had my doubts about using 2 tablespoons of sugar in the sauce, it proved to be an exceptional dish. The sweetness of the sauce, augmented by prunes and onions, is tempered by the acidity of the vinegar.

Serve, if you like, with Baked Rice (page 127).

serves 4

12 pearl onions

2 tablespoons olive oil

2 tablespoons red or white wine vinegar

2 tablespoons sugar

2 pounds boneless pork, preferably tenderloin, cut into 1-inch cubes

3 garlic cloves, minced

1 medium onion, preferably Vidalia or other sweet onion, slivered

Kosher or sea salt

Freshly ground pepper

$1/2$ cup chicken broth

8 pitted prunes

Bring a pot of water to a boil, then add the pearl onions and boil for 3 minutes. Rinse under cold water and slip off the skins. In a small bowl, combine 1 tablespoon of the oil with the vinegar and sugar and stir until the sugar is dissolved.

Heat the remaining tablespoon oil in a deep pot. Add the pork, garlic, and the slivered onion and sauté over medium-high heat, stirring and sprinkling with salt and pepper, until the onion is softened. Add the broth, the vinegar mixture, and the prunes. Cover and simmer for 1 hour. Add the pearl onions and simmer for 15 minutes more.

LOMO DE CERDO ASADO A LA NARANJA ✥
PORK TENDERLOIN IN ORANGE SAUCE

This recipe comes from several sources in Castilla, Extremadura, and Andalucía and even has a close equivalent in a recipe from the sixteenth century. The pork acquires a slight sweetness and a rich flavor from the orange juice, and it is a dish in which all elements meld perfectly. Although already a tender cut of meat, the pork tenderloin is further tenderized by the orange juice. Serve with Baked Rice (page 127).   serves 4

2 tablespoons olive oil

Two $^3/_4$-pound pork tenderloins

Kosher or sea salt

Freshly ground pepper

$^1/_2$ medium onion, slivered

6 garlic cloves, minced

1 tablespoon minced fresh parsley

1$^1/_2$ teaspoons fresh thyme, or $^1/_4$ teaspoon dried

$^1/_2$ cup plus 2 tablespoons freshly squeezed orange juice

$^1/_2$ cup plus 2 tablespoons chicken broth

Scant $^1/_8$ teaspoon crumbled thread saffron

Preheat the oven to 350°F. In a shallow casserole, heat the oil and brown the meat all over, sprinkling with salt and pepper as it browns. Remove to a warm platter. Add the onion and garlic and sauté until the onion is softened. Return the meat to the pan and add the parsley, thyme, orange juice, broth, and saffron. Bring to a boil, cover, and bake for about 1 hour, until the meat's internal temperature reaches 160°F. Slice the meat at an angle, about $^1/_2$ inch thick, and spoon on the sauce.

LOMO RELLENO A LA MALLORQUINA ❧
BREADED PORK CUTLETS FILLED WITH *SOBRASADA*

I am quite amazed that a recipe this easy can deliver such complex flavors. It is, of course, the cutlet filling of *sobrasada*—a soft, spreadable chorizo from the Balearic Islands—that is responsible for making this dish of so few ingredients into something so special that you would enjoy serving it to guests—and with so little effort on your part. You will need *sobrasada*, which is available from mail-order sources (if you buy it, be sure to try it also in the tapas recipe on page 30 or, as I love it, placed between two slices of sandwich bread and grilled). Otherwise, a soft cooking chorizo, casing removed and beaten to a paste in a food processor, will give similar results. Serve with Pilar's Spinach Sautéed with Raisins and Pine Nuts (page 74).   serves 4

$1/4$ pound *sobrasada* (see Pantry, page 16), cut into $1/8$-inch slices

$1 1/2$ pounds thinly sliced pork cutlets (about $1/4$ inch thick)

About 1 cup bread crumbs, preferably a mixture of dried bread crumbs and crumbled Japanese-style panko crumbs

$1/4$ teaspoon dried thyme

$1/4$ teaspoon dried oregano

$1/4$ teaspoon dried parsley flakes

2 large eggs, lightly beaten

3 tablespoons olive oil

Arrange the slices of *sobrasada* over half of the pork cutlets. Cover with the remaining cutlets and press lightly to seal. Combine the bread crumbs with the thyme, oregano, and parsley. Dip the cutlets in the egg, then coat well with the crumb mixture. Let sit for 20 minutes on a wire rack.

Heat the oil in a skillet and add as many cutlets as will comfortably fit. Turn the heat to medium-high and sauté until golden, turning once. Drain on paper towels and repeat as necessary for the remaining pork. Serve.

LOMO EMPANADO DE CLARA OROZCO ❧ CLARA'S BREADED PORK TENDERLOIN

"There were only three people—me, my mother, and Grandfather—living in our house in Madrid in the forties," recalls my husband, Luis, "but we always had at least twelve for lunch every day. My grandfather would come home from work, and I would return from school for a midday break. Madrid at this time was filled with refugees from wartorn Europe, and although Spain was neutral in World War II, we were still recovering from the ravages of our Civil War in the 1930s. Our house became the place for European intelligentsia-in-exile to gather for a free meal and fine conversation. My mother, Clara, who was an extraordinary cook, often prepared these simple pork fillets coated with white sauce, breaded, and pan fried." Serve with Fernando's Sherry-Infused Baked Sliced Potatoes (page 88).

serves 4

White Sauce

2 tablespoons unsalted butter

3 tablespoons olive oil

6 tablespoons flour

$3/4$ cup chicken broth

$3/4$ cup milk

Kosher or sea salt

Freshly ground pepper

$1/8$ teaspoon ground nutmeg

2 tablespoons olive oil

1 pound pork tenderloin, cut into $3/8$-inch slices

Kosher or sea salt

2 large eggs

1 tablespoon grated cheese, such as Manchego or Parmesan

$1/2$ teaspoon dried parsley flakes

1 cup bread crumbs, preferably a mixture of dried bread crumbs and crumbled Japanese-style panko crumbs

Mild olive oil for frying

To make the white sauce, melt the butter with the oil in a saucepan, add the flour, and cook over low heat for a minute or two. Gradually stir in the chicken broth, milk, salt and pepper to taste, and nutmeg. Cook, stir-

MEATS   227

ring constantly, until the sauce is thickened and smooth. Cool, stirring occasionally.

In a large skillet, heat the oil and add as many pork slices as will comfortably fit. Quickly sauté, until lightly browned and cooked through, sprinkling with salt and turning once. Remove to a warm platter and repeat for the remaining pork.

Dip the meat slices in the white sauce, coating them completely on both sides. Place on a plate or tray and refrigerate until the sauce solidifies, at least 1 hour.

In a dish, beat the eggs, cheese, and parsley with a fork. Dip the pork in the egg, then coat with the crumbs. Pour oil to a depth of $^1/8$ inch in a large skillet and heat to the smoking point. Reduce the heat to medium-high, add as many pork slices as will comfortably fit, and fry until lightly golden, turning once. Drain on paper towels and serve right away, or keep warm briefly in a 200°F oven.

LANDRILLA DE LAGARTERA DE PEPITA ALÍA ✿ PEPITA'S PORK STEW

At first glance Lagartera appears no different from any of the hundreds of villages dotting the arid sun-drenched plains of Castilla–La Mancha. But as we discovered years ago, this village of only two thousand people is responsible for much of Spain's finest needlework, and just about every female engages in the traditional skills of embroidery and drawn-thread work. There is precious little time for the kitchen, and the women of Lagartera are the first to admit that cooking is not their forte.

Nevertheless, Lagarteranas, among them our friend Pepita, do make some tasty dishes that require little effort. Pepita's pork stew is made with a minimum of ingredients—it does not even include an herb or a spice. But the flavor is still exceptional because of the last-minute addition of wine and garlic. Certainly this simple dish hardly takes time away from Pepita's labor of love, but surely it gives great pleasure to her family. You can serve this stew with small boiled new potatoes and Fray Juan's Sautéed Chicory with Ham and Cumin (page 77).   serves 4

2 tablespoons olive oil

2 pounds pork loin, cut into 1-inch cubes

Kosher or sea salt

1 medium onion, slivered

1 medium tomato, finely chopped

2 garlic cloves, minced

$1/2$ cup dry white wine

Heat the oil in a deep casserole or pot. Add the meat and sauté, sprinkling with salt, until browned all over. Add the onion and sauté until it is wilted, then stir in the tomato and cook for a minute. Cover and simmer slowly for 45 minutes, adding a little water if the pot dries out.

Meanwhile, mash the garlic to a paste in a mortar, then stir in the wine. Add to the meat and simmer for 15 minutes more. Serve.

RAXÓ DE PORCO EN ZORZA DE DIGNA PRIETO
DIGNA'S GALICIAN-STYLE MARINATED PORK TENDERLOIN

Digna, the matriarch of the family restaurant Crisol in Galicia's seaside village of El Grove, grandly sits at her reception post every afternoon and evening, greeting clients and directing operations, as she has done since she was a young bride so many years ago. Her daughter Susi takes charge nowadays of the kitchen. El Grove comes to life in summer and once again in fall during the local fiesta called La Exaltación del Marisco, a celebration showcasing the exquisite shellfish for which this northwest coast is celebrated. Although the restaurant centers almost exclusively on seafood, the recipes Digna gave me include both surf and turf, and this marinated pork is one of my all-time favorites.

I have never understood how paprika (pimentón) became such an essential part of Galician cooking, but some of the region's most typical dishes, like this one, rely on it. Indeed, dishes called "a la gallega" (Galician style) are usually so named because of the inclusion of paprika. Digna's version is especially good and most versatile. "You can roast it with pearl onions, if you like," she says, "slice it thin and grill it, or cut in fillets, coat with bread crumbs, and sauté." I might add that when grilled and placed on a slice of bread it makes a great tapa. As is often the case, Spanish smoked paprika will make a noticeable difference.

Little boiled new potatoes are typically served with this dish, and a green salad is also a good accompaniment.

serves 4

5 garlic cloves, minced

1 bay leaf, crumbled

2 tablespoons minced fresh parsley

1 1/2 teaspoons dried oregano

1/4 teaspoon kosher or sea salt

5 tablespoons olive oil

1 tablespoon sweet paprika, preferably Spanish smoked (see Pantry, page 14)

1/2 teaspoon hot paprika, preferably Spanish smoked (see Pantry, page 14)

3 tablespoons dry white wine

Two 3/4-pound pork tenderloins

1 small onion, slivered, or 8 pearl onions, blanched and peeled (see page 224)

Chicken broth

In a mortar or mini processor mash to a paste the garlic, bay leaf, parsley, oregano, and salt. Stir in the oil, sweet and hot paprikas, and wine. Transfer to a Pyrex pie plate or shallow casserole, add the meat, and turn to coat with the marinade. Cover and refrigerate for 3 days, turning occasionally.

Remove the meat from the refrigerator and preheat the oven to 375°F. Scatter in the onion and transfer to the oven. Cook until the meat is done, 25 to 30 minutes, or until it reaches an internal temperature of 160°F, adding a little broth if the dish dries out. Cut at an angle, in $1/2$-inch slices, and spoon on the sauce. Serve.

START PREPARATION 1 DAY IN ADVANCE

MEDALLONES DE SOLOMILLO IBÉRICO CON UNA MAJADA DE AJO Y PEREJIL

MARINATED PORK TENDERLOIN WITH GARLIC AND PARSLEY

We had been to some of Spain's finest restaurants on a trip to Andalucía with a group of Americans, but it was the simplest family fare served at the renowned olive oil estate of Núñez de Prado that captivated everyone and led some to proclaim the supper there the best meal of the trip.

This dish was part of that extraordinary meal, created entirely from time-honored family recipes, and all, of course—even the ice cream that ended the meal—featuring the family olive oil. The preparation of this pork tenderloin that came from native Iberian pigs, which are also the source of what food connoisseurs recognize as the world's best ham, is simplicity itself. The meat is marinated with garlic, parsley, and olive oil and lightly grilled. The perfect accompaniment is the spectacularly good Batter-Fried Vegetables (page 82) that were served with this pork at that memorable meal.

serves 4

8 garlic cloves, minced
1/2 cup minced fresh parsley
1/2 teaspoon kosher or sea salt
1/4 cup plus 2 tablespoons olive oil
Two 3/4 pound pork tenderloins, cut into 1/2-inch slices

In a mortar or mini processor, mash the garlic, parsley, and salt to a paste, then stir in the oil. Place the pork slices in a shallow flat-bottomed bowl and pour the mortar mixture over them. Turn the meat to coat well with the marinade. Cover and refrigerate overnight.

Drain the meat, reserving the marinade. Coat a stovetop griddle or large skillet with oil and heat. Remove the meat from the marinade, but let some marinade cling to it. Sauté in two or more batches as necessary, over medium-high heat, until very lightly browned and just cooked through, turning once and brushing with the marinade occasionally. Do not overcook—the meat should be slightly pink within. Sprinkle with salt and serve.

CORDERO CON LIMÓN DE MARÍA CARMEN Y CASTA ✤
MARÍA'S LAMB WITH LEMON

This lamb stew is made special by the nice tang of lemon that characterizes the sauce. It comes to me by way of my friend Carmen, who learned it from her friend María whose family is from the central plains of La Mancha. Serve, if you wish, with small boiled new potatoes and Sautéed Green Beans, Cáceres Style (page 76).   serves 4

2 tablespoons olive oil

3 pounds boneless lamb stew meat

Kosher or sea salt

Freshly ground pepper

2 garlic cloves, minced

1 medium tomato, skinned, seeded, and finely chopped

1 bay leaf

$^1/_4$ cup freshly squeezed lemon juice

2 tablespoons brandy

Heat the oil in a deep casserole. Brown the meat well, sprinkling with salt and pepper as it cooks. Add the garlic, cook for a minute, then stir in the tomato and bay leaf. Cook for 2 minutes more.

Pour in the lemon juice and brandy, bring to a boil, and taste for salt. Cover and simmer for $1^1/_2$ hours. Serve.

Baby Lamb at Its Finest

I am often tempted to count sheep when flying from New York to Madrid, but I know that would only make matters worse, for on my arrival I am anticipating a blissful indulgence in roast baby lamb. Already I can envision the exquisitely sensuous pleasure of nibbling each and every morsel from the tiny riblets, biting into the crackling skin, sopping up the delectable juices with big chunks of country bread, and watching the bones pile high on my plate, like a scene of medieval debauchery.

This is a passion I share with many Spaniards, who bestow on roast lamb something akin to cult status. Droves of Madrileños think nothing of traveling long distances into the countryside just to eat baby lamb at centuries-old inns in beautiful Castilian villages. We join them as we head into what is known as the "Region of the Roasts," a triangle in northern Castilla whose epicenter is the province of Segovia. In the distance we can make out a huge flock of sheep, nibbling on wheat stubble and aromatic wild herbs, attended by a lone shepherd and his trusty dog. Four centuries ago merino lamb's wool was the backbone of the Castilian economy, but today the sheep are a breed called *churra*, raised for their meat and for making sheep's milk cheese.

A car passes us with vine shoots strapped to its roof in preparation for a weekend *chuletada*, an outdoor lamb chop bash for which these aromatic shoots are the preferred fuel, and we flash back to a summer day over two decades ago when our car was similarly laden. We had met our good friend Pepe Sanz at Casa Tinín in Sepúlveda, our favorite inn for roasted lamb, for a late Sunday afternoon roasted lamb lunch. Accompanying him were two friends collectively known as "Los Gordos" (the Fat Ones), who proudly displayed their enormous paunches ("nourished," they declare, "on baby lamb and Spain's divine shellfish"). We polished off an entire lamb and were relaxing over coffee and brandy when Los Gordos announced, "It's time to prepare a *chuletada* for later this afternoon." "Impossible," we protested. "Don't worry," they insisted, "in a few hours you'll be hungry for lamb all over again."

We followed them a few miles north to Roa, where they bought freshly baked country bread, baby lamb chops, and *morcilla* blood sausage. In Mambrilla de Castrejón, one of Los Gordos (we never did learn their real names) gathered dried vine shoots from a nearby barn that belonged to a relative, and we continued to the outskirts of town, where they fired a grill. By then faint pangs of hunger had indeed begun, and we spent the next few hours grilling tiny chops and thick sausage slices, using chunks of bread instead of plates to catch the drippings. We made frequent trips to a nearby cave, bringing out homemade wine in spouted jugs called *porrones,* and it effortlessly slid down our open gullets. The local undertaker came by to join us in a round of something he called *la tarusa*—a kind of primitive bowling game—and the hours stretched on pleasantly under the warmth of the setting summer sun.

Lambs in La Rioja

CALDERETA DE CORDERO DE CARMEN SERRANO ✺
CARMEN'S LAMB STEW WITH NEW POTATOES

Although this recipe comes from my friend Carmen, it belongs to an acquaintance of hers who sometimes stops over for Saturday night card games. The ingredients are few, but the taste is exceptional—it's the dried red pepper (ñora) that makes the difference. Serve with Moorish-Style Green Salad with Cumin and Paprika (page 61).

serves 4

3 tablespoons olive oil

6 whole peeled garlic cloves

2 small *ñoras* (dried sweet red peppers; see Pantry, page 14) or 1 New Mexico–style dried red pepper, cores cut out with kitchen shears and seeded

2 to 2 1/2 pounds boneless leg of lamb, cut into 1 1/2-inch pieces

Kosher or sea salt

Freshly ground pepper

3/4 pound very small new potatoes, about 1 1/2 inches in diameter, peeled

1/3 cup dry white wine

3/4 cup chicken broth

Heat the oil in a deep pot, add the garlic and *ñoras*, and cook for a minute or two. Add the meat, sprinkle with salt and pepper, and sauté over medium-low heat until the meat loses its color. Cover and simmer for 30 minutes. Transfer the garlic and *ñoras* to a mortar, mash to a paste, and return to the pot. Add the potatoes, wine, and broth, cover, and continue cooking until the potatoes are tender, about 30 minutes. Serve.

CORDERO MOZÁRABE DE JULIA PIÑEDO ❧ JULIA'S MOORISH LAMB STEW

Julia owns and operates a lovely restaurant in Cazalla de la Sierra in the province of Sevilla with her sister Lucía and enjoys serving dishes from her town's Moorish past. One of Julia's favorite recipes is this wonderful lamb stew with its Moorish touches of spice—cinnamon, nutmeg, and ginger—and the inclusion of dried fruits, in this case, prunes, figs, and raisins. Serve with a green salad.

serves 4

1 1/2 pounds leg of lamb

2 cups dry red wine

1 teaspoon sugar

1/4 teaspoon cinnamon

1 small onion, chopped

1 bay leaf

6 peppercorns

1/2 teaspoon minced peeled fresh ginger

1/8 teaspoon nutmeg

2 tablespoons brandy

Kosher or sea salt

8 pitted prunes

6 dried figs, cut into 1/4-inch crosswise slices

1 tablespoon raisins

Freshly ground pepper

Bone the lamb (or have your butcher do it for you) and keep the bone. In a deep pot, combine the lamb bone, wine, sugar, 1/8 teaspoon of the cinnamon, the onion, bay leaf, peppercorns, ginger, nutmeg, brandy, 2 cups water, and salt to taste. Bring to a boil, cover, and simmer for 1 hour. Uncover and boil down until considerably reduced and slightly thickened. Strain, pressing with the back of a metal soup ladle to extract as much liquid as possible. Return the sauce to the pot and add the prunes, figs, and raisins. Bring to a boil, cover, and simmer for 10 minutes. Reserve.

Preheat the oven to 450°F. Place the meat (tied with kitchen twine if necessary) in a greased shallow oven-proof casserole or roasting pan. Sprinkle the meat with salt, pepper, and the remaining 1/8 teaspoon cinnamon. Brush with a little of the broth and transfer to the oven, reducing the temperature to 325°F. Roast for about 1 hour, until the meat is slightly pink inside, about 165°F. Reheat the sauce. To serve, slice the meat and spoon the sauce over it.

A Passion for Moorish Cooking

We have come to the delightful Andalusian town of Cazalla de la Sierra for just one reason: to taste the cooking of sisters Julia and Lucía, who preside over a charming, immaculately kept hotel, La Posada del Moro (The Inn of the Moor). The hotel's restaurant is famous in the entire province of Sevilla for its excellent and unusual food with a distinctive Eastern accent. But as luck would have it, the restaurant is closed evenings during the summer months. Instead, we find a barbecue set up on the hotel's terrace, and we thoroughly enjoy a magnificently fresh salad, a smooth partridge and venison pâté, and marinated pork skewers, well known in Spain by the name *pincho moruno* (Moorish kabobs), served with a delicious baked potato topped with a dollop of green *alioli* and a side of sweet red peppers. It was a simple but memorable meal, and I would return in a heartbeat just to repeat it.

We strike up a conversation with the two women at the next table and express our disappointment that we have come so far but cannot dine in the restaurant or chat with Julia and Lucía. To our surprise and good fortune, the two ladies are none other than Julia and Lucía, enjoying the out-of-doors on their night off. Lucía, it turns out, is somewhat retiring, while Julia is animated, bursting with Andalusian charm, style, and flair.

"As poor as the ingredients in many Spanish recipes may seem, they often have magic," says Julia. "Often the spark comes from Andalucía's five centuries of Moorish influence that brought sweet-sour combinations and Eastern herbs and spices to Spanish cooking. Fried eggplant with honey, mint, and sesame seeds; greens with quince preserves and toasted sesame seeds; and lamb with cinnamon, ginger, nutmeg, prunes, figs, and raisins are three wonderful examples." All three recipes were explained to me in great detail over coffee by Julia and appear here in *La Cocina de Mamá*.

"Interest in the cooking of the past," says Julia, "goes hand in hand with healthy eating. That's one reason why traditional cooking endures." Indeed, Julia's burning passion is unearthing recipes from Andalucía's Moorish past, and you can just imagine her excitement when a few years ago a cousin of hers, who works at the town's courthouse, found among the papers of a woman who died in the 1800s an impressive collection of handwritten recipes. To Julia, it was a culinary treasure trove beyond compare, and many of the recipes found their way to her restaurant menu.

CHULETAS DE CORDERO CON AJO Y PEREJIL DE CÁNDIDA ACEBO ✺
CÁNDIDA'S GRILLED LAMB WITH GARLIC AND PARSLEY

In Cándida's tiny village of Compludo, family cooking is uncomplicated but full of flavor, as is the case in this recipe for grilled lamb. Although Cándida's recipe calls for a whole leg of lamb, lambs are so small in Spain that using a much larger lamb would not be an adequate substitute, so I have used loin lamb chops instead.

As an accompaniment, very small red potatoes, unpeeled, halved, sprinkled with salt and pepper, and tossed in olive oil can be arranged on a piece of greased foil and placed on the grill a few minutes before the lamb (they will need about 25 minutes).

serves 4

4 garlic cloves, minced

1/4 cup minced fresh parsley

Kosher or sea salt

2 tablespoons extra virgin olive oil plus some for brushing

2 tablespoons dry red wine

8 loin lamb chops, about 2 pounds, 1 to 1 1/4 inches thick

In a mortar mash to a paste the garlic, parsley, and 1/4 teaspoon salt. Stir in the oil and wine.

Brush the chops on both sides with oil and sprinkle with salt. Grill, preferably on a covered barbecue, and when almost done to taste, spoon the mortar mixture over the chops, give a brief turn, sprinkle with salt, and serve.

CORDERO ESTILO SAN VICENTE DE DIGNA PRIETO
DIGNA'S ROAST LAMB AND POTATOES

'This roast lamb, prepared in an earthenware casserole, was once made in village wood-burning bakery ovens in Galicia on festive occasions, well before village kitchens had their own ovens," recalls our friend Digna. The lamb is first marinated, then roasted with potatoes—among the best potatoes I have ever tasted.

Earthenware casseroles (see Equipment, page 18) are generally sold without lids, because in Spanish cooking these casseroles are either used for roasting or for dishes that do not require long, slow cooking.

serves 4

14 garlic cloves, minced

2 bay leaves, crumbled

2 tablespoons minced fresh parsley

Kosher or sea salt

8 tablespoons olive oil

6 tablespoons dry white wine

$1^1/2$ to 2 pounds boneless leg of lamb, cut into 2-inch cubes

$1/4$ cup chicken broth

2 cloves

Freshly ground pepper

1 pound baking potatoes, peeled and cut into $1/2$-inch cubes

$1/8$ teaspoon crumbled thread saffron

In a mortar, mash to a paste one-quarter of the minced garlic cloves with the bay leaves, parsley, and $1/4$ teaspoon salt. Stir in 4 tablespoons of the oil and 2 tablespoons of the wine. Transfer to a large bowl, add the meat, and stir to coat well. Marinate overnight or longer in the refrigerator.

Preheat the oven to 375°F. Heat 2 tablespoons of the oil in a large shallow casserole, preferably earthenware. Add the meat with its marinade and brown over high heat. Remove the casserole from the heat and add the remaining 2 tablespoons olive oil, the remaining 4 tablespoons wine, the broth, the remaining garlic, the cloves, and salt and pepper to taste. Place in the oven and roast for 30 minutes, uncovered. Add the potatoes, sprinkle them with salt and the saffron, and continue cooking for about 30 minutes more, until the potatoes are tender. Serve.

LOMITO DE CORDERO RELLENO DE HONGOS DE FÉLIX DURÁN ❧
FÉLIX DURÁN'S RACK OF LAMB STUFFED WITH MUSHROOMS AND SCALLIONS

Although the ingredients in this splendid recipe are traditional Spanish—baby lamb, scallions, mushrooms, and sherry, chef Félix Durán at the Parador in Plasencia has put them all together to create an elegant, sophisticated dish. The number of servings for each rack will depend upon the size of the lamb. I used very small New Zealand lamb—similar in size to baby Spanish lamb. Serve with Asparagus Salad with *Piquillo* Peppers, Egg, and Anchovy (page 66).   serves 4 to 6

2 baby racks of lamb (³/4 to 1 pound each)

2 tablespoons olive oil plus some for drizzling

¹/2 cup minced scallions

1¹/2 cups minced mushrooms (stems trimmed), such as
    brown or shiitake

Kosher or sea salt

Freshly ground pepper

¹/4 cup medium-sweet oloroso sherry

About 2 tablespoons fresh thyme, or 1 teaspoon dried

3 tablespoons dry white wine

1¹/2 tablespoons freshly squeezed lemon juice

With a very sharp knife, slit the chops of each rack of lamb in the meatiest part, following the center of each bone and cutting about halfway through. Heat the oil in a skillet and slowly sauté the scallions and mushrooms, sprinkling with salt and pepper, until the mushrooms are softened. Add the sherry and cook it away. Fill each slit in the racks of lamb with about 1¹/2 teaspoons of the scallion and mushroom mixture. Tie the racks with kitchen twine across the slit portion.

Preheat the oven to 400°F. Arrange the racks in a greased roasting pan, drizzle them with oil, then sprinkle with salt, pepper, and thyme. Roast for 15 minutes. Add the wine and lemon juice and cook for about 10 minutes more, until the meat reaches an internal temperature of about 145°F for medium-rare, adding a little water or broth if the pan dries out. To serve, slice between the bones into individual chops and spoon on any pan juices.

FRICANDÓ AL ESTILO ANTIGUO ✤
OLD-FASHIONED VEAL STEW WITH ALMONDS, HAZELNUTS, AND MUSHROOMS

"A very old recipe," says our friend Cinta Gutiér-rez, "handed down from our forefathers" (or mothers, as the case may be). In Cinta's region of Catalunya the addition of nuts to sauces is the secret of so many fine dishes, and the tomato sauce in this exceptional stew has a flavor unlike any other because it includes dried mushrooms, mashed almonds, and hazelnuts (the nuts are key ingredients in the typical last-minute flavor enhancement in Catalan cooking known as *la picada*). Serve with a green salad.   serves 4 to 6

$1\frac{1}{2}$ ounces dried mushrooms, such as porcini

2 tablespoons olive oil

One $\frac{3}{8}$-inch bread slice, cut from a French-style loaf

2 pounds veal stew meat, cut into $\frac{1}{2}$-inch steaks

Kosher or sea salt

Flour for dusting

2 medium onions, preferably Vidalia or other sweet onions, finely chopped

$\frac{2}{3}$ cup canned tomato sauce

Freshly ground pepper

$1\frac{1}{4}$ cups homemade or canned vegetable broth

$\frac{1}{2}$ cup chicken broth

Picada

8 blanched almonds

6 hazelnuts, shelled

$\frac{1}{4}$ teaspoon kosher or sea salt

Freshly ground pepper

1 teaspoon olive oil

1 teaspoon flour

6 tablespoons dry white wine

Soak the mushrooms in hot water until softened, about 30 minutes. Heat the oil in a shallow casserole and sauté the bread slice over medium-high heat, turning once, until golden. Transfer the bread to a mortar or food processor and reserve. Sprinkle the veal with salt and dust with flour. Add the meat to the casserole and sauté until lightly browned on both sides. Remove to a warm platter.

Drain the mushrooms and dry on paper towels. Sauté the mushrooms briefly in the casserole and reserve with the meat. Add the onions to the casserole and sauté for a minute or so. Cover and cook slowly for 20 minutes.

Stir in the tomato sauce and salt and pepper to taste. Cover and continue cooking slowly for another 10 minutes. Add the reserved meat and mushrooms and the vegetable and chicken broths. Cover and simmer for 45 minutes.

Meanwhile, make the *picada*. Preheat the oven to 400°F and toast the almonds and hazelnuts on a cookie tray until golden, about 5 minutes. Cool the nuts and transfer to the mortar with the reserved bread. Mash, adding some salt and pepper to taste, until as fine as possible. Mash in the oil and then the flour. Stir in the wine and add the mortar mixture to the meat. Cover and cook for 15 minutes more.

Maruja's Fish Fillets Layered with Tomato, Capers, Bread Crumbs, and Cheese, page 179

Fish Baked with Potatoes, Onions, Saffron, and Paprika, page 185

Chicken and Sparerib
Stew, page 198

José Manuel's Stuffed
Pork Loin, page 220

Félix Durán's Rack of Lamb Stuffed with Mushrooms and Scallions, page 242

Mallorcan Lamb and
Sobrasada Pie, page 256

Rufino's Hot Chocolate
with Fritters, page 262

Mari Carmen's Orange Cake, page 269

TERNERA CON CEBOLLITAS DE LA ABUELA MARÍA ❧
GRANDMA MARÍA'S BEEF STEW WITH PEARL ONIONS

This recipe comes from my friend Cinta in Empúries, who attributes it to her grandmother. She was from the village of Cassà de la Selva in the Bajo Empordà region of the Catalan province of Girona. "She was an extraordinary person," Cinta recalls, "and when she was widowed at a young age, supported her family by working in a textile factory. She knew how to take the poorest ingredients and create meals that were truly exquisite."

The stew's hint of cinnamon gives an interesting twist to this excellent meal-in-a-pot. Cinta says that instead of onions, her grandmother sometimes put peas or snow peas in the stew. A green salad is all you need with this dish.

serves 4

30 medium pearl onions (about $3/4$ pound)

2 pounds boneless stew beef, cut into $3/4$-inch cubes

3 tablespoons olive oil

8 to 12 very small new potatoes, about $1^1/2$ inches in diameter, peeled

3 tablespoons brandy

One $1^1/2$-inch piece cinnamon stick

2 bay leaves

Kosher or sea salt

12 peppercorns

Chicken broth

Bring a pot of water to a boil, add the onions, and boil for 3 minutes. Rinse under cold water and slip off the skins.

In a deep pot, combine the onions, beef, oil, potatoes, brandy, cinnamon, bay leaves, salt to taste, and peppercorns. Cover tightly and simmer slowly for 2 hours, adding a little chicken broth as necessary to keep the pot from drying out and to have enough sauce when serving.

TERNERA ESTILO COTO DOÑANA ❧ BEEF STEW WITH CUMIN AND CORIANDER

Although today Coto Doñana is a magnificent wildlife preserve in southwestern Spain with little population, it was once home to fishermen, hunters, and cattlemen. As such, it had its own gastronomy, much of which has been lost. But through the efforts of Juan Martínez Lao and his book *La cocina de Doñana–El Rocío*, which highlights recipes from these marshlands, the region's cooking has been brought back to life.

Coriander is a spice (its leaf is called cilantro) that thrives here in Doñana, and the cumin and coriander that season this fragrant stew are a heritage of the Moors and frequently appear in Andalusian cooking.

Coriander seeds can be difficult to find. If need be, cut the coriander and increase the amount of cilantro to 5 tablespoons, plus another tablespoon for garnish, and you will also produce a very tasty stew. Very small boiled white potatoes are a nice accompaniment.   **serves 4**

2 tablespoons olive oil

1^1/$_2$ to 2 pounds beef stew meat, cut into 1-inch cubes

Kosher or sea salt

2 medium onions, preferably Vidalia or other sweet onions, thinly sliced

4 garlic cloves, minced

1 pound tomatoes, finely chopped

1^1/$_2$ teaspoons ground cumin

1^1/$_2$ teaspoons ground coriander seeds

3 tablespoons minced fresh cilantro

^{1}/$_2$ teaspoon crushed red pepper, or to taste

^{1}/$_2$ cup beef broth (low-salt if canned), or chicken broth

Heat the oil in a deep pot and quickly sauté the meat, sprinkling with salt as it cooks, until well browned. Add the onions and garlic to the pot and slowly sauté until the onions have softened. Stir in the tomatoes, 1 teaspoon of the cumin, the coriander, 2 tablespoons of the cilantro, and the red pepper, and cook for another 2 minutes. Add ^{1}/$_4$ cup water and the broth, bring to a boil, cover, and simmer for 1^1/$_2$ hours. Stir in the remaining ^{1}/$_2$ teaspoon cumin and simmer for 30 minutes more. Serve, sprinkled with the remaining tablespoon cilantro.

Roman aqueduct and
Mesón de Cándido, Segovia

Cows in the mountains
of Cantabria

ESTOFADO DE TERNERA DE ANTONIA ROLLÓN ❧
ANTONIA'S BEEF STEW WITH MUSHROOMS AND *PIQUILLO* PEPPERS

This *delicious* stew *followed* Antonia's *potatoes with pork ribs* (page 110), *the ones that swept us off our feet when we visited* Bodegas Fariña *in* Toro *with a group of Americans a few years ago. The ingredients are not unusual, but the mortar mash of sautéed onion and garlic, for example, gives extra flavor and consistency to the stew, and the piquillo peppers lend a superb touch of color and flavor. Out of loyalty and in recognition of the fine quality of Fariña wines,* Antonia *adamantly affirms, "I will use nothing but Fariña's Colegiata white wine in my cooking!"*

Serve, *if you wish, with small boiled new potatoes and a green salad.*   serves 4 to 6

3 tablespoons olive oil

1 medium onion, preferably Vidalia or other sweet onion, slivered

6 garlic cloves, minced

1$\frac{1}{4}$ cups dry white wine

2 pounds boneless beef stew meat, cut into 1-inch cubes

Kosher or sea salt

Freshly ground pepper

2 medium carrots, scraped and cut into $\frac{1}{8}$-inch crosswise slices

1 teaspoon dried oregano

2 tablespoons minced fresh parsley

$\frac{1}{4}$ pound small mushrooms, such as cremini, brushed clean, stems trimmed, and quartered

1 cup thin strips of *piquillo* peppers (see Pantry, page 15), or pimientos

2 teaspoons tomato paste

Heat 2 tablespoons of the oil in a deep pot and slowly sauté the onion and garlic until the onion is softened. Transfer the onion and garlic to a large mortar, leaving the oil in the pot. Mash to a paste and stir in the wine.

Reheat the pot, adding the remaining tablespoon oil, and brown the meat, seasoning with salt and pepper as it browns. Stir in the mortar mixture, carrots, oregano, and parsley. Cover and simmer for 1 hour.

Add the mushrooms, *piquillo* peppers, and tomato paste and simmer for $\frac{3}{4}$ to 1 hour more.

ALBÓNDIGAS DE MARISÉ ZUBIZARRETA ❧
MARISÉ'S MEATBALLS WITH GREEN PEPPER AND TOMATO

An egg coating (a trick our friend Marisé at Casa Julián in Asturias uses often), brief cooking, and the addition of onion, green pepper, and tomato to both the meatballs and the sauce makes these meatballs tasty and uncommonly succulent. Serve with Spanish-Style Mixed Salad (page 58).

serves 3 to 4

Meatballs

3 tablespoons olive oil

1 garlic clove, minced

$1/4$ medium onion, finely chopped

$1/2$ medium green bell pepper, finely chopped

$1/4$ pound tomato

1-pound mixture of ground pork and veal

About $1 1/2$ teaspoons kosher or sea salt

Freshly ground pepper

3 large eggs

3 tablespoons dried bread crumbs

Flour for dusting

Sauce

$1/4$ medium onion, finely chopped

1 garlic clove, minced

$1/2$ medium green bell pepper, finely chopped

1 teaspoon flour

1 tablespoon canned tomato sauce

$1/4$ cup dry white wine

1 cup chicken broth

Kosher or sea salt

Freshly ground pepper

To make the meatballs, heat 1 tablespoon of the oil in a shallow casserole, and very slowly sauté the garlic, onion, and bell pepper. Remove the vegetables to a bowl and wipe out the casserole.

Cut the tomato in half crosswise and holding it over the bowl, grate the tomato with a coarse grater down to the skin. Add to the bowl the meat, salt, a generous amount of pepper, 1 egg, and the bread crumbs. Work with your hands until well mixed, then shape into $1^{1}/_{2}$-inch balls. In a dish, lightly beat the remaining 2 eggs.

Heat the remaining 2 tablespoons oil in the casserole. Dust the meatballs with flour, dip in the egg, then place directly in the hot pan. Sauté over medium heat until browned on all sides and barely cooked through. Remove to a warm platter, leaving the oil in the casserole.

To make the sauce, in the same oil (add a little more if necessary) sauté the onion, garlic, and bell pepper until softened. Stir in the flour, then the tomato sauce, wine, broth, and salt and pepper to taste. Cover and simmer for 20 minutes. Return the meatballs to the casserole, heat, and serve.

ALBÓNDIGAS EN SALSA DE LIMÓN DE PILAR MONTEOLIVA ❧
PILAR MONTEOLIVA'S MEATBALLS IN LEMON SAUCE

Another great recipe from my friend Pilar Vico's mother—pork and veal meatballs in an unusual lemon, egg yolk, and saffron sauce, quite unlike any other sauce I've come across in Spanish cookery. Serve with very small boiled new potatoes.

serves 4

6 tablespoons dried bread crumbs

1/4 cup milk

1 1/2-pound mixture of ground veal and pork

2 tablespoons finely chopped Serrano or prosciutto ham

5 tablespoons minced fresh parsley

3 garlic cloves, minced

Kosher or sea salt

1/2 teaspoon freshly ground pepper

3 tablespoons plus 1 teaspoon freshly squeezed lemon juice

2 large eggs

Flour for dusting

2 tablespoons olive oil

1/4 cup finely chopped onion

3/4 cup chicken broth

3 tablespoons dry white wine

Scant 1/8 teaspoon crumbled thread saffron

2 large egg yolks

In a small bowl, combine the bread crumbs with the milk. In a large bowl, mix together the ground meats, ham, 2 tablespoons of the parsley, two-thirds of the garlic, 1 1/2 teaspoons salt, the pepper, 2 tablespoons plus 2 teaspoons of the lemon juice, the softened bread crumbs, and the 2 whole eggs. Shape into 1 1/2-inch balls and dust with flour.

Heat the oil in a shallow casserole and sauté the meatballs until browned all over. Add the onion and sauté until softened, then stir in the broth and wine. Bring to a boil, cover, and simmer for 40 minutes. Meanwhile, in a mortar or mini processor, mash to a paste 2 more tablespoons of the parsley, the remaining garlic, 1/8 teaspoon salt, and the saffron.

Remove the meatballs to a warm platter and strain the sauce, pressing with the back of a metal soup ladle to extract as much liquid as possible. Return the sauce to the casserole and add the remaining 2 teaspoons lemon juice and the mortar mixture. In a small bowl, combine the egg yolks with a little hot broth and add to the casserole, gently simmering and stirring until thickened (if too thick, add a little more broth or water). Return the meatballs to the sauce and simmer for a minute. Sprinkle with the remaining tablespoon parsley and serve.

PASTEL DE TRES CARNES DE LA CUÑADA DE PILAR ⚜
THREE-MEAT LOAF FROM PILAR'S SISTER-IN-LAW

This recipe comes by a roundabout route from our friend Carmen Serrano, who in turn got it from the sister-in-law of her friend Pilar. A dish made by the family cook, this is somewhere between a meat loaf and pâté—the chopped meats are attractively sandwiched between chicken cutlets and enclosed in bacon—giving this *pastel* (a word that may refer either to a dessert pastry or to a pâté) a much more refined and delicate flavor than a common meat loaf. Be sure to spoon on the juices when serving—they give lots of extra flavor. Serve with boiled sliced potatoes, spooning the juices over the potatoes as well.

The loaf is also excellent cold as a luncheon meat, accompanied by cornichon pickles and a red berry fruit preserve, such as currant. serves 4

$^1/_4$ pound thin-sliced bacon

$1^1/_4$ pounds thin-sliced chicken cutlets

Kosher or sea salt

Freshly ground pepper

2 tablespoons dried bread crumbs

2 tablespoons milk

$1^1/_4$-pound mixture of ground veal and pork

1 large egg

2 garlic cloves, minced

2 tablespoons dry fino sherry

3 tablespoons minced fresh parsley

Line the bottom of a $9^1/_4$ x $5^1/_4$-inch loaf pan with half the slices of the bacon. Arrange half of the chicken in the bottom of the pan, piecing to fit if necessary. Sprinkle with salt and pepper.

Soak the bread crumbs in the milk. In a bowl, mix well to combine the ground meats, egg, garlic, $1^1/_2$ teaspoons salt, $^1/_4$ teaspoon pepper, the sherry, parsley, and soaked crumbs. Spread out evenly in the loaf pan, top with the remaining cutlets, sprinkle with salt and pepper, and cover with the remaining bacon. Place the loaf pan in a pan of hot water and bake at 450°F for 1 hour.

Loosen the loaf around the edges, then drain off and reserve the juices. Turn out the loaf onto a board or plate and slice. Spoon the juices over the meat and serve.

PASTEL DE CARNE Y PATATA ❧ SPANISH-STYLE HASH CASSEROLE

This is the Spanish take on hash, a recipe that came to me from several friends, but all the recipes are remarkably similar (one goes by the charming name of *"Puré Chufles,"* a transposition into Spanish of the French words *purée* and *soufflé*). A touch of brandy and nutmeg gives the meat a distinctive flavor, and the egg, cheese, and crumb topping a finished appearance, making this hash worthy of a company meal. I like to serve it with sautéed *piquillo* peppers (see Pantry, page 15) and a green salad. serves 4 to 6

4 tablespoons olive oil plus some for greasing

2 medium onions, finely chopped

1^1/2 pounds ground beef

Kosher or sea salt

Freshly ground pepper

1 medium tomato, finely chopped

3 tablespoons minced fresh parsley

1 teaspoon freshly ground nutmeg

^{1}/4 cup brandy

2 pounds medium Idaho potatoes, peeled and halved crosswise

2 whole peeled garlic cloves

About 1 cup warm milk

Dried bread crumbs

2 large eggs

Unsalted butter

Grated Manchego or Parmesan cheese

Heat 2 tablespoons of the oil in a large skillet and sauté the onions for 2 minutes. Cover and sauté over low heat for another 10 minutes. Turn the heat to high, add the meat, and sauté, breaking it up with the edge of a wooden spoon and seasoning with salt and a generous amount of pepper as it cooks, until it loses its color. Add the tomato, parsley, nutmeg, and brandy and sauté for about 5 minutes more.

Bring the potatoes to a boil in salted water to which the garlic cloves have been added and cook until tender. With an electric mixer, puree the potatoes and garlic with the remaining 2 tablespoons olive oil and as much warm milk as required. Season with salt and pepper.

Heat the oven to 350°F. Grease an 8 x 12-inch baking dish (preferably Pyrex) with oil and sprinkle with bread crumbs. Starting with the potato, make several layers of potato and meat, ending with potato.

Beat the eggs with an electric mixer until thick, creamy, and lemon colored. Pour over the dish. Dot with butter and sprinkle with bread crumbs and grated cheese. Bake for about 30 minutes until brown. Loosen the edges and cut into portions, removing them with a metal pancake turner. Serve.

EMPANADA MALLORQUINA ❧ MALLORCAN LAMB AND SOBRASADA PIE

Lard is the shortening of choice in Mallorca, and in combination with orange juice and olive oil, it makes an excellent crust for this tasty meat pie that puts together lamb and Mallorca's typical sausage, *sobrasada*. *Sobrasada* tastes very much like chorizo but is softer and spreadable (the island's climate is not suitable for long periods of curing). With a green salad, this makes a nice supper dish.

serves 6

Pie Crust

2 1/2 cups unbleached flour

1/4 teaspoon kosher or sea salt

6 tablespoons chilled lard (see Pantry, page 12), or vegetable shortening, cut into several pieces

3 tablespoons mild olive oil

3 tablespoons freshly squeezed orange juice

1/4 cup ice water

Filling

2 tablespoons olive oil

1 pound lean lamb, from the leg or shoulder and cut into 1/2-inch dice

Kosher or sea salt

Freshly ground pepper

2 medium onions, preferably Vidalia or other sweet onions, slivered

2 garlic cloves, minced

1/2 cup dry white wine

Scant 1/8 teaspoon crumbled thread saffron

1/4 pound *sobrasada* (see Pantry, page 16), or soft cooking chorizo, skinned and finely chopped

1 large egg, lightly beaten

To make the pie crust, combine the flour and salt in a food processor. Pulse in the lard until it is fully incorporated into the flour, then gradually pulse in the oil, juice, and water. Shape into two smooth balls, cover with plastic wrap, and let sit at room temperature.

To make the filling, heat the oil to the smoking point in a shallow casserole and sear the lamb, sprinkling with salt and pepper as it cooks. Remove to a warm platter. Add the onions and garlic (and a little more oil if necessary) to the casserole and sauté for 2 minutes. Lower the heat, cover, and let the onion cook very slowly for about 20 minutes.

Return the meat to the casserole, stir in the wine and saffron, and reduce the liquid to half. Mix in the so-brasada, cook for 2 minutes, and cool.

Heat the oven to 350°F. Roll the dough between wax paper into two 13-inch circles. Place one on an ungreased cookie tray and spread with the meat mixture to within 1 inch of the edge. Cover with the second dough circle, roll up the edges, and press well to seal. With a knife make a small hole in the center of the crust and brush with the beaten egg.

Bake for about 30 minutes, until nicely browned. The empanada is best served when warm but is also good at room temperature.

CHAPTER 9

POSTRES
desserts

AS ODD AS IT MIGHT SOUND, SPANISH SWEETS AND religion go hand in hand. Dessert making was once the domain of nuns. They inherited the tradition from the Moors, who favored sweets made with almonds, honey, sugar, and egg yolk. Serendipitously, Spanish wine makers needed large quantities of egg whites to clarify their wines but had no use for the yolks. They donated them to convents and the nuns built thriving businesses selling their sweets. Today there is no shortage of desserts and candies in Spain, but Spaniards nevertheless go out of their way to buy from convents, because such confections have the seal of purity and motherly love. These cherished recipes are never written down; rather they are passed down from the mother superior to the next in line. Among them are *yemas*, rich egg yolk and sugar syrup candies that have made convents like San Leandro in Sevilla famous.

Spain, however, is not especially well known for its desserts. Until recently a meal typically ended with fruit, and desserts were reserved for celebrations and afternoon snacks. Many are specifically associated with certain festivals and holidays: fried pastries bathed in honey, pastry puffs, and *torrijas* (sugared toast, page 261) appear during Holy Week; doughnuts and *churros* (fritters, page 262) at local fiestas, fried in vats of hot oil; cookies, like *polvorones* and *perrunillas* (page 280), and *turrón* nougat candy are found at Christmas. And yet the variety and originality of the family dessert recipes I gathered were truly a revelation. I found fried pastries scented with anise and sesame, fruit tarts, a tart of almond and egg yolk, refrigerator cakes, as well as cheese and chocolate cakes, almond custards, rice puddings, crisp cookies and wafers, doughnuts, and cornmeal fritters. Some are based on little more than water, flour, and sugar, but with typical Spanish imagination and ingenuity are transformed into delightful treats. There are desserts here to complement every kind of meal. For a light finish you might choose something simple like custard, rice pudding flan, or cookies. For more elaborate finales, try apple custard tart, marzipan cake filled with custard, cheesecake made with exotic Torta de La Serena cheese, or meringue wafers with almond butter.

Sweet sherries made with the Pedro Ximénez grape, like those of Osborne and González Byass, are wonderful to accompany desserts, and outstanding Spanish muscatels are another fine choice—I especially like those made by Bodegas Fariña and Chivite.

Yemas: HEAVENLY SWEETS

The spring air in Sevilla is deliciously fragrant with the perfume of orange blossoms. My husband, Luis, daughter, Elisa, and I enter the convent of San Leandro through an airy plant-filled Andalusian patio, where the windows are barred and covered with wire mesh to protect the privacy of the cloistered nuns. We are here to buy *yemas*—sugar and egg yolk candies for which this convent is renowned—and the sale will take place between us and an unseen figure behind a beautiful, brass-studded eighteenth-century revolving shelf. We pull the bell cord.

"*Ave María Purísima*," sings an ethereal voice on the other side, and we place our order, put our money on the shelf, and give it a turn. A box of individually wrapped *yemas* is delivered to us by the same route. We find out that the owner of the bodiless, bubbly voice is Sister Carmen del Niño Jesús, who entered San Leandro when she was twenty, more than forty years ago, and has not seen her beloved Sevilla since. Yet she has lost none of her high spirits and zest for life, and she is hungry for conversation.

"How is my Sevilla? Is it as beautiful as ever?" she inquires. We assure her it most certainly is. Her attention turns to our daughter and she asks, only half in jest, "Do you think she might consider joining our order? It's so difficult to attract young girls these days!" Sister Carmen del Niño Jesús does not persist and tells us instead about the convent's famous *yemas*. "We've made *yemas* here since the year 1500, but not until King Alfonso XIII paid a visit at the turn of the twentieth century did our *yemas* become famous throughout the country." How are they made, we ask. Apparently it's a tightly guarded secret. "Only three of us know the magic formula."

We leave and nibble on our *yemas* as we walk. Each and every bite reminds us of the enterprising nuns who began making *yemas* so many centuries ago.

LAS TORRIJAS DEL PADRE DE PEDRO SUBIJANA ⚜
"FRENCH TOAST" FROM PEDRO SUBIJANA'S FATHER

"I remember how well my grandmother used to make torrijas," master chef Pedro Subijana of Akelaře restaurant in San Sebastián told me, *"but the one who did them best was, without doubt, my father, who was a pastry maker by trade, and I can still smell the wonderful aromas of sweet breads and pastries wafting from his oven. He was a man of uncommon sensibility, who delighted in preparing food for family events, thinking only of the pleasure it would bring to his guests. He gave his distinctive touch to torrijas, just as he did with everything else that passed through his hands in the kitchen."*

Although torrijas are quintessentially Spanish, they are similar to what we know as French toast. Bread slices are soaked in a custard-like milk mixture, coated with beaten eggs, and fried. They emerge crisp on the surface and creamy within. A nice crusty bread works best, and torrijas should be eaten when freshly made. **serves 8**

2 cups milk

6 tablespoons sugar plus more for sprinkling

1 cinnamon stick

Zest of 1 lemon, in several pieces

Mild olive oil for frying

Sixteen 3/4-inch bread slices, cut from a day-old French-style loaf

2 large beaten eggs

Ground cinnamon for sprinkling

Heat the milk, sugar, cinnamon stick, and lemon zest in a saucepan. When it reaches a boil (watch carefully so that it does not boil over), reduce the heat to a slow boil and cook for a minute. Return to a full boil, then reduce the heat again as before. Repeat four to five times until the milk is slightly thickened. Simmer for 5 minutes and cool down until barely warm.

Pour the oil to a depth of at least 1 inch in a skillet (or better still, use a deep-fryer set at 360°F) and heat until the oil quickly browns a cube of bread. Place the bread slices in the warm milk and soak for about 1 minute on each side. Coat with the egg and pass directly to the hot oil. Fry until golden, turning once. Drain on paper towels. Arrange on a serving dish and sprinkle generously with sugar and cinnamon. Serve as soon as possible warm or at room temperature.

CHOCOLATE CON CHURROS DE RUFINO LÓPEZ ❧
RUFINO'S HOT CHOCOLATE WITH FRITTERS

I adore the long narrow Spanish fritters called *churros* and love to buy them in Spain for breakfast. But I never seem to find the time at home to make *chocolate con churros*—the quintessentially Spanish breakfast, afternoon snack, and typical treat at outdoor fiestas, served with thick rich hot chocolate in which the *churros* are typically dunked. Nor can I find the right time of day to indulge—the combination is too heavy for breakfast and too filling for between meals. Our friend Rufino López, owner of Solera, New York's premier Spanish restaurant and Galician by birth, has found the perfect solution. He serves *chocolate con churros,* as a dessert, reducing the hot chocolate to an intense chocolate sauce and presenting it in an espresso cup—a playful nod to its breakfast origins.   serves 6

Hot Chocolate

$^1/_4$ cup sugar

1 cup good-quality semisweet chocolate bits

$^1/_4$ cup bittersweet chocolate bits

1 tablespoon good-quality cocoa powder

$^1/_4$ cup milk

Churros

$1^1/_2$ teaspoons mild olive oil

$^1/_4$ teaspoon kosher or sea salt

1 cup unbleached flour

Mild olive oil for frying

Granulated sugar for dusting

To make the hot chocolate, bring $^1/_2$ cup water and the sugar to a boil. Add the semisweet and bittersweet chocolate, cocoa, and milk and lower the heat. Stir constantly with a wooden spoon until the chocolate is thick and smooth, about 5 minutes. Reserve.

To make the *churros,* bring 1 cup water, the oil, and the salt to a boil in a saucepan. Add the flour all at once and stir vigorously with a wooden spoon until a smooth ball forms. Lower the heat and cook, flattening and turning the dough for 2 minutes. Cool and transfer to a pastry bag equipped with a $^3/8$-inch star tip (the fluted edge is essential), or use a special device to make *churros* (see Equipment, page 18).

Pour the oil to a depth of at least 1 inch in a skillet (or better still, use a deep-fryer heated to 360°F) and heat until the oil quickly browns a cube of bread. Squeeze 5-inch lengths of dough through the pastry tube into the oil—as many as will comfortably fit. Reduce the heat to medium-hot and fry until the *churros* puff and have barely begun to turn golden, about 20 seconds. Do not overcook—the *churros* should be crunchy outside and still soft within. Drain on paper towels. Keep them warm briefly, if necessary, in a 200°F oven until ready to serve.

To serve, reheat the chocolate over very low heat and divide into 6 espresso cups placed off center on 6 dessert plates. Dredge the *churros* in the sugar and arrange 4 on each plate.

ROSQUILLAS ELOISA ❧ ELOÍSA'S SPICED DOUGHNUTS

Wonderfully crisp on the outside, tender within, and subtly fragrant with anise, nutmeg, and cloves, these doughnuts are somewhat like crullers but with a decidedly Spanish flair. They come to me by way of my friend Carmen Serrano, who in turn got the recipe from her friend Mari Carmen, daughter of Eloísa, who makes them for birthdays and other festive occasions. makes about 15 doughnuts

1 1/2 cups unbleached flour

1/8 teaspoon kosher or sea salt

1 tablespoon baking powder

1/2 teaspoon freshly ground nutmeg

6 cloves, finely crushed

1/2 teaspoon finely crushed anise seeds

1 large egg

1/4 cup granulated sugar

1 1/2 tablespoons cold milk

2 tablespoons melted unsalted butter, cooled

Mild olive oil for frying

Confectioners' sugar for dusting

In a bowl, sift together the flour, salt, and baking powder. Stir in the nutmeg, cloves, and anise.

In another bowl, beat the egg and granulated sugar with an electric beater for about 20 minutes, until very light colored and fluffy. Beat in the milk and butter, then add the flour mixture and stir until incorporated. Turn out on a floured work surface and knead for about 5 minutes, adding more flour as necessary, until the dough no longer sticks to your hands (do not add more flour than necessary).

Roll out the dough on a floured surface to 1/4 inch. Cut with a doughnut cutter and let sit for 10 minutes.

Pour the oil to a depth of at least 1 inch in a skillet (or better still, use a deep-fryer) and heat until moderately hot (about 350°F). Add as many doughnuts as will comfortably fit and fry until golden, turning once. Drain on paper towels. Cool, then dust with confectioners' sugar. The doughnuts can be stored in a cookie tin but are best when eaten the same day.

TORONJAS DE XÁTIVA QUE SON ALMOJÁVANAS ❧
"CITRONS FROM JÁTIVA THAT ARE REALLY FRITTERS"

This recipe, with its odd name, appears in the six-teenth-century cookbook *El Llibre del Cuiner* by Ruperto de Nola, who was chef to Spanish King Fernando of Naples, when Naples was a Spanish possession. *Toronja* refers to the size and shape of these fritters (citrons are small citrus fruits) and *almojábana* (as it would be spelled today) in Moorish times meant cheese tortes, although to-day the word refers to a fritter that typically does not include cheese.

These wonderful fritters, with a hint of mint and bathed in honey, are creamy within, crunchy on the outside, and are made—as they originally were—with cheese.

makes 12 to 14 fritters, to serve about 4

$^1/_3$ cup unbleached flour

$^1/_8$ teaspoon kosher or sea salt

$^1/_2$ teaspoon baking powder

$^1/_2$ pound farmer's cheese, crumbled

5 tablespoons sugar

1 large egg

4 teaspoons minced fresh mint

Mild olive oil for frying

$^1/_2$ cup honey thinned with 1 tablespoon water

Cinnamon for dusting

Combine in a bowl the flour, salt, and baking powder. Stir in the cheese, sugar, egg, and mint.

Pour the oil in a skillet to a depth of at least $^1/_2$ inch (or better still, use a deep-fryer) and heat until the oil is moderately hot (about 350°F). Drop the cheese mixture by heaping teaspoons into the oil and fry until the frit-ters are, in the words of Ruperto de Nola, "the color of gold." Drain on paper towels and keep warm briefly, if necessary, in a 200°F oven. Arrange on individual dessert plates. Heat the honey and spoon over the frit-ters. Dust with cinnamon and serve warm.

SOPLILLOS DE SERY BERMEO ❧ SERY'S SUGAR-DUSTED PASTRY PUFFS

Sery Bermeo and her husband, Eugenio, have dedicated most of their lives to Mesón de la Villa, their restaurant in Aranda de Duero in the heart of northern Castilla. As is often the case with Castilian cooking, ingredients are basic and preparation simple, but the results are eminently appealing. Sery, in charge of the kitchen, lends her magic to these traditional pastries that puff as they fry. They have a haunting hint of anise and oranges.   makes about 30 pastries

2 tablespoons mild olive oil

2 tablespoons dry white wine

2 tablespoons dry or sweet anise liqueur

2 tablespoons freshly squeezed orange juice

1 teaspoon freshly grated orange zest

$1/4$ teaspoon vanilla extract

About 1 cup unbleached flour

Mild olive oil for frying

Granulated sugar for dusting

In a bowl, combine the oil, wine, liqueur, orange juice, orange zest, and vanilla. Gradually add the flour to form a soft dough. Turn out on a work surface and knead briefly, incorporating more flour as necessary so that the dough is not sticky. Enclose in plastic wrap and let sit at room temperature for about 20 minutes.

Roll out the dough on a floured surface, in a roughly rectangular shape, to less than $1/8$ inch. Cut the dough diagonally at 1-inch intervals with a thin sharp knife, then repeat in the opposite direction, at 3-inch intervals, crisscrossing to form rhombus shapes.

Pour oil to a depth of $1/2$ inch in a skillet (or better still, use a deep-fryer heated to 360°F) and heat until the oil quickly browns a cube of bread. Add as many pastries as will comfortably fit and fry until well browned, turning once. Drain on paper towels and while still warm, roll in sugar. *Soplillos* will keep for several days on a platter, covered with foil.

HOJALDRE DE MANZANA ❧ SPICED STEWED APPLES IN PUFF PASTRY

Apples appeared in Spain during the rule of the Romans and found their ideal climate in Asturias and in the adjoining province of León. Spanish reineta apples are similar to our Golden Delicious, which I have used in this first-rate dessert.

The use of puff pastry goes back centuries in Spain and was traditionally made with lard rather than butter. If you choose to make your own puff pastry, you can find recipes for both puff pastry made with lard (masa hojaldrada) and puff pastry made with butter in my book Tapas: The Little Dishes of Spain.

serves 4 to 5

6 ounces puff pastry, homemade or good-quality purchased

$1/2$ cup plus 2 tablespoons granulated sugar

8 tablespoons apple juice

$1/2$ cup white wine

1 cinnamon stick

Peel of $1/2$ lemon yellow part only

$1/4$ teaspoon freshly ground nutmeg

5 cloves

2 large Golden Delicious apples, peeled, quartered, and cored, then cut into $1/4$-inch wedges, and each wedge into $3/4$-inch pieces

Melted vanilla ice cream, or sweetened heavy cream

Confectioners' sugar for dusting

Preheat the oven to 450°F. Roll the puff pastry to $1/8$ inch, then cut into 4 x 3-inch rectangles. Arrange on a greased cookie tray and bake for 8 minutes, or until puffed and golden brown. Turn off the oven, leave the door slightly ajar, and keep the pastry in the oven for about 5 minutes more to further crisp the leaves.

Place the granulated sugar in a saucepan with 3 tablespoons of the apple juice. Cook over high heat, stirring constantly, until syrupy and lightly golden. Turn off the heat and carefully stir in the remaining 5 tablespoons apple juice, then add the wine, cinnamon stick, lemon peel, nutmeg, and cloves. Bring to a boil, lower the heat, and simmer for 10 minutes. Add the apples, bring again to a boil, and simmer for about 30 minutes, uncovered, until tender. Raise the heat and gently boil down for about 2 minutes, until the liquid is syrupy. Cool. Discard the lemon peel, cinnamon stick, and cloves.

When ready to serve, split the puff pastry in half and fill with about 2 tablespoons of the stewed apples. Serve over a pool of melted ice cream or sweetened heavy cream. Dust with confectioners' sugar.

CHARLOTE DE XOCOLATE DE IRENE ESPAÑA ❧ IRENE'S CHOCOLATE CHARLOTTE

The beauty of this elegant dessert from my good friend Irene in the Spanish Pyrenees is its simplicity and utter purity of ingredients. The ladyfingers that line the cake mold can be arranged very close together or with some spaces to create chocolate swirls. If this seems similar to French charlotte desserts from just across the border, that is not surprising, since this region of the Catalan Pyrenees, by a quirk of history, opens geographically into France rather than Spain.   serves 8

About 9 ladyfingers, split in halves

$^1/_4$ pound (1 stick) unsalted butter

5 ounces good-quality bittersweet chocolate

$^1/_2$ cup sugar

3 large eggs, separated

Line a $1^1/_2$-quart charlotte mold (or bowl of a similar capacity, about $6^1/_2$ inches across the top, 4 to 5 inches tall, and 4 to 6 inches across the bottom) with the ladyfingers. Melt the butter and chocolate together in a large saucepan. Add the sugar and continue cooking, stirring constantly, until the mixture is smooth and the sugar dissolved. Turn off the heat and cool slightly.

Place the egg yolks in a small bowl and stir in some of the chocolate mixture. Return to the saucepan. Leave the heat off and stir vigorously.

In a bowl, beat the egg whites until stiff but not dry. Gently fold them into the chocolate mixture. Pour into the lined mold and refrigerate overnight. Loosen with a knife and turn out onto a serving dish. Keep chilled.

BIZCOCHO DE NARANJA DE MARI CARMEN MARTÍN ❧
MARI CARMEN'S ORANGE CAKE

A golden, moist cake perfumed with orange. According to our friend Mari Carmen, the secret to its success is adding the ingredients in precisely the order indicated and beating well after each addition. The cake is excellent served with coffee or tea, or to dress it up, combine 2 tablespoons apricot jam and 2 teaspoons orange liqueur. Simmer for 2 minutes, then brush over the finished cake. You can also serve it with a scoop of ice cream and fresh strawberries. For a cake with a wetter texture, heat 4 tablespoons ($^1/_2$ stick) butter, $^2/_3$ cup sugar, and $^1/_3$ cup freshly squeezed orange juice until the sugar is dissolved. Pour over the cake while it is hot and in the pan. Allow to cool thoroughly before removing from the pan.

makes an 8-inch Bundt cake

3 large eggs

1 cup granulated sugar

1 cup freshly squeezed orange juice

1 tablespoon freshly grated orange zest

$^1/_2$ cup mild olive oil

2 cups unbleached flour

1 tablespoon baking powder

Confectioners' sugar for dusting

Grease and flour an 8-inch fluted Bundt pan. Preheat the oven to 350°F. In a bowl, beat the eggs with an electric mixer until thickened and light colored. Gradually beat in the granulated sugar, then—in order—the orange juice, orange zest, and oil. Beat in the flour and, finally, the baking powder.

Pour the batter into the pan and bake for about 45 minutes, until a toothpick inserted in the cake comes out clean and the cake springs back to the touch. Cool slightly, then turn out onto a serving dish. Dust with confectioners' sugar, or finish in any of the ways described in the headnote.

PONCHE SEGOVIANO ⚜ SEGOVIA'S CUSTARD AND MARZIPAN CAKE

I always look forward to visiting Segovia for historical as well as culinary reasons. The two-thousand-year-old Roman aqueduct never ceases to amaze me, the town specialty, roasted suckling pig is prepared here as nowhere else, and Ponche Segoviano is one of my favorite desserts, found only in this ancient city. Moistened with rum-flavored syrup, filled with custard, covered with a thin coating of almond paste, and dusted with confectioners' sugar, it is found in just about every restaurant and pastry shop. Nowhere is it more traditional than at Mesón de Cándido, a culinary institution like no other in Spain.

Typically a design is burned into the sugar coating of the cake, making a very attractive presentation. Although the recipe may look involved, it is really quite simple. The cake can be assembled in 15 minutes, and the custard and syrup can be prepared while the cake bakes and cools. Almond paste is found in tubes in the baking section in supermarkets. Be sure the label reads "Pure Almond Paste."

serves 6

Cake

4 large eggs, separated

$1/2$ cup granulated sugar

$1/4$ teaspoon kosher or sea salt

2 tablespoons melted unsalted butter, cooled

$1/4$ teaspoon freshly grated lemon zest

1 cup unbleached flour

Syrup

6 tablespoons granulated sugar

1 small cinnamon stick

1 tablespoon dry light or dark rum

Custard

1 cup milk

Zest of $1/2$ lemon

3 large egg yolks

$1/4$ cup granulated sugar

2 tablespoons cornstarch

2 teaspoons unsalted butter

4 ounces pure almond paste

Confectioners' sugar for dusting

Preheat the oven to 350°F. Grease and flour an 8-inch square baking pan. With an electric mixer, beat the egg yolks, granulated sugar, salt, butter, and grated lemon zest until pale yellow and spongy. Gradually beat in the flour.

In a separate bowl, beat the egg whites until stiff but not dry. Gently fold into the batter. Pour into the baking pan and bake for about 20 minutes, until a toothpick inserted in the cake comes out clean and the cake springs back to the touch.

Meanwhile, make the syrup. Combine in a small saucepan the granulated sugar, 6 tablespoons water, and the cinnamon. Bring to a boil and simmer for 10 minutes. Remove from the heat and stir in the rum. Cool.

When the cake is done, remove from the oven and shake to loosen it in the pan. While the cake is still hot, pour half of the syrup over it, then invert onto a plate and pour the rest of the syrup over the other side. Cool.

While the cake is cooling, make the custard. Heat the milk and lemon zest in a saucepan, cover, and simmer for 10 minutes. Discard the lemon zest. In a bowl, whisk the egg yolks, then whisk in the granulated sugar and cornstarch. Gradually pour in the hot milk, return to the saucepan, and cook over moderate heat, stirring constantly, until thickened and smooth. Remove from the heat and stir in the butter. Cool, stirring occasionally.

Split the cake in half. Using the top half as the bottom of the cake, spread the cut side with the custard, then cover with the other half of the cake. On a work surface, roll the almond paste to $1/8$ inch (it should be slightly larger than the cake). Carefully lift with a dough scraper and place the almond paste over the cake. Trim to size with a sharp knife. Gently press so that the almond paste adheres to the cake. Sprinkle generously with confectioners' sugar. Heat a metal skewer over a flame, holding the end with a pot holder. When it is very hot, hold it diagonally over the cake to burn a line in the sugar. Wipe off and continue heating and burning to make a rhombus design over the cake. Store in the refrigerator, but bring to room temperature before serving.

Galician cheeses,
Santiago de Compostela

TARTA DE LA SERENA DE FÉLIX DURÁN ⚬⚭
FÉLIX DURÁN'S EXTREMADURA-STYLE CHEESE TART

A divine creamy cheesecake from Félix Durán at the delightful Plasencia Parador in the region of Extremadura. The secret to its slightly exotic flavor is the wonderful cheese from here, Torta de La Serena—very similar to another cheese from Extremadura, Torta del Casar, which has received accolades from cheese aficionados in the United States. Both of these extraordinary cheeses are soft and runny, like a Brie or Camembert, but made with sheep's milk cheese and with a flavor all their own.   serves 8

1 cup (10 ounces) small-curd cottage cheese

6 ounces cream cheese

2 ounces Torta de La Serena (see Pantry, page 16), Torta del Casar, Camembert, or Brie, without rind

1 cup sugar

4 large eggs

2 large egg yolks

3/4 cup heavy cream

Raspberry Puree, optional

1 1/3 cups fresh or frozen raspberries

1/4 cup sugar

1 1/2 teaspoons fruit-flavored orujo (a Spanish liqueur similar to grappa), aquavit, kirschwasser, orange liqueur, or water

Fresh raspberries, optional

Preheat the oven to 350°F. With an electric mixer, beat together the cottage, cream, and Serena cheeses with the sugar. Beat in the whole eggs and yolks, one at a time, until the mixture is smooth and creamy. Gradually stir in the cream.

Lightly grease a 9-inch cake pan, then line the bottom and sides of the pan with parchment paper or foil. Pour in the cheese mixture and bake in a pan of hot water for 1 hour and 20 minutes to 1 1/2 hours, until fairly firm to the touch. Remove from the pan of water and cool completely. Invert onto a plate, remove the parchment paper, and turn over again. Chill thoroughly, preferably overnight.

To make the raspberry puree, if using, combine the raspberries, sugar, and liqueur in a food processor and blend until smooth. Strain.

Spoon the raspberry puree onto individual dessert dishes. Place a slice of the cheese tart on top and scatter the fresh raspberries, if using, around the dish.

TARTA VASCA DE MANZANA DE BASERRI MAITEA ❧
BASERRI MAITEA'S BASQUE APPLE CUSTARD TART

Baserri Maitea is a stunning eighteenth-century country house on an isolated hilltop just north of Guernica in Spain's Basque Country, and its dining room is cozy and rustic, hung with cornstalks, dried red peppers, and braids of garlic. Among their desserts is this extraordinary tart, the recipe for which was given to me by vivacious Alexia, the restaurant's pastry chef. It is a tart common to the Basque Country and found in many versions, but this is by far the best I have ever tasted. It begins with a wonderfully short crust filled with creamy custard and topped with sliced apples marinated in spiced apple syrup. It involves several steps, but all are short and easy. The tart is best when eaten the same day, unrefrigerated and preferably slightly warm. If you must refrigerate, warm briefly before serving.

The recipe makes a 9-inch tart, but Alexia also likes to make individual tartlets, a lovely and most elegant presentation. For tartlets, use six 4-inch tartlet pans with removable bottoms, roll the dough a bit thinner, and bake for 2 or 3 minutes less.

serves 6

2 Golden Delicious apples, peeled, cored, quartered, and cut into scant $1/8$-inch slices

$1^{1}/2$ cups apple juice

3 tablespoons sugar

2 cloves

$1/4$ teaspoon freshly ground nutmeg

Pastry Crust

1 cup unbleached flour

2 tablespoons sugar

$1/2$ teaspoon baking powder

6 tablespoons chilled unsalted butter

1 tablespoon egg yolk

2 tablespoons heavy cream

Pastry Cream

1 cup milk

$1/2$ cinnamon stick

Zest of $1/2$ lemon

2 large egg yolks

$1/4$ cup sugar

2 tablespoons cornstarch

2 teaspoons unsalted butter

2 tablespoons apricot preserves

Arrange the apples in a flat-bottomed bowl. In a saucepan combine the apple juice, sugar, cloves, and nutmeg and bring to a boil. Simmer, reducing to half. Pour the syrup over the apples and let sit at room temperature for several hours.

Preheat the oven to 350°F. To make the pastry crust, combine in a bowl the flour, sugar, and baking powder. Work in the butter with your fingers, then stir in the egg yolk and cream with a fork. Turn out on a work surface and work lightly to form a ball. Sprinkle lightly with flour and roll out between sheets of wax paper into an 11-inch circle (chill briefly if the dough becomes too soft). Fit into the bottom and up the sides of a 9-inch tart pan with a removable bottom, trimming any excess by pressing and cutting off at the rim. Prick all over with a fork and bake for about 15 minutes, until lightly browned. Turn off the oven.

To make the pastry cream, bring the milk with the cinnamon stick and lemon zest to a boil in a saucepan. Cover and simmer for 20 minutes. Cool briefly, then discard the cinnamon and lemon.

In a bowl, whisk together the egg yolks and sugar, then whisk in the cornstarch and gradually stir in the warm milk. Return to the saucepan over medium heat, stirring constantly, until thickened and smooth. Remove from the heat and add the butter. Cool, stirring occasionally.

Preheat the oven to 450°F. Pour the custard into the prepared crust. Remove the apples from the syrup and arrange in tightly overlapping rows on top. Bake for 10 minutes.

Heat the apricot preserves until they have liquefied and brush over the tart. Cool, remove the sides of the tart pan, and serve, preferably warm.

ALMENDRADOS DE LA SIRGA ❧ SUGARED PUFF PASTRY STRIPS WITH ALMONDS

If you use prepared puff pastry, these simple yet elegant pastries can be made in no time. They come from the rustic timber-beamed, centuries-old restaurant Los Templarios in the town of Villalcázar de Sirga, an important stop on the pilgrimage route known as El Camino de Santiago. Owner Pablo El Mesonero, already in his nineties when we first met him, used to dress as a pilgrim in his brown cape with scallop shells on the shoulders (the shells from the coast of Galicia, a symbol of the city of Santiago de Compostela), with a staff from which a water gourd dangled. His outfit was completed by a wide-brimmed hat and a red-striped wool *serape* over one shoulder. He would sound a bullhorn, then bless the meal by reciting poetry or whatever struck his fancy. He always ended his discourse with the words, "And if you don't like the food, there's the door!" With that diners invariably burst into cheers and wild applause.

Pablo has passed on, but in his memory his staff and cape adorn a corner of the restaurant and his children carry on. The dishes are the very same ones the family has been serving for generations.

makes about 20 pastries

½ pound puff pastry, homemade or good-quality purchased

1 egg white, lightly beaten with a fork

4 to 5 tablespoons sugar

4 to 5 tablespoons finely chopped sliced almonds, skin on

Preheat the oven to 450°F. Roll the puff pastry to ⅛ inch and cut into $2^{3}/4$ x $1^{1}/2$-inch rectangles. Arrange on a greased cookie tray. Brush with the egg white and sprinkle each pastry with about ½ teaspoon of the sugar and about ½ teaspoon almonds. Bake for 8 minutes, or until golden brown. Turn off the oven, leave the door slightly ajar, and let cool in the oven for about 5 minutes until the pastries are thoroughly crisped. Store in a cookie tin.

BRAZO DE FABIOLA ❧ COFFEE-FLAVORED REFRIGERATOR LOG

"This recipe has been in my family for many years," says our friend Reme Domínguez, who takes charge of the kitchen at Tasca del Puerto in Castellón de la Plana. *"I remember my grandmother making it, but I have no idea why it is called Fabiola's Arm."*

Made with María cookies layered with coffee frosting and covered in meringue (a more sophisticated version of our chocolate wafers and whipped cream log), this dessert is so simple to make, but its taste and appearance would make anyone think you had spent hours in the kitchen. It is very rich—serve small portions—and it tastes best when refrigerated overnight and served cold, or even slightly frozen.   **serves 6 to 8**

$1/2$ pound (2 sticks) unsalted butter, at room temperature

8 tablespoons sugar

2 teaspoons instant espresso coffee

$1/2$ cup fresh espresso, regular coffee, or liquid instant espresso, cooled

$1/2$ package María biscuits (about 14 cookies; see Pantry, page 12)

1 large egg white

With an electric mixer, cream the butter and 6 tablespoons of the sugar. Add the instant coffee and 2 teaspoons of the liquid coffee and beat until smooth.

Pour the remaining coffee into a dish and dip each cookie quickly in the coffee (don't leave the cookies in the coffee any longer or they will break up).

Spread about 2 teaspoons of the butter mixture on each cookie, pressing the cookies together to form a log.

In a small bowl, beat the egg white and the remaining 2 tablespoons sugar with an electric mixer until stiff peaks form. Using a spatula, cover the log with the meringue, forming swirls and soft peaks. Refrigerate overnight. To serve, cut on the bias into thin slices.

TÉCULA MÉCULA · FÉLIX DURÁN'S ALMOND AND EGG YOLK TART

I have no idea where the name Técula Mécula comes from (neither word appears in a dictionary) that describes this rich, candy-like tart that I find addictive. It is typical of the region of Extremadura and the recipe was passed to me by Félix Durán, chef at the magnificent Plasencia Parador, who advises that one of the secrets of this tart is to add the ingredients one at a time and in the specified order.

The parador, which features several other traditional recipes from Extremadura, like *Patatera*, a smoked paprika and potato spread (page 32), and *Félix Durán's Extremadura-Style Cheese Tart* (page 273), is as delightful as the food. Once a sixteenth-century palace and convent, it has been magnificently restored, and in spring and summer hundreds of storks swoop low over the interior patios, a sight to behold.

If you don't have homemade puff pastry around (I always keep some in my freezer), and since the pastry is merely a bottom crust, purchased puff pastry works just fine. The tart will keep at room temperature for several days.

serves 8 to 10

1/2 pound puff pastry, homemade or good-quality purchased

1/4 pound blanched almonds

3 tablespoons unbleached flour

1 1/4 cups granulated sugar

1 tablespoon unsalted butter, softened

2 tablespoons pure fresh lard (see Pantry, page 12), or
    another 2 tablespoons unsalted butter, softened

5 large egg yolks

1 1/2 tablespoons lightly beaten large egg

Sugar Glaze

1/2 large egg white

1/2 cup confectioners' sugar

Preheat the oven to 400°F. Roll the pastry into an 11-inch square, then trim the corners to make a circle. Fit into an 8-inch fluted tart pan with a removable bottom, continuing up the sides and trimming any excess by pressing at the rim to cut off the excess. Be sure the pastry adheres to the sides—if not, dampen the underside and press lightly. Prick all over with a fork and bake until lightly browned, about 15 minutes.

Meanwhile, in a food processor grind the almonds with the flour until the almonds are as finely ground as possible. In a large saucepan, bring to a boil the granulated sugar and $^1/_2$ cup water and boil for 2 minutes. Cool slightly.

Add to the saucepan—one at a time and in the following order—the almond mixture, the butter, stirring until melted, then the lard, stirring again until melted, the egg yolks, and finally the whole egg. Cook over medium-low heat until the mixture begins to bubble, stirring occasionally, about 15 minutes. Pour into the tart pan and bake for 13 to 15 minutes, until lightly browned on top. Cool briefly, then remove the sides of the tart pan.

In a small bowl, whisk the egg white until foamy, add the confectioners' sugar, and whisk until smooth and thickened. While the tart is still warm, paint the top (there will be extra glaze that you can use, if you wish, for some other confection). Serve at room temperature in small portions.

PERRUNILLAS DE RUPERTO BLANCO ❧
RUPERTO'S CINNAMON- AND LEMON-SCENTED COOKIES

Remarkably light and flaky, these cookies rely on lard (which has less saturated fat than butter) for their texture and typically Spanish flavor. You could, of course, substitute butter, but then these cookies would lose their distinctiveness. It is imperative, however, to use pure fresh lard, not the insipid hydrogenated kind sold in supermarkets. Aside from its uses in Spanish cooking, lard makes incredibly good biscuits and pie crusts. Like all of the other delicious recipes my friend Ruperto provided for this book, this one is outstanding, as well as quick and easy to prepare, as is his style. Note that these are fairly thick cookies, and you can shape them as you wish, although I particularly like them cut with a round scalloped-edge cookie cutter.

makes about 30 cookies

$1/2$ pound pure fresh lard (see Pantry, page 12)

$1/2$ cup sugar plus more for sprinkling

$1/2$ teaspoon cinnamon

$1/2$ teaspoon freshly grated lemon zest

1 large egg, separated, plus $1 1/2$ tablespoons beaten large egg

2 cups unbleached flour

Preheat the oven to 425°F. With an electric mixer, beat the lard and sugar until light and fluffy. Stir in the cinnamon, lemon zest, egg yolk, beaten egg, and flour, working with your hands until fully incorporated and adding more flour if the dough is sticky. Roll on a floured surface to a thickness of $3/8$ to $1/2$ inch. Cut with a $1 3/4$-inch scalloped-edge cookie cutter.

Line a cookie sheet with foil and arrange the cookies on it, well spaced. Brush with the egg white, lightly beaten with a fork, sprinkle well with sugar, and bake until well browned, 13 to 15 minutes. Store in a cookie tin.

ANTIGUAS TORTAS DE ACEITE ❧ OLD-FASHIONED OLIVE OIL WAFERS

Once more the cooking of Spain takes the most basic ingredients and transforms them into an irresistible treat. Bread dough (pizza dough from your local pizzeria is a perfect substitution for effortless preparation), into which olive oil and aromatic crushed seeds have been incorporated, makes large flaky wafers that are not overly sweet and are usually eaten for breakfast or as an afternoon snack. They are also a nice accompaniment to simple custard or frozen desserts. Traditionally they are individually wrapped in wax paper to maintain freshness and to protect them from breakage. But surely they will not last long enough to warrant the extra effort!

Tortas de Aceite are direct descendants of Moorish *alcorzas*, little wafers made with flour, yeast, oil, and sugar that were baked or fried. To this day they are still made where they have been made for centuries, in the town of Castilleja de la Cuesta, just outside of Sevilla.   **makes 6 large wafers**

1 tablespoon sesame seeds

2 teaspoons anise seeds

$1/4$ cup mild olive oil

Peel of $1/4$ lemon, yellow part only

$1/4$ pound uncooked pizza dough

$1 1/2$ teaspoons sweet anise liqueur

About $1/2$ cup unbleached flour

About 2 tablespoons sugar

Preheat the oven to 350°F and toast the sesame and anise seeds on a small oven tray until lightly browned, about 8 minutes. Transfer to a mortar or mini processor and pound to break up the seeds.

In a small skillet, heat the oil with the lemon zest over high heat until the zest is blackened. Discard the zest and cool the oil.

In a bowl combine the crushed seeds, the pizza dough, oil, and anise liqueur. Gradually work in the flour until the dough holds together. Turn out on a work surface and knead lightly, incorporating more flour if necessary. Roll to the thinness of a nickel. Cut in $4 1/2$-inch circles, using a small inverted bowl of that size as a guide.

Raise the oven temperature to 375°F. Pass the rolling pin over the circles to return them to their $4 1/2$-inch size (the circles tend to shrink once cut). Transfer to a greased cookie tray and sprinkle about 1 teaspoon of the sugar over each wafer. Bake for about 12 minutes, until the bottoms of the wafers are lightly browned. Place the cookie tray briefly under the broiler, about 5 inches from the heat, until the tops are golden and the sugar melted. Cool, then store individually wrapped in wax paper.

LÁMINAS DE MERENGUE CON MANTEQUILLA DE ALMENDRA DE IRENE ESPAÑA
✿ IRENE'S MERINGUE WAFERS WITH ALMOND BUTTER

Heavenly! Light as air, simple to make, and totally irresistible. Meringues have always been popular in Spain, and my husband, Luis, still recalls with delight dressing in his Sunday best to accompany his grandfather to El Riojano pastry shop—a place as popular today as in the past—to buy meringues for the afternoon meal. His favorites were the miniature strawberry meringues—crisp, two-tiered affairs that when pulled apart revealed a creamy interior.

Irene's, however, are not the typical meringues of Luis's youth, but sophisticated creations, constructed like napoleons and, like everything else that I have ever eaten from Irene's kitchen in the village of Artiés, they are first-class. The best way to achieve well-shaped meringue wafers and limit breakage is to use a piece of cardboard cut like a picture frame as a guide (a trick I learned from *Gourmet* magazine). The almond and butter filling should be spread on shortly before serving; otherwise the meringues become chewy (which is fine if you like them that way). If you do choose to assemble in advance, refrigerate but bring to room temperature before serving.

serves 8

4 large egg whites, at room temperature

$1/2$ teaspoon cream of tartar

$1/2$ cup superfine sugar

1 cup sifted confectioners' sugar

5 ounces blanched almonds, whole or slivered

6 ounces ($1^1/2$ sticks) plus 2 tablespoons unsalted butter

Sliced almonds, skin on

Preheat the oven to 200°F. Line two lightly greased cookie trays with parchment paper. Cut a piece of heavy cardboard to $5^1/2$ x 4 inches. With a razor blade or similarly sharp tool, cut out a $3^1/2$ x 2-inch rectangle from the center of the cardboard, leaving a 1-inch frame.

Beat the egg whites with an electric mixer until they are foamy, add the cream of tartar, and gradually beat in the superfine sugar. Continue beating until stiff peaks form. Fold in the confectioners' sugar. Place the cardboard frame on the parchment paper and with a rubber spatula, fill the frame with a $1/4$-inch layer of egg white mixture. Carefully remove the frame and repeat to make 16 rectangles, using two cookie trays. If there is extra meringue, make a few more to allow for breakage.

Bake for 2 hours, until the meringues are crisp and

dry all the way through (they should not brown). Turn off the oven, leave the door slightly ajar, and leave the meringues in the oven for 15 minutes more. Remove from the oven and cool. Carefully lift the meringues from the parchment.

Increase the oven temperature to 400°F. Place the blanched almonds on a cookie tray and toast for about 5 minutes, until well browned. Cool, then transfer to a food processor. Pulse until very finely chopped. Pulse in the butter and refrigerate until ready to use.

To serve, with a narrow rubber spatula spread about 2 tablespoons of the almond butter, slightly softened, over half of the meringues. Cover each with a second meringue and spread a very thin coating of the almond butter on top. Sprinkle with the sliced almonds.

DULCE DE NUEZ DE MIGUELA ❧
MIGUELA'S WALNUT AND EGG WHITE FLAN IN CARAMELIZED CUSTARD SAUCE

When our longtime friend Mari Carmen Martín was growing up, she recounts, this delightful dessert was often served in her household, prepared by Miguela, the family cook. It is a flan made only with egg whites, walnuts, sugar, and a touch of sherry, but the yolks appear in the accompanying custard sauce. Note that the custard sauce has no sugar but will be sweetened when mixed with part of the caramelized sugar.

serves 6

Caramelized Sugar

$1/2$ cup sugar

7 tablespoons hot water

Flan

5 large egg whites

5 tablespoons sugar

$1/4$ cup grated walnuts (use a Mouli-style grater)

1 tablespoon oloroso sherry, or port

Custard Sauce

5 large egg yolks

1 cup milk

$3/4$ teaspoon vanilla extract

2 dozen walnut halves

Preheat the oven to 325°F. To make the caramelized sugar, combine the sugar and 3 tablespoons of the water in a small saucepan. Cook over high heat, stirring constantly, until the mixture is syrupy and turns a light golden color. Turn off the heat. Slowly and very carefully stir in the remaining 4 tablespoons water. Pour into a greased 8-inch Bundt pan or savarin mold.

To make the flan, beat the egg whites in a large

bowl until stiff but not dry. Beat in the sugar, the grated nuts, and the sherry. Spoon into the pan, place the pan in another pan of hot water, and bake until set, about 25 minutes. Remove the pan from the water and cool.

Meanwhile, make the custard sauce. Whisk the yolks in the top of a double boiler until pale yellow. Gradually stir in the milk. Cook, stirring constantly until thickened to a soft custard consistency. Remove from the heat and stir in the vanilla.

Unmold the flan onto a dish, returning to the mold any caramelized sugar that is still liquid. Pour the custard sauce into the mold and mix with a spoon to loosen and blend any remaining sugar.

To serve, spoon the custard sauce on 6 dessert dishes. Cut the flan into 6 portions and place over the custard. Garnish with the walnut halves.

SOPA DE ALMENDRA DE PEPITA ALÍAS ✥ PEPITA'S ALMOND "SOUP"

Because her time is so occupied with the fine pulled thread work that her hometown of La-gartera is famous for, our longtime friend Pepita favors the simplest of recipes. This almond "soup" is in reality an almond custard, topped with sugar-coated fried bread for a nice crunch. A similar recipe given to me by Rafaela Ortiz from Zuheros in Andalucía goes by the name gachas. In her version the almonds are toasted and a dash of anisette is added when the custard is removed from the heat.   serves 4 to 6

$^1/_2$ pound blanched almonds

$^1/_2$ cup sugar plus more for sprinkling

4 cups milk

Zest of 1 lemon, cut into several pieces

2 cinnamon sticks

Mild olive oil for frying

Eight $^1/_4$- to $^3/_8$-inch bread slices, cut from a French-style
   loaf

In a food processor pulse together the almonds and the sugar, until the almonds are as finely ground as possible. In a saucepan, bring the milk to a boil with the lemon zest and cinnamon sticks. Lower the heat and simmer for 10 minutes. Add the almond and sugar mixture, return to a boil, and then reduce the heat and simmer until the mixture is thickened to the consistency of a soft custard, about 3 minutes. Cool to room temperature, remove the lemon zest and cinnamon stick, and pass the custard through a fine strainer, pressing with the back of a metal soup ladle to extract as much liquid as possible.

Shortly before serving, pour the oil to a depth of at least $^1/_4$ inch in a skillet (or better still, use a deep-fryer set at 360°F) and heat until the oil quickly browns a cube of bread. Add the bread slices and fry until golden, turning once. Drain on paper towels and sprinkle with sugar. (Alternatively, you can brush the bread with oil and bake until golden in a 350°F oven, then sprinkle with the sugar, but the bread is far better when fried.)

Serve the custard at room temperature or chilled, preferably in small flat-bottomed earthenware dishes, garnished with the fried bread slices.

CREMA DE LIMÓN CON MIEL ⚘ FROZEN LEMON CREAM IN LEMON SHELLS

All natural, commercially prepared sorbets frozen in fresh fruit shells are found all over Spain as far back as I can remember, and recently even exported to America. In this version from Mesón La Ráfaga in Andalucía the filling is soft and smooth, more of a cream than an ice cream or sorbet, and takes on an intense lemon flavor as it sits overnight in the lemon shells. The presentation is splendid and naturally requires large, unblemished lemons. The number of servings depends on the size of the lemons.   serves 4 to 5

4 to 5 large unblemished lemons

2 cups milk

Zest of $1/2$ lemon, cut into several strips, plus $1/2$ teaspoon freshly grated lemon zest

1 cinnamon stick

2 large egg yolks

$1/4$ cup honey

$1^1/2$ tablespoons granulated sugar

$1/3$ cup flour

Confectioners' sugar for dusting

Small raspberries or blueberries

Slice off the tops of the lemons and scrape the pith and membrane from the tops with the aid of a grapefruit knife or a very small spoon into a bowl. Scrape out the rest of the lemon in the same way and transfer to the bowl, trimming with kitchen shears any remaining membrane so that only the shells remain. Strain the juice and reserve 2 teaspoons (save the rest for another use). Slice off a small piece from the bottoms of the lemons, if necessary, so that they stand upright.

To make the lemon custard, in a saucepan, heat the milk with the strips of lemon zest and cinnamon stick until the milk barely comes to a boil. Reduce the heat and simmer for 10 minutes. Discard the lemon zest and cinnamon.

In another saucepan, whisk the yolks with the grated lemon zest, honey, granulated sugar, and reserved lemon juice. Stir in the flour, then gradually add the hot milk. Cook over moderate heat, stirring constantly, until the custard is thickened and smooth and begins to bubble and no flour taste remains. Cool completely, stirring occasionally.

Fill the lemon shells with the custard, cover with the caps, and refrigerate overnight. To serve, sift confectioners' sugar over 4 to 5 dessert dishes and place a lemon in the center of each dish. Remove the caps and arrange some berries over the custard, then partially cover with the caps. Scatter more berries around each plate.

NATILLAS DE LA ABUELA CON NUECES Y TORTOS DE MAÍZ ❧
GRANDMA'S SOFT CUSTARD WITH WALNUTS AND CORNMEAL FRITTERS

Corn arrived in Spain after the discovery of America and never gained much acceptance as a cooking ingredient (it was and still is more likely to be used as feed for livestock). Nevertheless, it does occasionally appear in old recipes, especially those from Spain's northern regions of Galicia, Asturias, Cantabria, and the Basque Country, where corn found an ideal climate (see also Basque Chorizo and Cornmeal Fritters, page 50). Young chef Javier González Martínez is indeed from northern Spain, specifically from Torrelavega in the lushly green mountains of Cantabria, and through the good cooking of his grandmother and his culinary investigations, came up with this dessert.

The crispness and unique flavor of the cornmeal puffs perfectly complement this soft custard that is as silky smooth as velvet. With a sprinkling of walnuts on top and a splash of *orujo* (Spain's version of grappa) you have a first-rate dessert. Do not make the fritters more than a few hours before serving or they will lose their crunch, although they can be crisped in a 350°F oven.

serves 4

Custard

2 cups plus 2 teaspoons milk

$1/2$ cup sugar

Peel of $1/4$ lemon, yellow part only, in one piece

One 1-inch piece of cinnamon stick

$2^1/2$ teaspoons cornstarch

3 large egg yolks

Fritters

$3/4$ cup stone-ground yellow cornmeal

$1/4$ cup unbleached flour

$3/4$ cup sparkling water

$1/4$ teaspoon kosher or sea salt

1 tablespoon olive oil

Mild olive oil for frying

6 walnuts, cut into quarters

Ground cinnamon

1 teaspoon Spanish orujo, or grappa, optional

Bring the 2 cups milk to a boil with the sugar, lemon zest, and cinnamon stick and simmer for 10 minutes. Dilute the cornstarch in the remaining 2 teaspoons cold milk. Whisk in the egg yolks, add a few tablespoons of the hot milk, then stir this mixture into the saucepan. Simmer for about 2 minutes more without boiling, stirring constantly until thickened and smooth. Cool, stirring occasionally. Discard the cinnamon stick and lemon zest.

To make the fritters, combine the cornmeal, flour, sparkling water, salt, and the tablespoon of oil in a bowl and stir until smooth. Pour the frying oil to a depth of 1 inch in a skillet (or better still, use a deep-fryer set at 360°F) and heat until the oil quickly browns a cube of bread. Drop the batter by heaping teaspoons into the oil and fry until golden. Drain on paper towels.

Pour the custard into flat-bottomed dessert bowls, preferably earthenware, and arrange the fritters and several walnut pieces over the custard. To serve, sprinkle with cinnamon and a splash of the liqueur.

PASTEL DE ARROZ CON LECHE AL RON DE PEDRO SUBIJANA &

PEDRO SUBIJANA'S RICE PUDDING FLAN WITH RUM

Pedro Subijana of Akelaře restaurant in San Sebastián cuts a dashing figure with his handlebar mustache and jovial demeanor. He attributes this singular dessert—a winning fusion of Spanish-style rice pudding and Spanish flan—to his father, a baker who was passionate about food. "My father's love of pastry making and all other kinds of cooking awoke in me a strange fascination for everything related to the world of food, and was certainly my inspiration to become a chef," says Pedro.   serves 6

5 tablespoons golden raisins

2 tablespoons dry light or dark rum

4 cups milk

$1/2$ cup Valencian short-grain rice (see Pantry, page 15), or
    Arborio

$1/2$ cup sugar

1 cinnamon stick

Zest of $1/2$ lemon

Caramelized Sugar

$1/2$ cup sugar

7 tablespoons hot water

2 large eggs

4 large egg yolks

In a small bowl, soak the raisins in the rum. In a large saucepan, combine the milk, rice, sugar, cinnamon stick, and lemon zest. Bring to the boiling point, then simmer for 30 minutes, stirring frequently. Cool for 10 minutes. Discard the lemon zest and cinnamon stick.

Preheat the oven to 350°F. To make the caramelized sugar, combine in a saucepan the sugar and 3 tablespoons of the water. Bring to a boil and continue boiling, stirring constantly, until the sugar is lightly caramelized. Remove from the heat and very carefully stir in the remaining 4 tablespoons water. Pour into the bottom of an 8-inch Bundt pan or savarin mold.

In a large bowl, lightly whisk together the whole eggs and the egg yolks. Stir in the milk mixture, raisins, and rum. Pour into the caramelized flan pan, place the pan in another pan of hot water, and transfer to the oven. Cook for 45 to 60 minutes, until the custard is set. Loosen the sides and invert onto a serving dish.

SOURCES FOR SPANISH PRODUCTS

LA TIENDA

Tel: 888–472–1022; Fax: 757–566–9603

www.latienda.com

A complete line of Spanish foods (some exclusive, like the tiny fresh sweet green peppers, *pimientos de Padrón*), cooking equipment, Spanish cookbooks, beautiful hand-painted ceramics, traditional fans, and a small but select wine list. Friendly knowledgable staff to assist you.

THE SPANISH TABLE

Tel: 206–682–2827; Fax: 206–682–2814

www.tablespan.com

Everything you need for Spanish cooking, including excellent cheeses and olive oils, plus a great selection of Spanish music and an astonishing six hundred wines.

LA ESPAÑOLA

Tel: 310–539–0455; Fax: 310–539–5989

www.donajuana.com

Excellent domestically made Spanish-style sausage, plus many imported foods from Spain.

DESPAÑA BRAND FOODS

Tel: 718–779–4971; Fax: 718–779–7438

www.despanabrandfoods.com

An unusual selection of Spanish artisanal cheeses, frozen baby eels and octopus, fish roe, wooden forks for baby eels, and traditional wooden plates in several sizes.

DIETRICH'S MEATS AND COUNTRY STORE

Krumsville, PA

Tel: 610–756–6344

A good source for top-quality lard.